The Lesbian Health Book

CARING FOR OURSELVES

Jocelyn White, M.D.
and
Marissa C. Martínez

Seal Press
Seattle

Seal Press
3131 Western Avenue, Suite 410
Seattle, Washington 98121
sealprss@scn.org

Acknowledgments: Versions of the following pieces previously appeared in the following publications: "Lesbian Denial and Lesbian Leadership in the AIDS Epidemic" in *Women Resisting AIDS: Feminist Strategies of Empowerment,* edited by Beth E. Schneider and Nancy E. Stoller (Temple University Press, 1994); "My Life as a Volcano" in *Off the Rag: Lesbians Writing on Menopause,* edited by Lee Lynch and Akia Woods (New Victoria Publishers, 1996); "Leah's Passing" in *Sinister Wisdom* (Winter/Spring 1996); and "Homophobia and the Health Care System,"with co-authors, in the *Journal of the Gay and Lesbian Medical Association* (March 1997). *The Mourners' Kaddish,* English translation by Rabbi Burt Jacobson, is used by permission of Kehilla Congregation, Berkeley, California.

Library of Congress Cataloging-in-Publication Data
White, Jocelyn
The lesbian health book : caring for ourselves / Jocelyn White and Marissa C. Martínez
Includes bibliographical references and index.
1. Lesbians—Health and hygiene. 2. Lesbians—Medical care.
I. Martínez, Marissa C. II. Title
RA778.2.W47   1997   613'.086'643—dc21   97–18091
ISBN 1-878067-31-1

Printed in Canada
First printing, November 1997
10 9 8 7 6 5 4 3 2 1

Distributed to the trade by Publishers Group West
In Canada: Publishers Group West Canada, Toronto
In Europe and the U.K.: Airlift Book Company, London
In Australia: Banyan Tree Book Distributors, Kent Town

Cover design by Kate Thompson
Text design by Rebecca Engrav
Text composition by Rebecca Engrav and Laura Gronewold

Acknowledgments

Jocelyn: I cannot say enough in gratitude to my partner of seventeen years, Lynn Nakamoto, who in her quiet, steady way has given me an abundance of love, patience and encouragement, enabling me to bring this book to fruition.

Marissa: I would like to thank my partner, Kathleen Benson, for sharing our relationship for three years with this book. I appreciate her stalwart belief in the necessity for this project and her personal resolve in supporting me despite my reckless disregard for her warnings. I would also like to thank Carlos for the boundless joy he has added to our relationship, and my family for the way they still cringe at my writing endeavors, despite their best efforts not to.

We would both like to thank Holly Morris, our editor at Seal Press, for her patience and willingness to work with us on this project. We also thank Evelyn White and Naomi Shihab Nye for sharing their experiences of editing with us, Judith Barrington for her teachings on the art of the memoir and Ruth Gundle for her counsel on editing, publishing and the lexicon of contracts.

*To all the lesbians who have chosen
silence in a medical setting*

CONTENTS

Life's Cycle

Living True

Looking Forward

Introduction

Jocelyn: This book has its roots back in my college days: My small group of lesbian friends sat in a circle late at night, our hands cupped around mugs of tea, and told each other the terrible experiences we had had with doctors. My friends were helping me decide whether to become a physician. Sharing our stories and the pain we had felt helped me understand how important it was that I become not just a physician, but an openly lesbian physician who could provide other lesbians with a safe place to get health care. My friends and I drew comfort and learned skills from one another. Those evenings taught me another lesson: Sharing life stories with someone who will listen is possibly the most powerful healing act there is.

Marissa: "Are you sexually active?" asks the doctor. I am in the college medical clinic for something totally unrelated to sexual activity. I have been to doctors hundreds of times because of chronic knee problems and have never been asked this question before. Unbeknown to me, I have passed that magical age where I am now more statistically likely to engage in sex. Unbeknown to the doctor, I have indeed recently had sex for the first time, but it was with a woman. I think about the other women in my living group who are also sexually active, but with men. I hypothesize that this question will lead to one about birth control methods. How much do I want to engage with this man about my newly discovered sexuality and "guaranteed" birth control? I am still newly out to myself, not out to my parents, and continue to go through an anxious, sometimes painful, coming-out process in my living group.

"Are you sexually active?" the doctor asks again, looking up from the list for the first time.

I don't want to explain about birth control. I don't want to argue that I am very confident that I will not get pregnant. I do not want to come out to this man.

"No," I respond.

Jocelyn: Health care for lesbians was still an abstraction for me until I went for a checkup while in medical school. The nurse asked me about birth control. I responded, "I don't use birth control. I'm a lesbian." When the female doctor I had specifically requested came in, she asked me about birth control. Again I responded, "I don't use any. I'm a lesbian." She never looked up from the chart, and she gave me the most uncomfortable pelvic exam I've ever had and scolded me rudely for taking aspirin for cramps. At that moment the importance of good health care for lesbians came to life for me. That experience galvanized my decision to make a difference in lesbian health care, to help counteract not only sickness but the pain and silent suffering of discrimination as well.

Marissa: "Are you sexually active?" I am seated in the doctor's office, rather than on an exam table. This is my first meeting with this doctor. My partner has given me a hard time because I have not had a pelvic exam in several years, and I have finally made an appointment. I am enrolled in a new health plan, and I have selected this woman carefully from the hundreds in the plan directory. She is in a practice with five other women. Her office is close to my home. Another woman in her practice is a lesbian, but that doctor is not taking new patients. I am fully prepared to find another doctor if this does not work out.

"Yes, I am. I'm a lesbian."

"Have you ever had sex with men?"

"No."

She skips the question about birth control.

Six years later, I have moved to a new house, she has moved to a new office, and I am still with this same doctor. On my recent visit, I showed her our latest family portrait. She noted that my son was getting bigger.

Jocelyn: When Seal Press asked us to edit a book on lesbian health, I saw the book as a catalyst for thousands of lesbians to sit with mugs of tea and share stories on lesbian health as I and my friends had. I hoped we could learn from one another by sharing our experiences and come to understand ways in which we can grow stronger in the health care system. I hoped we could all find some healing. Marissa and I have worked over the past three years to make that vision a reality.

Marissa: We asked the contributors to *The Lesbian Health Book* to relive their stories in such a way that every reader will sit next to them at the doctor's office or lie with them on the exam table, struggle with them in their embarrassment and laugh with them as they discover humor in the midst of pain.

The first section, "Past Tense, Present Challenge," provides background information on the lesbian health movement and offers an up-to-date perspective on the impact of homophobia on health and health care. Building on this background, "Through Health and Illness" presents stories of lesbians' transformative experiences with illness or the medical system. Each of these women grapple with the gravity of being a lesbian and being sick, wanting optimal health care while navigating the maze of health care in the United States. "Life's Cycle" comprises experiences with health and families, having and raising children and grieving the loss of a family member. "Living True" explores the challenges of several mental health issues. The book's final section, "Looking Forward," offers a blueprint for the future of lesbian health advocacy and research, and provides a wealth of resources on lesbian and women's health. These resources are meant to give you a starting place for finding more information about your unique health needs.

This book is a testimony to our belief that lesbians deserve competent, compassionate health care and that homophobia, which prevents access to that care, must be overcome. These essays not only record the challenges we must face, they also show us how to meet and surpass those challenges. In reading these women's stories, we learn the skills we need to cope with illness and the health care system. For some of us those skills merely need refinement or updating. For others, this book may represent a beginning to gaining them.

The Lesbian Health Book continues a national conversation among lesbians—initiated in dorm rooms and at kitchen tables—on the state of lesbian health and its future. We want this book to provide a healing catharsis for women in pain and a source of comfort and strength for lesbians negotiating the health care system. We hope it helps change that system and supports us on our path to wellness.

Jocelyn White, M.D.
Marissa C. Martínez
March 1997

The Lesbian Health Book

Past Tense, Present Challenge

RISA DENENBERG, R.N.

A History of the Lesbian Health Movement

When I was asked to write about the history of the lesbian health movement for this book, at first I felt limited by my own experience and vantage point. I thought sadly of my friend and comrade, Frosty Grey, who lived her life in support of others' health struggles but who died herself of breast cancer. A feminist and antiracist activist, Frosty had no health insurance when she found her breast lump. She delayed seeking care for several months. Finally she fought with all her might, trying chemotherapy and holistic medicine. She continued to work at the Feminist Women's Health Center in Tallahassee, Florida, providing abortion, prenatal and well-woman services to mostly poor women until the last weeks of her life. It seems to me, horribly, that lesbians take care of everyone but ourselves.

So, to start the task of writing about our history, I gathered books, articles, reports and other evidence. As I read, I discovered that we are more than I realized. I saw the threads of a movement, intertwined inextricably with the threads of other movements: books and articles, surveys and published accounts, lesbian health fairs and clinics, conferences and programs addressing lesbian health concerns, lesbian insemination and parenting classes, lesbians in recovery reaching out to lesbian addicts, lesbian cancer support groups and political activists, safe sex forums and lesbian HIV projects, lesbians running groups for lesbians in prisons and shelters—we are a movement, small, but expanding. Vulnerable, but powerful. Unsupported and unrecognized perhaps, but capable of undermining and unhinging the status quo of the medical establishment and its assumptions about us. We are a movement toward health. Health for lesbians. Wow, what a concept!

The Women's Health Movement

The women's health movement dates back to the "second wave" of feminism in the 1960s in the United States. As women disclosed the intimate details of their lives to one another in consciousness-raising groups, a body of knowledge began to emerge about women's health care experiences. The early women's health movement, which fought primarily for women's autonomy in reproduction and in opposition to medical authority, was resisted with all the force that the patriarchal medical profession could muster. Despite that resistance, the women's health movement thrived and helped to usher in an era in which women have a greater knowledge and sense of ownership of their bodies than they have had in any previous generation.

As a participant in both the women's movement and the early women's health movement, I know that many of the leaders were lesbians. During the years of struggle to create an autonomous health movement—fighting for abortion rights, learning about our bodies by doing as well as reading, creating feminist clinics—a mere handful of projects and programs were developed and designed for lesbians. Our issues were subsumed within the more visible agenda of heterosexual women's rights. Over the next two decades, the women's movement both faltered and flourished. It undertook the complex task of broadening to include issues of race and class; single-issue battles such as reproductive control became calls for prenatal care and childcare, wages for housework, and elimination of discrimination and abuse in the arenas of work, education and health care.

An early moment in the women's health movement occurred at a women's conference in Boston in the spring of 1969. A workshop on women's bodies spawned a group of twelve women who continued to meet and work together on common issues of women's health. This group, the Boston Women's Health Book Collective, published its first edition of *Our Bodies, Ourselves* in 1970. During this same time, the first women's self-help groups were forming in Los Angeles. Carol Downer and Lorraine Rothman, early pioneers of the feminist self-help movement, traveled around the country in 1971, demonstrating cervical self-examination and menstrual extraction. Hundreds of self-help groups formed during the 1970s. Common to all were dissatisfaction with the way women were treated in the health care system, and a desire to demystify medicine and seize control of power and technology that could free women from patriarchal control over their lives and bodies.

Abortion was legalized by a Supreme Court decision in 1973. Prior to that, each year unwanted pregnancy had placed large numbers of women at risk of stunted education, forced marriage, abandonment of children they had conceived and borne, and damage and death from illegal abortion. In response to this burden, women all over the United States participated in abortion referral and counseling and clandestine abortion procedures. One very effective group worked out of Chicago, using the code name "Jane." Jane members, angry that doctors charged so much and provided so little caring, learned to do abortions themselves. Self-help groups also developed the menstrual extraction procedure, which can be performed by trained laywomen, for termination of very early pregnancy. After the legalization of abortion, many such groups opened feminist-owned and -operated clinics, providing abortion and other health care services in a woman-controlled setting.

Also during the 1970s, feminists wrote about health care and started national organizations to deal with health care abuses and neglect. Childbirth, the birth control pill, the morning-after pill, menopause and sterilization abuses were documented, described and given public attention. The National Women's Health Network, founded in 1975, is still active today and serves as a clearinghouse of women's health information as well as a monitor for women's health policy nationwide. As the women's health movement grew, other groups emerged, including the National Black Women's Health Project (NBWHP), Hysterectomy Educational Resources and Services (HERS) and the Campaign for Women's Health, to name a few. In retrospect, it is clear that the women's health movement provided a model and crucible for radical change in health care not only for women but for everyone.

The Gay and Lesbian Health Movement

The lesbian and gay health movement in the United States resulted from several important political and social forces in our country; specifically, the civil rights movement of the 1950–60s, the modern feminist movement of the 1960–70s, and the newly visible gay and lesbian movement following the Stonewall riots in 1969. In addition, the movement for better health services, particularly for minorities, low income people and others grossly underserved because of immoral and inhuman reasons, contained many lesbian and gay individuals. The way these forces and their antecedents interacted so as to produce the gay and lesbian health movement remains for students of the history of social change to explicate.

One factor stands out clearly: the long-standing, pervasive and intense hostility of mainstream health services and practitioners toward the issue of homosexuality, in general, and to homosexual men and women, in particular. That hostility bred in lesbians and gay men a necessary secrecy and segregation of any sexual or personal issues when dealing with the mainstream health care system. Certainly, such secrecy was not new in the early 1970s when the lesbian and gay health movement began. What was new was that the homophobia of the health care system and the need for secrecy had become intolerable in the face of other major social change occurring at that same time in history. The response was the gay and lesbian health movement.

— Bopper Deyton and Walter Lear, "A Brief History of the Gay/Lesbian Health Movement in the USA," in *The Sourcebook on Lesbian/Gay Health Care*

In 1973, following years of political protest from gay and lesbian mental health activists, the American Psychiatric Association changed its definition of homosexuality, no longer designating it as a mental illness. By 1973, the civil rights and feminist movements were established, and gay liberation was dawning. Gay liberation found much to criticize in the care and mental health systems' treatment of gay and lesbian people.

Professional associations of gay and lesbian nurses, social workers, medical students, mental health workers and others formed as caucuses within larger professional organizations in the early seventies. The Gay Public Health Workers Caucus of the American Public Health Association, for example, was organized in 1975. By 1978, the first national Gay Health Conference had been held in Washington, D.C.

Gay-identified health services were an outgrowth of the "free clinics" and "people's clinics" which arose as part of the

counterculture movements of the sixties and more or less welcomed gay and/or lesbian clients. Feminist clinics appeared in the
early seventies and, at first, placed their highest priority on es-
tablishing low-cost, safe, accessible abortion services. Later, opposition to governmental population-control policies and reclaiming
pregnancy and childbirth experiences from medicalization and co-
optation headed the feminist health agenda. The leadership of
feminist clinics in the seventies and eighties was largely lesbian
women, but no lesbian-identified health concern visibly emerged.
In fact, many feminist clinics that offered "for lesbians only" well-
woman sessions during the seventies later stopped offering this
service. A handful of clinics developed specifically for lesbians
appeared in the seventies and eighties, including the St. Mark's
Women's Health Collective in New York City and the Lyon-Martin
Women's Health Clinic in San Francisco.

In the early 1970s, some urban communities could identify gay
male physicians known to provide sensitive health care to gay
clients and to be knowledgeable about infections sexually transmitted among men. Independent gay-identified clinics also arose
in the seventies in Boston, Los Angeles, New York City and Philadelphia. The impetus to start such clinics was the need for gay
men to have a safe place for treatment of sexually transmitted
diseases (STDs). Mental health and alcohol abuse services were
also among the early priorities of gay clinics. Lesbian-specific
mental health, gynecological and substance abuse services were
generally either absent or minimally operative. When the AIDS
epidemic appeared in gay men in the early 1980s, the twin structures of openly gay male doctors and gay "STD clinics" became
the magnifying glass that rendered HIV visible in gay men. (In
hindsight, it is clear that HIV was present in men and women,
gays and straights, in the late seventies. It was only *noticed* in gay
men first.) By the mid-eighties, AIDS had consumed the gay and
lesbian health agendas.

In the early eighties, mainly as a response to the AIDS

epidemic, the health departments of New York City and San Francisco created offices for gay and lesbian health issues and concerns. Although initially engrossed with the epidemic, both offices still exist, providing an official template for opposing homophobia, and both have staff devoted to addressing issues of lesbian health.

AIDS Activism

> Lesbians were and still are in the vanguard of the women's and lesbian and gay liberation movements. Without us, there would be no rape crisis centers, no women's foundations or buildings, no awareness of domestic violence, no women's music festivals or women's radio programming. There would be no National March on Washington, AIDS quilts, AIDS food banks or many other AIDS services, especially those for women. Without us, the women's movement would not have addressed homophobia and heterosexism and the lesbian/gay movement would not have addressed sexism. Indeed, without us, these movements would have remained one-dimensional reform movements. With us, they become dynamic forces for social change.
>
> — Jackie Winnow, "Lesbians Evolving Health Care: Our Lives Depend on It," in *Cancer as a Women's Issue*

Like my friend, Frosty Grey, Jackie Winnow died of breast cancer. And like many lesbians, both were AIDS activists. Lesbians have been part of the AIDS activist movement in the United States since the beginning of the epidemic, paralleling a strong lesbian presence in the earlier civil rights and women's movements. Lesbians involved in AIDS activism have both personal and political impetuses: They, like gay men, have experienced the increasing homophobic bigotry and violence that have accompanied the epidemic, and they often have strong personal ties to gay men, as friends, political allies, family and as co-parents or sperm donors.

Prior to the epidemic, lesbians and gay men worked together

as natural allies in the gay liberation movement, and lesbians struggled with gay men for visibility and against sexism in ways that were similar to those of women struggling with men about sexism in prior movements. During the years that AIDS was identified primarily as a disease affecting gay men, feminists and other lesbians often criticized lesbian AIDS activists for abandoning "women's issues." At the same time, within AIDS activism, lesbians, who were sometimes told (by gay men) that AIDS was not a lesbian issue, often raised issues of inclusivity, gender and race. While most lesbians have been affected personally—losing friends, colleagues, comrades and family—some have felt excluded and marginalized because of the breadth of human and financial resources that the epidemic has required of the lesbian and gay community.

While working with, socializing with and caring for gay men with AIDS, lesbians were among the first to advocate for recognition of HIV-positive women. Lesbians recognized that the epidemic affected many different groups: gay men, injection drug users, lesbians, heterosexual men and women, children and poor women of color. Often, lesbians have been important in creating bridges between groups and adding to the dialogue on the desperate need for a cure for AIDS, in the context of long-term social change within the health care system.

Lesbians who had been involved in the development of the women's health movement brought the perspective of that movement to AIDS activists; the gains made for women in the seventies, such as a sense of body ownership and knowledge, demystification of medicine, informed consent and professional-client partnership, have been greatly elaborated by AIDS activists.

For example, when HIV-positive men created an agenda that demanded immediate access to AIDS drugs (prior to completion of clinical trials), women recalled the horrors of decades of unregulated and experimental drug use in women's bodies (for example, the birth control pill and the synthetic hormone DES) that resulted in far more harm than good.[1] Women from the women's health movement who had demonstrated at the Food and Drug Administration (FDA) in the seventies against unsafe, poorly researched female hormones, found ourselves protesting with gay men for the early release of toxic and poorly researched AIDS drugs. While these perspectives appear contradictory, the synthesis of both positions has resulted in new and fruitful ways of forcing regulatory agencies to acknowledge constituencies and heed their perspectives.

As the epidemic continues, more women and more lesbians have been diagnosed with HIV/AIDS, and lesbians have been critical in making these women visible: The ACT UP/New York Women and AIDS Book Group published *Women, AIDS, and Activism* in 1990; lesbian HIV/AIDS projects, such as the Lesbian AIDS Project of the Gay Men's Health Crisis in New York City, have been created; the New York State AIDS Institute held a roundtable meeting on lesbians and AIDS in 1993 and produced a booklet that reprinted more than fifty articles about lesbians and HIV/AIDS; and in the spring of 1995, the Centers for Disease Control invited lesbian "experts" to Atlanta, Georgia, to advise on issues related to HIV transmission in lesbians.

The Lesbian Health Movement

One doesn't have to look far to realize that many people, specifically women and minority communities, are dissatisfied with the U.S. health care system. As efforts are undertaken to make the necessary large scale changes in this system, the issues of sexism and heterosexism must be dealt with. With this in mind, we see as a necessary beginning point, the education of our own lesbian community on matters of our health. . . . In the realm of health care, it is important for lesbians to challenge and re-direct the interpretation and teaching of medicine,

science and psychology. Biased interpretation of research con-
tinues to perpetuate notions of female inferiority and of homo-
sexual perversion. . . . [W]e want this booklet to be a part of
building strength and solidarity among lesbians. Learning ac-
curate information about our bodies, ourselves, and our com-
munity is one of the many tools necessary to relate to our health
and lives in a powerful way.

— Santa Cruz Women's Health Collective,
Introduction, *Lesbian Health Matters!*

As in the gay men's health movement, many vanguards of the
lesbian health movement have died, often of reproductive cancers
(breast and ovarian cancer). One example is Pat Parker, a poet and
co-director of the Feminist Women's Health Center in Oakland,
California, who died of breast cancer in 1988. The poet Audre
Lorde published *The Cancer Journals* in 1980 and died of a reoccurrence of her cancer in 1992. In a deeply feminist and radical voice, Lorde spoke universal truths about illness, death and
silence that have resonated among and given voice to all women,
all cancer survivors, all lesbians and all AIDS activists.

I was going to die, if not sooner then later, whether or not I
had ever spoken myself. My silences had not protected me.
Your silence will not protect you. But for every real word spoken, for every attempt I had ever made to speak those truths
for which I am still seeking, I had made contact with other
women while we examined the words to fit a world in which
we all believed, bridging our differences. . . . The fact that we
are here and that I speak now these words is an attempt to
break that silence and bridge some of those differences between us, for it is not difference which immobilizes us, but
silence. And there are so many silences to be broken.[2]

As I have already described, lesbians have been an integral part of evolving health movements, but not one of these movements has definitively addressed their health care concerns. For the most part, lesbians are an invisible constituency in the health care system, either entering the system incognito or opting out of the system altogether. Some would even question that specific "lesbian health" concerns exist. Yet, when lesbians' health care needs are the same as those of other women for screening, prevention, treatment, education and crisis intervention, they are less well met than those of heterosexuals. And when lesbians present unique problems and needs, the medical system generally can't or won't meet them.

Individual lesbian responses to a hostile health care system have included distrust of all providers, distrust of male providers or non-gay providers, opting out of the health care system and failing to obtain preventive or screening services, skepticism toward all Western health care strategies, denial of risk, perception of lesbians as being

Highlights of the Lesbian Health Movement

1969 The Stonewall riots in New York City are the catalyst for a more visible gay and lesbian liberation movement.

1969 A workshop on women's bodies at a Boston women's conference brings together the original group of twelve women who later formed the Boston Women's Health Book Collective.

1970 The Boston Women's Health Book Collective publishes the first edition of *Our Bodies, Ourselves*.

1971 Carol Downer and Lorraine Rothman, early pioneers of the feminist self-help movement, travel around the country demonstrating cervical self-examination and menstrual extraction.

1973 The United States Supreme Court legalizes abortion in *Roe v. Wade*.

1973 The American Psychiatric Association removes homosexuality from its official list of mental illnesses.

1974 The National Women's Health Network is founded; it provides a clearinghouse for women's health information and monitors national women's health policy.

1978 The first national Gay Health Conference is held in Washington, D.C.

OVER

1979 The Santa Cruz Women's Health Care Collective publishes *Lesbian Health Matters!*

Early
1980s In response to the AIDS crisis, the New York and San Francisco Health Departments create offices for gay and lesbian health issues.

1987 *The National Lesbian Health Care Survey,* conducted by Caitlin Ryan and Judith Bradford, is published by the National Gay and Lesbian Health Foundation.

1990 *Women, AIDS and Activism* is published by the ACT UP/NY Women and AIDS Book Group.

1990 The Chicago Lesbian Community Cancer Project, one of the first of many such organizations, is created.

1992 The first annual New York City Lesbian Health Fair is held.

1993 The New York State AIDS Institute holds a roundtable meeting on lesbians and AIDS and produces a booklet of articles on lesbians and HIV/AIDS.

1995 The Centers for Disease Control invites lesbian experts to speak on woman-to-woman transmission of HIV.

at increased risk, and increased use of alternative health care practitioners (such as chiropractors, naturopaths and acupuncturists). In addition to personal coping strategies, lesbians have responded by creating lesbian health care projects and programs in many communities, as well as writing, researching and teaching about lesbian health care issues. It has been an act of courage and perseverance that, in the face of an invisible problem and overt hostility, lesbians have created a health care movement.

Research and Lesbian Health

Substantial informal and scholarly research regarding lesbian health issues exists, yet a body of knowledge regarding lesbian health has yet to be delineated. While most authors of articles on lesbian health decry the paucity of research, their lengthy reference sections suggest the opposite. The problem is not a lack of inquiry or investigation (almost exclusively by lesbian researchers), but rather a lack of incorporation of this wisdom into other disciplines. It is the *mainstreaming* of this research into the body of knowledge about women's health that has yet to be accomplished. Subgroups of lesbians are not identified in large studies that include women, nor are the concerns of lesbians articulated in the body of research into women's sexual and reproductive health. This failure is thematic of the practice of discrimination against lesbians in general.

Some important research studies have been conducted and analyzed, but never formally published. Much of the existent research also suffers from certain methodological flaws, such as lack of a random sample, lack of a control population or small sample size. These problems are due primarily to a lack of access to the resources necessary for conducting research and publishing scientific data. Still, it is important to recognize that this research and documentation represent a significant foundation of the lesbian health movement.

A number of lesbian researchers have emphasized the need to gather information about lesbians—who we are, where and how we live, our health and mental health problems, our personal health strategies and relationship to the health care system, and our relationships with each other and with our families of origin. *The National Lesbian Health Care Survey,* published in 1987 by the National Gay and Lesbian Health Foundation, was the first large-scale publication of national data about lesbian health and health care needs.[3] Other important surveys have since been conducted in various communities, including San Francisco, Los Angeles, New York City and Dallas.

Organizational and Individual Response

Battling racism and battling heterosexism and battling apartheid share the same urgency inside me as battling cancer. None of these struggles are ever easy, and even the smallest victory is never to be taken for granted. Each victory must be applauded, because it is so easy not to battle at all, to just accept and call that acceptance inevitable.

— Audre Lorde, *A Burst of Light*

Lesbian Health Matters!, a prescient booklet first published in 1979 by the Santa Cruz Women's Health Care Collective, outlined the agenda of the lesbian health care movement, with chapters on sexuality, gynecology, research, cancer prevention, alcohol, menopause, menstrual cramps, feminist therapy, artificial insemination and long-term strategies.

Clinical programs for lesbian health are still few in number and most often associated with other, nonlesbian services. Still, programs exist, some functioning since the 1970s. Some programs have a primary care model; others only provide gynecology and infection screening; some programs have counseling, peer counseling and group counseling services; a few have insemination and prenatal services; most offer referrals, advocacy and education.

The strengths lesbians possess as activists, healers and advocates have come together in the form of lesbian cancer projects. As Jackie Winnow pointed out:

I am both a cancer activist and an AIDS activist. As a lesbian feminist, I have been involved with the AIDS crisis since the early 1980s. In 1985 I was diagnosed with breast cancer, founded the Women's Cancer Resource Center in Berkeley, California, in 1986, and was diagnosed with metastatic breast cancer in my lungs and bones in 1988. I have lost friends, acquaintances, and colleagues to cancer and to AIDS. Both of these diseases are life-threatening, and yet I have seen my community rally around one and overlook the other.[4]

The Mautner Project began as the vision of Mary-Helen Mautner, a lesbian attorney who was diagnosed with a reoccurrence of breast cancer in 1986. Before she died in 1989, she described her idea of a project for lesbians with life-threatening illnesses. Her lover, Susan Hester, organized and now directs the project, which provides education, support, advocacy and direct services to lesbians with cancer. Nancy Lanoue, a karate teacher in Chicago and a breast cancer survivor, started the Lesbian Community Cancer Project in 1990. Other projects have created seminars and conferences for lesbians with life-threatening illnesses.

A single-day event, the Lesbian Health Fair, is a recent creation of the lesbian health movement. Lesbian health fairs have taken place in New York City, San Diego, Baltimore and San Francisco. The New York City Lesbian Health Fair Organizing Committee held its fifth annual fair in May 1996 with more than six hundred women attending. The fair offered free Pap smears, mammograms and other health screenings as well as workshops, demonstrations, videos, a journal, refreshments, massage therapy and body work. This type of organizing is now possible because of the smaller projects and consistent organizing of lesbians over the past twenty-five years.

Of course, books, articles, journals and magazines have been written that focus on lesbian health. An aspect of the lesbian health movement greatly enhanced by publications is the promotion and eroticization of lesbian sex. *On Our Backs* and other "irreverent" magazines extol the virtue of positive, safe, pro-woman and pro-lesbian sexuality. Susie Bright, Pat Califia, JoAnn Loulan and Joan Nestle are a few of the authors of books that describe, explore, teach and challenge lesbians to enrich our sexual health. As Susie Bright puts it, "Sexual illumination is as precious as any human connection."[5]

There are journals that describe lesbians' experiences of cancer and other life-threatening illness, books about having children, substance use and recovery, sexual trauma and domestic violence, mental health and many more.

Lesbian recovery groups exist in most urban areas, creating their own model of health for participants. Lesbian support groups, coming-out groups, parenting groups, self-help groups, singles groups, incest recovery groups, tobacco cessation groups, Al-anon groups, exercise and sports clubs and a myriad of other collections of lesbians for support, social contact and healing are now a part of the lesbian health movement.

The movement has its "insiders" as well, and they have been quite effective in the past few years. Dr. Suzanne Haynes, a cancer specialist at the National Institutes of Health (NIH), forecast an epidemic of breast cancer in lesbians, based on epidemiological statistics generated by the National Cancer Institute. Noting that 45 percent of lesbians don't obtain regular gynecological care and 70 percent have not had children before the age of thirty (considered to be an important risk factor for breast cancer), she presented her predictions at a lecture given at the 1992 Lesbian and Gay Health Conference. Somewhat out of context, lesbian journalists began to state that as many as one in three lesbians would develop breast cancer (in contrast to the current one in nine prediction for women in general). Increasing awareness of risk of reproductive cancers in lesbians (including possible increased risk for ovarian and endometrial cancers, based on the same risk factors) has had a positive impact on governmental agencies that address women's health issues. The NIH-sponsored Women's Health Initiative (which will study long-term health indicators for more than 160,000 women) includes a question regarding sexual orientation, which will allow researchers to study disease difference by sexual orientation. The Office of Research on Women's Health has offered supplemental money to all NIH-funded projects that identify and include minority women, including lesbians, in their research. And the Centers for Disease Control convened a meeting in April 1995 inviting lesbian "experts" to advise them regarding woman-to-woman HIV transmission. CDC researchers published "Assessing HIV Risk among Women Who Have Sex with Women: Scientific and Communication Issues" in the *Journal of the American Medical Women's Association*.

■

Conflicts Within a Movement

*[A] factor that can create conflict is the intense demand for
sameness, for a common and collective identity that is typical
of many communities. This demand for sameness in lesbian
communities makes differences uncomfortable and suspect, as
if dissimilarity could erode cohesiveness. The contradiction is
that lesbians happen to be a remarkably diverse group. What
lesbians share, aside from gender, is a decision to act on a preference, the preference to relate both emotionally and sexually
to women. All the rest can be differences—race, ethnicity, class,
politics, education, work, living styles, bisexual inclination, role
identity, differences in sexual/political coming-out, early or late
awareness of attraction to women.*

— Sarah F. Perlman, "The Saga of Continuing
Clash in Lesbian Community, or Will an Army of
Ex-Lovers Fail?" in *Lesbian Psychologies*

*Don't give up. Don't let yourself say "we tried to invite people
of color into the organizing committee but no one showed up"
or "there aren't any 'out' older lesbians in our community."
Every time a group of white people say we tried—no one came,
let's go on with the meeting anyway, let's vote anyway, let's
publish the magazine anyway, let's march anyway—we guarantee the perpetuation of racist, ageist, and ablest events and
systems.*

— Dana Greene, "Rules to Live By,"
in *Lesbian Health Fair Manual*

The conflicts and difficulties experienced within the lesbian health
movement parallel conflicts within the women's movement in
general. The path toward multiculturalism, inclusivity and enjoyment of both sameness and difference has been uneven and difficult. External oppression generally results in some internalized

oppression. Internalized sexism and homophobia lead to distrust of the lesbian self and of lesbians in general. Internalized supremacist values result in racist and class-biased behaviors. None of this is unique to lesbians.

Like most oppressed groups, lesbians wish to separate at times in order to heal, organize and create. Lesbian separatism, in extreme, has allowed for exclusion of all males, even male babies. Naturally, lesbian mothers of male children take exception to this type of separatism, calling it elitism. Still, lesbians need not apologize for taking and creating women-only space for the purpose of furthering our health.

The issue of women-only space leads to conflict over "who is a woman?" and lesbian-only space creates division over "who is a lesbian?" When tolerance of difference is narrow in a community of lesbians, division can occur over issues of monogamy, definitions of lesbian sex, butch/femme roles, S/M sexuality, bisexuality, being "out" or "in the closet," and male-to-female and female-to-male transexuality. The tendency for lesbians to judge other lesbians based on what we do in bed is acknowledged in the phrase "lesbian sex police."

Conflict may occur when lesbians with different cultural backgrounds clash over issues related to gay and lesbian visibility. Lesbians of color often feel that lesbian visibility is a matter of white, middle-class privilege. Terminology (for example, lesbian versus gay) and issues of primacy of identity (for example, ethnicity versus sexual identity) often create conflict rather than a healthy curiosity and dialogue about difference. And, within the lesbian health movement, deciding which issues most deserve attention can cause conflict. In the 1980s, many lesbians who became AIDS activists were criticized for that choice by other lesbian health activists. And, when these same middle-class lesbian AIDS activists were concentrating on the issue of woman-to-woman transmission of HIV and creating safer-sex forums for lesbians, lesbians who contracted HIV through their own injection drug use, or through sex with men, were virtually being ignored.

Conflict over "professionalism" and battling "outside" versus "inside" the system for change is part of any health movement. Lesbians are not the exception. Coming out of the women's movement, self-help, demystification, body ownership, informed consent and health care alternatives are basic tenets of a lesbian health agenda. But conflicts of strategy are familiar to the lesbian health movement landscape. Whether or not to work with gay men, with men at all, within government agencies, or to accept funding from various sources are all points of potential conflict. Lesbian groups are often similar to feminist groups in that they rely heavily on group process and consensus for decision-making; so, while conflict can be the origin of healthy dialogue, debate and good decision-making, it can also, when coupled with rigid ideas and structures within a group, result in stalemate and inaction. Lesbian health activists have had our share of conflict, stalemate and difficulty in organizing. We have also had magnificent successes.

A Lesbian Health Agenda

Lesbians clearly experience health and illness differently from both gay men and heterosexual women, and our differing needs constitute a lesbian health agenda that is becoming increasingly visible through the lesbian health movement. The agenda demands, first and foremost, the elimination of homophobia, lesbian-phobia, heterosexual assumption, sexism, racism, class bias and discrimination within the larger health care system and within other health movements. The education of professionals toward this goal should not have to be the responsibility of lesbians, but should be mainstreamed within medical, nursing, social work and health educational programs.

The highest priority concerns of lesbians presently include access to basic health care and prevention services as well as to alternative choices in health care, cancer prevention and research, support for childbearing and achieving family goals, effective substance-use education and treatment, mental health services, research and guidance regarding female-to-female sexually transmitted infections and treatment for gynecological problems. In all of these identified concerns, lesbians deserve and expect access to lesbian-sensitive services, lesbian-informed research, professional education, public health education, funding, support and participation.

Notes

1. For a good historical discussion of these issues, see Barbara Seaman and Gideon Seaman, *Women and the Crisis in Sex Hormones*, (New York: Bantam Books, 1978).

2. Audre Lorde, *The Cancer Journals* (San Francisco: Aunt Lute, 1980).

3. Judith Bradford and Caitlin Ryan, *The National Lesbian Health Care Survey: Final Report* (Washington, D.C.: National Lesbian and Gay Health Foundation, 1987).

4. Jackie Winnow, "Lesbians evolving health care: Cancer and AIDS," in *One in Three: Women with Cancer Confront an Epidemic*, Ed. Judith Brady (Pittsburgh, PA: Cleis Press, 1991).

5. Susie Bright, *Susie Sexpert's Lesbian Sex World* (San Francisco: Cleis Press, 1990).

KATE O'HANLAN, M.D.

Homophobia and the Health Care System
Solutions for the Future

Recognizing the Problem and Its Multiple Effects

Homophobia is the "irrational fear of, aversion to, or discrimination against homosexuality or homosexuals."[1] This ubiquitous antipathy derives from the misperception of gay men and lesbians as child molesters, immoral individuals or threats to commonly held family values or the "natural order." A review of the psychiatric literature over the last fifty years reveals no major differences in levels of maturity, neuroticism, adjustment, goal orientation or criminality between heterosexual and homosexual people. Indeed, no credible evidence has ever been developed to pathologize homosexuality, yet homophobia persists, is legal and is widely socially unchallenged. Unlike racism, sexism, anti-Semitism, ageism and ableism, there is no federal or state mandate to reduce or eliminate homophobia. So it persists.

It must be recognized that homophobia operates both internally and externally. Internal homophobia represents antihomosexual prejudices that all individuals learn (internalize) from their families, friends, teachers, religious institutions, government and the popular media. It keeps all people from experiencing real warmth toward same-sex others, and it teaches self-loathing to all who come to recognize their same-sex attraction. The effect is to socialize all youth to believe they are either heterosexuals or pariahs. Among homosexual youth, such chilling constraints frequently cause shame, isolation and depression, or repression of the recognition of their homosexuality, with latency periods extending decades. When the individual develops enough personal strength to overcome the social stigma and self-loathing, recognition occurs, often after misspent years in attempted heterosexual relationships, often including marriages.

External homophobia is the overt expression of those learned biases, and ranges from social avoidance, to legal and religious proscription, to violence. Media reports of violence toward homosexuals, court challenges to homosexuals' parental rights, the battle over homosexuals in the military, the religious right's efforts to prevent homosexual marriages and spousal rights teach any observer that homosexuals are, at best, undeserving on every level. The result: Approximately 90 percent of homosexual men and women experience public verbal derision, and about a third experience some form of violent physical assault.[2]

It is not surprising that some studies have shown higher lifetime rates of depression, attempted suicide, psychological help-seeking and substance abuse among homosexuals, attributing such problems to chronic stress from societal hatred or to the loss of personal status that homophobia imposes. For the homosexual, these life stresses may have more significant mental health implications because homosexuals have frequently lost their familial support systems.[3-6] Furthermore, these stresses are compounded by isolation due to concealment and suppression of their homosexual feelings and thoughts.[7]

■

Social and Educational Propagation of Hatred

There is little balance or accuracy in reporting or teaching about homosexuality in American culture. The fear is that exposure to homosexuality will result in higher rates of "conversion" to homosexuality; however, this has been roundly refuted in the psychiatric and psychologic literature.[8] Comparing children raised in gay or lesbian households with children raised in heterosexual households, no difference in self-concept, locus of control, moral judgment, intelligence, sex-role behavior or orientation was observed.[9]

The virtual absence of gay and lesbian role models in society limits the ability of gay and lesbian youth to develop a positive self-identity and gain respect and understanding from their peers.[10] Negative stereotypes of homosexuality pervade television, theater and print media and go unchallenged. As an example, news articles about the proscription against homosexuals in the military consistently omit reporting the abundant data documenting the absence of security risk or any evidence of performance inadequacy among homosexual service members.

Few parents and few religious or educational institutions teach children about issues of sexual orientation, and not at the early ages most youths begin to discern their orientation. In one study of gay youth, awareness of sexual orientation typically occurred at age ten; however, disclosure to another person did not occur until six years later.[11] Suicide attempts were acknowledged by 42 percent of this sample, particularly during this critical time. In contrast, the Centers for Disease Control reports that 8 percent of a random sampling of American teenagers in 1991 (presumably including some gay or lesbian youth) had attempted suicide.[12]

In pediatric interviews, the children who experience homosexual feelings typically report isolation from their family, perceiving that heterosexuality is the only acceptable "norm."[13] Some children are "kidnapped" and sent to camps for reparative therapy, treatment aimed at changing an individual's sexual orientation. Reparative or conversion therapy has been found to be ineffective, unethical and harmful because it further stigmatizes the individual as defective.[14,15] Risk factors for gay and lesbian youth suicide have been identified and include societal and familial disapproval, with parental disapproval of critical importance.[16]

Additional sources of psychological stress among homosexuals derive from the anxiety, depression and guilt associated with being perceived as immoral and deviant, an effect that has been compounded by—and further compounds—the HIV epidemic. Individuals who carry multiple socially marginalized statuses, for example, race, ethnicity and sexual orientation, may carry an even higher risk of depressive distress.[17] Stress and difficulties in identity development are significant cofactors that increase rates of high risk behavior for acquiring HIV infection.[18]

"Coming out" has been associated with significant amelioration of anxiety and depression, conferring a higher self-concept, greater relationship satisfaction, sense of community and integration into family and society.[19, 20] Despite this, many homosexuals have not disclosed their orientation to everyone in their lives because of persistent fears of loss of job, community respect and family love.

Socioeconomic Consequences of Homophobia

Socioeconomic stratum and medical insurance are important health correlates. Homosexual couples cannot file for government low-income housing assistance or inherit each other's estates tax-free as married spouses can. Anticipated homophobic discrimination inhibits homosexuals from seeking many jobs,[21] and barriers to medical insurance, such as low income and lack of domestic partner coverage, may keep lesbians and gays from obtaining yearly screening tests or seeking care early in the course of a disease.

■

Health Care System Bias

Health care providers are not immune to misinformation received in their early socialization, and they typically are not educated about gay and lesbian health issues in their medical training, with the possible exception of HIV/AIDS. A 1987 questionnaire study of Midwest bachelor-degree nursing-school faculty revealed that many believed lesbianism was a disease, immoral, disgusting and unnatural. In a 1986 questionnaire study of the San Diego County Medical Society, nearly one-quarter of the 930 respondents scored as "severely homophobic."[22] Thirty percent reported that they would not admit a highly qualified gay or lesbian applicant to medical school, and 40 percent stated they would discourage a gay or lesbian medical student from entering a pediatric or psychiatric residency. Forty percent stated they would not refer patients to a gay or lesbian colleague, and 40 percent reported being uncomfortable providing care to gay or lesbian patients. Among obstetricians/gynecologists and family practice/internists, the primary care providers and gatekeepers in most comprehensive health care plans, one-third self-reported hostile attitudes toward gay and lesbian patients.

In the 1994 survey of the membership of the Gay and Lesbian Medical Association, an association of United States and Canadian physicians and physicians-in-training, over one-half of the 711 respondents reported observing heterosexual colleagues deny care or provide reduced or substandard care to gay or lesbian patients because of their orientation, with 88 percent reporting that their physician colleagues made disparaging remarks in public about gay or lesbian patients relating to their sexual orientation.[23] While 98 percent of respondents felt it was medically important for patients to inform their physicians of their orientation, 64 percent believed that in so doing, patients risked receiving substandard care.

The attitudes of nurses, medical students and physicians are perceived by patients and can negatively affect their health care experience, including the likelihood of obtaining necessary follow-up care. Many homosexual patients report experiencing ostracism, rough treatment and derogatory comments, as well as disrespect for their partners from their medical practitioners. Many homosexual patients withhold information about their sexual behavior from their health care providers, fearing sanctions or repercussions if they reveal their homosexuality. As a result, some homosexuals are hesitant to return to their physicians' offices for new complaints and are less likely to receive medical screening tests, including Pap smears, blood pressure checks, cholesterol panels and stool blood assays.

Detoxification and rehabilitation programs often show little sensitivity to issues of sexual orientation and generally do not encourage disclosure. It has been shown that failure to acknowledge gay or lesbian identity issues in alcoholism treatment makes recovery more difficult and increases the likelihood of relapse.[24]

Considering all of these factors, lesbians may be at greater risk of developing cancer or heart disease than other women and experience greater morbidity or mortality, especially if they defer seeing a physician until symptoms become severe.

What Can Be Done?

In psychological, social and medical respects, the broad process of homophobia—the socialization of heterosexuals against homosexuals and concomitant conditioning of gays and lesbians against themselves—must be recognized by Americans as destructive to all individuals, as is every other bias. When hatred keeps the oppressed group limited, the dominant group also suffers from the constrictions and limitations.

Certainly, the education of well-meaning but uninformed individuals will reduce hatred to some extent. But many factors inhibit well-informed and progressive academic and lay individuals from taking public stands in support of homosexual civil rights.

As observed in the McCarthy era's rooting out of communists, taking a stand for a group's rights can implicate one as a member. Some heterosexual people and some closeted homosexuals believe it is insulting to be considered homosexual and will not take a public or activist stand. Additionally, many subscribe to the myth that informing children about homosexuality, even in an age-appropriate manner as advocated, can liberate them to experiment and potentially become a homosexual.

It will be admittedly difficult to illuminate those in governing positions who believe homosexuality is a "morals" issue and must be repressed and denied. Those in government who oppose dissemination of science-based educational plans on sexual orientation present a large challenge to progress. Their antiacademic bias needs to be illuminated for what it is by grassroots educational endeavors. Only after effective dissemination of accurate information can it be expected that the national, state and local governments will gradually reflect a nonbiased protection of all people in our laws.

Progress has already been made. Most of the cabinet departments of the presidency have included sexual orientation in their nondiscrimination policies. Eight states prohibit discrimination based on orientation. Most of the top universities and many Fortune 500 industries are now providing domestic partner insurance benefits. Even the American Medical Association (AMA), at its 1993 annual meeting, voted to include the words "sexual orientation" in its nondiscrimination statement, after having rejected this motion for four consecutive years. Recently, the AMA revised its policy statement on homosexuality to reflect the scientific literature, but it refused to take further leadership in advocating specific educational and legislative health-related changes essential to reducing homophobia. However, the American Medical Women's Association (AMWA) passed, without opposition, a policy statement urging the enactment of national, state and local legislation "to end discrimination based on sexual orientation in housing, employment, marriage and tax laws, child custody and adoption laws; to redefine family to encompass the full diversity of all family structures; and to ratify marriage for lesbian, gay and bisexual people . . . [to support the] creation and implementation of educational programs . . . in the schools, religious institutions, medical community, and the wider community to teach respect for all humans."[25]

Initiating Change in the Health Care System

Physicians and health care workers are in a unique position in our culture in their responsibility to provide quality care for all and to understand and transmit new scientific information to the public. Physicians (and, indeed, everyone) must recognize that as much as 6 percent of the population—some fifteen million Americans—is gay, lesbian or bisexual, and that these individuals express part of the normal range of human sexuality. Such information must come from organized curricula in medical school and/or residency training programs. The American Psychiatric Association, for example, has sponsored "A Curriculum for Learning About Homosexuality and Gay Men and Lesbians in Psychiatric Residencies," which describes educational objectives, learning experiences and implementation strategies for sound clinical practice.

Health care providers can do much to reduce homophobia within their individual practices. The need for a trusting, supportive and open provider-patient relationship is critical. And just as they do for their married patients, physicians should provide support for the stability of their lesbian patients' relationships.

Educational pamphlets in gynecologists', pediatricians' and family practitioners' offices could provide life-affirming information to youth and an educational source for parents, possibly lessening rates of youth suicide as well as public violence and discrimination.

But simply *having* a nonjudgmental, nonhomophobic attitude

is not enough. The responsible practitioner must *convey* a nonjudgmental attitude to all patients. With this awareness, practitioners can serve as leaders and positive examples in both the medical and the larger community in reducing homophobia.

Teaching Our Youth

It is impossible to predict which youth are struggling with issues of sexual orientation, but all youth benefit from the nonbiased demonstration of a positive attitude toward orientation issues by parents, peers and teachers. While gender-atypical youth may ultimately develop a homosexual orientation, negative attitudes serve only to alienate and isolate these children. It is irrational to classify such behavior in youth as abnormal when homosexuality in adults is not considered abnormal. The American Academy of Pediatrics (AAP), recognizing homosexuality as a natural sexual expression, recommends psychotherapy for gay and lesbian youth who are uncertain about their orientation or who need help addressing personal, family and environmental difficulties *that are concomitant* with coming out.[26] The AAP also recognizes that families may experience some stress and need information while supporting an individual's newly expressed orientation, and recommends that families contact organizations such as Parents, Family and Friends of Lesbians and Gays (P-FLAG) or obtain therapy.[27]

Homophobia must be addressed during the age ranges in which it is initially recognized—the elementary school years—by school-based family-counseling programs and school and social support programs for gay and lesbian youth. Promotion of the positive image of gay men and lesbians begins with educational programs directed initially toward educators, clergy and professionals and, later, toward the youth themselves and society at large. Familiarity with issues of orientation as well as the openly respectful attitudes of teachers, parents, local organizations, peers and friends may help frightened youth come to grips with their fears about sexual identity and begin to confront their own internalized homophobia as their self-concept strengthens. While many school counselors and classroom teachers believe they should be more proactively supportive of the welfare of their gay and lesbian students, their professional intervention and support are negligible because of community prejudice, ignorance and fear.[28]

Youth need access to accurate information in their school libraries and in social studies classes as well as in sex education curricula. To facilitate acculturation of gay and lesbian youth as well as the children of gay and lesbian parents, school libraries need to include storybooks of positive role models that resemble their families. Educators are urging that multicultural diversity training programs in elementary schools must include sexual orientation issues in their curricula.[29] The state of Massachusetts requires schools to write policies protecting students from harassment, violence and discrimination because of orientation, to train teachers in crisis intervention and violence prevention, to create school-based support groups for gay and lesbian as well as heterosexual students, to provide information in the school libraries and to write curricula which include gay and lesbian issues.[30]

Parents and teachers should provide a supportive atmosphere at home and school and not allow taunting about orientation or gender identification. There may not be a more powerful source of support for children than their parents' acceptance and love. All children would benefit from hearing their parents say, "No matter whom you love, I will love you."

Taking Responsibility

Efforts are being made to obtain and disseminate accurate information about gay men and lesbians, but obstacles are plentiful. There is some important progress in health research: The principal investigators of the National Institutes of Health Women's

Health Initiative, the largest study (160,000 participants) on women's health ever planned, had initially declined to ask participants their sexual orientation out of fear that respondents would quit the study. However, after a review of information on recruitment and retention of lesbians in health trials and after piloting the question to test groups, the NIH included a sexual orientation question.[31] The investigators of the Nurses' Health Study have also decided to stratify their ongoing longitudinal study by sexual orientation to determine morbidity differences. At the Department of Health and Human Services Secretary's Conference for a National Action Plan for Breast Cancer, the Committee for Access to Mammography recommended that all future and ongoing studies be stratified by orientation because of the presence of multiple risk factors for breast cancer within the lesbian community. If studies show a higher incidence of or mortality from cancers or heart disease among lesbians, then screening and/or health education programs could be instituted to target them.

Very likely the most important and profound effect our government can have on improving the lives of homosexuals would be to conduct a National Institutes of Health Consensus Development Conference as it does on many other controversial health topics. For example, only about eighteen thousand women yearly develop ovarian carcinoma, but because there are a myriad of methods to treat this cancer, a Consensus Development Conference was held to standardize information about the best treatments and to discourage use of less helpful treatments. Homosexuality directly affects some 3–6 percent of United States citizens, or seven to fifteen million Americans and their families. A Consensus Development Conference would shed light on the facts that are known about homosexuality and on the absence of any basis for homophobia. It could create a valid academic stand for the departments and cabinet of the government to take, based only on the scientific research. The proceedings from such a conference could be used as a basis for future legislation, providing a rationale as well as a sense of safety for legislators to use in creating laws that help all Americans to be treated equally, to enjoy "life, liberty and the pursuit of happiness," as intended by the Constitution of the United States. Against such research-based information, the radical religious right could not object.

The Consensus Development Conference information, when viewed as a government policy, would enable legislation to: 1) allow equal marriage rights for all, 2) make discrimination against gay men and lesbians illegal and 3) allow equal access to serve in the military. Such courageous legislation would be the most effective solution to the psychological, sociological, financial and interpersonal problems that result from homophobia. A 1992 subcommittee report regarding domestic partner benefits at Stanford University, the first university to offer identical benefits packages to all employees, provides encouragement for a progressive stand:

> One imagines, for example, that a decision by Stanford forty years ago to take the lead in eradicating discrimination against blacks, women or Jews in admissions, hiring, memberships in sororities and fraternities, etc., would have been politically unpopular with many alumni, as well as with the larger political community. One also imagines that had Stanford taken such a leadership role, few in the Stanford community would look back on that decision now with anything but pride.[32]

Conclusion

Each of us, regardless of our sexual orientation or political or religious affiliation, must examine our attitudes about homosexuality and recognize that the views we hold that are not consistent with facts. We each have a unique opportunity to influence others in our society to align their attitudes with objective information. It is everyone's responsibility to reduce racism, sexism, ageism, ableism and now homophobia. A National Consensus Development Conference sponsored by the National Institutes of Health should be held to illuminate the facts and to serve as a basis for future legislation and educational reform. Civil rights legislation proscribing discrimination and providing legal recognition for the unions of lesbian and gay families will restore legal, societal and financial equity to this marginalized population. Public education of both adults and children about the diversity of orientation will reduce the pervasive, unfounded disdain for homosexuals and maintain lesbian and gay individuals' self-respect.[33] The resultant increased visibility of lesbians and gays will increase their familiarity in the community and promote more understanding.

We must all take responsibility, all the time, at every opportunity. Each effort will begin to decrease the oppression of lesbians and gays in society, as well as learned self-oppression. Improved access to health care, increased integration into family and society and heightened life-satisfaction, productivity and health will result when homophobia is recognized as the major health hazard of gay and lesbian individuals.

Notes

1. *Merriam-Webster's Collegiate Dictionary,* 10th ed., s.v. "homophobia."

2. L. Gross and S. Aurand, *Discrimination and Violence Against Lesbian Women and Gay Men in Philadelphia and the Commonwealth of Pennsylvania: A Study by the Philadelphia Lesbian and Gay Task Force* (The Philadelphia Lesbian and Gay Task Force, 1992).

3. M. T. Saghir et al., "Homosexuality: III. Psychiatric Disorders and Disability in the Male Homosexual," *American Journal of Psychiatry,* vol. 127 (1970) 147.

4. M. T. Saghir et al., "Homosexuality: IV. Psychiatric Disorders and

Disability in the Female Homosexual," *American Journal of Psychiatry,* vol. 120 (1972) 477.

5. R. C. Savin-Williams, "Verbal and Physical Abuse as Stressors in the Lives of Lesbian, Gay Male, and Bisexual Youths: Associations with School Problems, Running Away, Substance Abuse, Prostitution, and Suicide," *Journal of Consultant and Clinical Psychology,* vol. 62 (1994) 261–69.

6. J. DiPlacido, "Stress, Behavioral Risk Factors, and Physical and Psychological Health Outcomes in Lesbians," APA Women's Health Conference (1994).

7. D. Larson and R. Chastain, "Self-Concealment: Conceptualization, Measurement, and Health Implications," *Journal of Social and Clinical Psychology,* vol. 9 (1990) 439–455.

8. C. J. Patterson, "Children of Lesbian and Gay Parents," *Child Development,* vol. 63 (1992) 1025–42.

9. Ibid., 1025–42.

10. American Academy of Pediatrics: Committee on Adolescence, "Homosexuality and Adolescence," *Pediatrics,* vol. 92 (1993) 631–34.

11. A. R. D'Augelli and S. L. Hershberger, "Lesbian, Gay, and Bisexual Youth in Community Settings: Personal Challenges and Mental Health Problems," *American Journal of Community Psychology,* vol. 21 (1993) 421–48.

12. Centers for Disease Control, "Attempted Suicide Among High School Students in the United States," *Morbidity and Mortality Weekly Report,* vol. 40 (1991) 1–8.

13. G. Remafedi, M. Resnick, R. Blum and L. Harris, "Demography of Sexual Orientation in Adolescents," *Pediatrics,* vol. 89 (1992) 714–21.

14. Council on Scientific Affairs, "Health Care Needs of Gay Men and Lesbians in the U.S.," *Journal of the American Medical Association,* vol. 275 (1996) 1354–58.

15. AAP Committee on Adolescence, "Homosexuality and Adolescence."

16. Ibid.

17. S. D. Cochran and V. M. Mays, "Depressive Distress Among Homosexually Active African American Men and Women," *American Journal of Psychiatry,* vol. 151 (1994) 524–29.

18. A. H. Grossman, "Homophobia: A Cofactor of HIV Disease in Gay and Lesbian Youth," *Journal of the Association of Nurses AIDS Care,*

vol. 5 (1994) 39–43.

19. Larson and Chastain, "Self-Concealment," 439–55.

20. AAP Committee on Adolescence, "Homosexuality and Adolescence," 631–34.

21. V. M. Mays, J. S. Jackson and L. S. Coleman, "Perceived Discrimination, Employment Status and Job Stress in a National Sample of Black Women," *Journal of Occupational Health Psychology* (1995).

22. W. C. Mathews, M. W. Booth, J. D. Turner and L. Kessler, "Physicians' Attitudes Toward Homosexuality—Survey of a California County Medical Society," *Western Journal of Medicine,* vol. 144 (1986) 106–10.

23. B. Schatz and K. O'Hanlan, *Anti-gay Discrimination in Medicine: Results of a National Survey of Lesbian, Gay and Bisexual Physicians,* The Gay and Lesbian Medical Association, 459 Fulton Street, Suite 107, San Francisco, CA 94102; 1994.

24. R. Cabaj, "Substance Abuse in the Gay and Lesbian Community," in *Substance Abuse: A Comprehensive Textbook,* 2nd ed., ed J. Lowinson, P. Ruiz, R. Millman, (Baltimore, Md: Williams and Wilkins, 1992) 852–60.

25. American Medical Women's Association. "Position Paper on Lesbian Health," *Journal of the American Mededical Womens' Assocociation,* vol. 49 (1993) 86.

26. AAP Committee on Adolescence, "Homosexuality and Adolescence," 631–34.

27. Ibid., 631–34.

28. D. F. Morrow, "Social Work with Gay and Lesbian Adolescents," *Social Work,* vol. 38 (1993) 655–60.

29. J. M. Goodman, "Lesbian, Gay and Bisexual Issues in Education," *Thrust for Educational Leadership* (April 1993) 24–28.

30. Massachusetts State House, Governor's Commission on Gay and Lesbian Youth, Room 111, (Boston: Massachusetts State House; 1993.)

31. K. A. O'Hanlan. "Recruitment and Retention of Lesbians in Health Research Trials," *Recruitment and Retention of Women in Clinical Studies* (National Institutes of Health, NIH Publication # 95-3756, 1995) 101–104.

32. B. Fried. "Report of the Subcommittee on Domestic Partners' Benefits," *University Committee for Faculty and Staff Benefits* (Stanford:1992) 37–38.

33. V. Uribe and K. M. Harbeck. "Addressing the Needs of Lesbian, Gay, and Bisexual Youth: The Origins of PROJECT 10 and School-based Intervention," *Journal of Homosexuality,* vol. 22 (1992) 9–28.

Through Health and Illness

MARJ PLUMB, M.N.A.

Butch Identity, Breast Reduction and the Chicago Cubs

The Effect of Gender and Class on Lesbian Access to Health Care

"It's 2:30 and Gloria's neck already hurts . . . " Anyone who has ever traveled the New York City subways is familiar with this headline on an ad for breast reduction—the ad is posted in just about every car in the system. A nice-looking woman with long hair is on one side of the ad, and a very long paragraph extolling the virtues of plastic surgery is on the other side. I am standing, holding onto the ceiling bar to stop from being flung about the speeding train, ever conscious of the jiggling of my triple-D breasts. I am looking at this ad for the first time. As I pull my briefcase under my left arm to stop one breast from flying about, I can't take my eyes off the words "breast reduction." Then I begin to wonder how I could make this happen for me. But the image being presented is clearly about femininity—breast reduction will make you look more attractive, more like a woman. That's not exactly what I have in mind.

When I saw that ad about Gloria's painful neck and the benefits of breast reduction, I was captivated. I realized that although I had had more than fifteen years of health care experience, I had never thought of breast reduction. Yes, I could claim a medical reason for the reduction and leave it at that; my neck and shoulders did always hurt from the weight of my breasts dragging my upper body toward the earth every time I stood. But I knew the real reason I wanted this operation was because I was a butch and had always hated my large breasts. Over the next year and a half, I slowly worked out all of the issues I had about the surgery and, in doing so, discovered who I was as both a female and a butch. The surgery also gave me an opportunity to deconstruct the concept of "barriers" to health care from my position as a working class woman and a lesbian.

On Being Lesbian

I have always thought that being gay saved my life. That small nagging (then unnamed) "difference" in me allowed me to escape the fate of my sisters—pregnant by high school. Not getting pregnant meant I had a chance to run away from home, or as many working-class dykes refer to it: graduate high school, get a sports scholarship and go to college. It was at college that I discovered the truth about myself and my sexual orientation. I was playing on a women's rugby team (I guess that should have said something right there, but we live very sheltered lives in the Midwest) when someone came up to me and said, "Stay away from them, they're lesbians." I ran to those lesbians so fast the other team thought the game had started. Hearing the word *lesbian*, at twenty years of age, was the first time in my life I felt normal—I had a name for myself. I came out personally and publicly shortly after that realization and never looked back.

Yet, fifteen years later, I still cringe at the very thought of sitting naked on an exam table and saying to a medical provider, "I don't want birth control. I only have sex with women." I always find my fear of this interaction fascinating as I am one of the most "out" lesbians I know. I am a professional "out" lesbian. I am the kind of lesbian who gets invited to meetings and asked to sit on committees because everyone knows I am a lesbian. I discussed lesbian "fisting" at a medical grand rounds in Davis, California, in front of the most conservative medical providers I had ever met. But having to correct the heterosexual assumptions of my own medical providers makes me physically ill. I call it "homophobiaphobia"—the fear of homophobia. And it still operates to stop me from getting care.

Because of this intense fear, I knew I was not going to be calling the medical providers who had helped the Gloria in the ad. I wasn't exactly sure what I wanted my breasts to look like, but I certainly wasn't going to explore this with some straight male physician. The first part of my journey was to find a lesbian, a lesbian-friendly female or a gay male medical provider—in that order!

I knew this wouldn't be easy. Many lesbian-feminists think plastic surgery is politically incorrect, so I didn't trust calling a lesbian health service for referrals. Then I remembered having seen an ad for a lesbian plastic surgeon in a gay publication in New York and having met the surgeon at a political function. I called her office, asked the receptionist if the doctor performed breast reductions and quickly hung up after she said, "Of course." I hung up because there were still many more barriers to overcome before I could get up the nerve to schedule an appointment. I now had to start looking at those barriers.

On Being Working Class

Every Christmas Eve my paternal grandmother would have her five children and their kids over to her home for dinner and presents. My aunts and uncles were in a slightly better financial bracket than my father and had much smaller families than ours. So every year for Christmas Eve they would pool their money to buy my grandmother something *big*, like new living room furniture or a dining room set or a washer/dryer. But with seven kids and scores of grandkids, my father's trucker salary could never stretch (even with my mom's waitress tips) to join this annual show of devotion. And I wondered as a little kid, did we love Grandma less because we were poor? Grandma would make a big deal about the wall cross we made of burnt match sticks or the ashtray of Play-Doh—as if it meant more to her than the furniture she had just gotten. But the shame of not being part of the joint gift-giving is one of the few memories I have of those evenings, another being telling my aunt I wanted a truck and not the doll she had given me!

I also noticed that as soon as we arrived at Grandma's an aunt would get up from her chair and quickly move to pick up the candy dishes, move the birdcage to another room and begin setting the table for dinner. I was young, but still I knew: We were not entirely wanted; we were a little feared. We were not only poor, we were uneducated, uncontrollable and wild.

In the lesbian movement, we rarely discuss class in any way other than as a synonym for poverty. Certainly someone like myself, with a master's degree and income from a professional job, is not struggling as I did growing up. But my working-classness, the class system I was raised in, is the molasses of insecurities I struggle through every day of my life. It does not change with a quick glance at my checkbook balance. I am, in part, how I was raised. And I was raised to believe that God would determine if you went to heaven or hell, that the Teamsters Union was as corrupt as the government, that the Chicago Cubs would someday win the World Series, that poor white was better than poor black, and not to expect much more than that out of life. Like my four sisters, I began training to be a waitress very early in life. I would sit in restaurants with my mother as she provided a running critique of the waitresses: Were they wiping the tables so the crumbs didn't fall on the floor? Were they bringing out food and taking back empty dishes (never on the floor empty-handed)? Did they understand the subtle clues that meant a customer was ready for a coffee refill? I was raised to be a waitress. Class does not allow poor people to believe in options.

I began to understand that during my first major relationship with a middle-class woman. I learned that class is about more than how much money you have; it is about socialization, about how you feel about yourself and how you interact with the world around you. Throughout our five-year relationship my partner consistently won the monthly "can" race. Every month we put the receipts from purchases for household items and food into a coffee can and at the end of the month added up each person's receipts to figure out who owed what to whom. I always owed my partner money. This seemed odd because we both made about the same amount of money each month and lived paycheck to paycheck. And then I realized that she didn't actually spend more on household expenses, but she always remembered to bring home the receipts—even for a gallon of milk! I realized then that it's not about money. It's about whether you were raised to believe you owed or were owed. These differences mean something in a relationship and in society, because ultimately class is about value—the value of each human being.

I still react when someone shifts away from me when I enter a room or when I overhear a subtle patronizing comment. I always wonder—is it because they know I don't belong? I fight these demons when I stand to give a speech or chair a meeting or go to a medical appointment. I can't shake the feeling that— no matter how many advanced degrees I get, no matter how well known I become, no matter what kind of fancy title or job I hold, no matter how many speeches I give—I am an impostor. There is a time clock in some greasy spoon somewhere outside of Chicago waiting for me to punch in. Every day I fight for the right to exist in the world as who I am, not who I was raised to be.

There are few places working-class people are made to fight more for their right to exist than in health care interactions. If you don't have health insurance, you enter the dehumanizing, over-crowded and underfunded public and community clinic system: Take a number, take a seat and take your chances. If you are lucky enough to have health insurance, you can choose a private doctor (if you can afford the deductible and co-payments), and if you can convince yourself that you deserve to be there, you can call for an appointment. But the molasses thickens: When I call the medical office, will I know what to ask? When I come in for an appointment, will the medical staff shift away from me? Will I be wearing the right clothes? Will I be laughed at? Will the staff think I can't afford the services? Even more importantly, can I afford the service?

Luckily, as I considered this surgery, I still had good health insurance from a previous job. I called the benefits office at the insurance company and received the typically unhelpful and non-committal response, "We don't pre-approve procedures. Have the surgery, if we believe it was medically necessary, we'll cover it—if not, we won't." My partner and I concluded, as our parents had and their parents before them, "Let's do it—we'll figure out how to pay for it later." And then it took me six months of thinning the rest of the molasses: to decide that I can do this, that I have the right to this, that I won't feel foolish. Only then could I gather the nerve to call for an appointment to see the lesbian plastic surgeon . . . whom I hoped I could afford.

On Being Butch

What a tomboy I was growing up! The great thing about having sisters was that I became less of a disappointment because they were eager to play the female roles within the family. The bad thing was, that with such close comparisons, my version of female began to look stranger and stranger every year. I think for a while my family believed I had either come from another planet or was at least switched at birth. I loved trucks, especially my father's real ones; I hated dolls, dresses, boys (except to play sports with), anything girly at all—yuck, yuck, yuck! I was the determined tomboy who snuck out of the house with pants under her dress, the legs rolled up, until safely out of her mother's sight. I hated the gender rules, rules like girls washed the dishes and boys took out the trash. And I can still remember how awful I felt when I wanted to play baseball with the neighborhood boys in the field next to our house and they wouldn't let me because I was a girl. That stung. I was being thrown off my own land because of something I couldn't control—simply because I was born a girl.

It wasn't a phase. I grew up to be the athletic teenager my family secretly disdained. High school was a blur of one sport after another, one injury after another. My gym teachers, the closest I could find to "my people," became my de facto guardians. I went to them for everything, and they took me in, but we never spoke of their "living arrangements" with other female gym teachers or of the possibility that I might be gay too. It was as if I had entered a home for the gay deaf—we never spoke aloud what was all around us. The gymnasium became my refuge. But it wasn't just the fun of athletics and competition; it was that the gender rules could be changed just a little. We could be aggressive and sweaty and dirty and yell and fight and openly plot out our battles. We didn't talk about boys, except to point out that the boys' teams still got better practice times and better equipment than we did. It was the only place in my life where the rules of who I was as a girl were relaxed. For just that little space of time.

Everywhere else there were lessons that I was not normal, that I was not girl enough. In line at the grocery store, my very short hair, jeans and a flannel shirt prompted the child behind me to ask, "Mommy, is that person a boy or a girl?" At times like that I would remember that I lived in a world where the answer to that question is still very important. Everything is fixed at birth. My anatomy dictates how I dress, what kind of jobs I'm interested in and who I date. It demands that I be feminine above all else. Throughout that period I would catch brief glimpses of my reflection and see myself as normal, as if the fun house mirrors were temporarily straightened. But the constant reminders of my being a gender outlaw were never far away and were very tiring.

And then I came out as a lesbian and began to meet others who came from the same planet I did. A community of women who did not (as far as I knew at the time) date boys, who ignored the gender rules and who spoke of a gender freedom that seemed like nirvana. It hurt even more, then, when shortly after the thrill of finding out I was a lesbian, I realized that while there wasn't a membership fee to be a part of this community of women, there was a dress code. The gender freedom discussed was really the freedom of androgyny. Too feminine meant you really weren't a lesbian—you hadn't disavowed the traditional version of female and probably harbored secret heterosexual fantasies. But too butch was bad for our media image—people might think we wanted to be men. Besides, I was told, butch/femme was a fad. Maybe older lesbians had pretended to be either butch or femme—because they had to, or because they didn't know any better. But it was not what a true, self-evolved, in-tune-with-her-inner-child's-third-chakra kind of lesbian did.

I had been left to fend for myself and my own gender identity throughout my life, and now I had to do the same thing in my own community. Butch was and still is reviled in the majority lesbian culture—just witness the significant butch-bashing in the letters section of the October 1995 issue of *Out* magazine. Ignoring that we are often painted with the same disdaining brush, two "lipstick lesbians" treated us "dykes" to a clear thrashing and outlandish generalizations: "man hating . . . in half-assed jobs . . . willing to be in physical altercations . . . hard-core . . . over forty."

That is not the butch I am, nor is it the butches I know. I love women; I love to hold open doors, pay for dinner, put my hand in the small of a woman's back and say what my dad used to say: "I'll take care of it," and "We'll be just fine." I hear my voice deeper and more powerful and I imagine I could get into a physical altercation, but only if I had to. Sure, I've been a short-order cook, I trained as a car mechanic and a gym teacher and I have the biggest toolbox on my block. I also have a master's degree and a professional job. I see myself as equal parts Arnold Schwarzenegger, James Dean and William Powell (minus the martinis). I sing the songs that men sing about the women they love—songs about picking my honey up for a date, bringing her home late and working double shifts to buy her all she needs and most of what she wants. I think of myself as charming and heroic and gallant. I am the perfect gentleman. I am not role-playing; this is who I am. So when did these become negative traits in a person's character?

When I came out I was told that lesbian meant sameness—that a woman makes love to a woman the way she would want to be made love to. We were all the same. Wimmin loving wimmin. I didn't know that I was part of a rich history and culture of women who desired women who were different from themselves. I didn't know that part of my erotic nature was the difference, the pull of opposites within the gender female.

If there were a quilt of my life, the one common thread would be my struggle with gender identity, my constant disharmony with the polar opposites of femininity and masculinity—attributes separately ascribed to the genders of female and male. Throughout this country, every single day, millions of women fill out medical intake forms and do something that I have trouble doing—they unquestioningly answer the question that asks if their gender is male or female. My anatomy is certainly female. But does that tell you how I see myself, how I carry myself in the world, what is important to me? Does it tell you how to treat me in a medical office? Does my being female tell you who I partner with? Who I am attracted to? Or what kind of sex I have? Does it tell you how I see my body or how I want my body to be seen by others?

Clarifying My Gender Identity

When I told a friend, a fellow butch, that I was going to have breast reduction surgery and that I was unsure what size I wanted my new breasts to be, she asked me a question that sliced through my idea of self surer than any scalpel might have: "Are you sure you want breasts? Maybe what you want is a chest." I had always thought that I just wanted smaller breasts, but this question compelled me to consider more thoroughly how I perceived my own gender identity. There is nothing like an option to open up the whole discussion.

The prospective surgery gave me an opportunity to answer my own questions: What does it mean that I call myself a butch, and how is being a female-butch different from being a female-to-male (FTM) transsexual? If I was butch, did that mean I really wanted to be a man? Was I really moving toward a sex-change operation? But if I had the breast reduction and allowed the surgeon to construct breasts, did that mean I wanted to be a girl and wasn't really a butch? How could I begin thinking about gender when gender is discussed as a binary code—either male or female? Like a toggle switch that is either off or on.

It is this formulation that I confronted as I considered my breast reduction. I believed I had to examine the "myths" of the links between biology, gender role, gender identity, sexual identity and sexual role so that I could answer my own questions as removed from societal conditioning as I could manage. I have little doubt the gender spectrum of female, which includes the masculine traits of butchness, has at one end female-to-male transsexuals. But whereas butchness is sometimes tolerated by the lesbian community, transgendered individuals are universally shunned and often excluded from the community by regulations such as the "women born women" rule of admission at the Michigan Womyn's Music Festival and the National Lesbian Conference. I would classify this exclusionary politic as the "traitor and the Trojan horse" syndrome: Women "passing" as men and men hiding in sheeps' clothing are not to be trusted.

The understanding of gender as being fluid or mutable is a stretch for most people, but an idea I began to give more and more weight to. In the October 1995 issue of *Out*, Donna Minkowitz reported on a young girl who lived as a boy and dated girls as a boy. Donna writes about Sean: "[He] doesn't use the words *transsexual* or *transgendered*. Instead his vocabulary is remarkably fluid. At one point, he offhandedly refers to himself as 'gay,' at other times as 'a girl'—but he asks people to identify him with male pronouns."[1] Another butch friend of mine tells the story of a young niece who asked her if she was a boy or a girl. She responded by saying "both." And both is how I often feel. I have both female and male traits: a female anatomy and a butch identity. This concept of fluidity, while controversial in the face of the rigid gender codes of our society, is comforting and authentic to me.

While transgenderism is not an idea I had previously given a great deal of thought to, I felt it was important for me to come to some resolution about it. Given that the surgery was an opportunity I would not ever have again, I wanted to give full consideration to whether the "male" part of my butchness wanted greater expression. I really had to consider whether I would rather have a double mastectomy (and possibly other FTM medical procedures) or not.

I thought about my sense of queerness and realized that it would in part be altered with a sex change operation; if I built my body as a masculine male and retained my sexual desire for feminine women, I would become, culturally at least, heterosexual.

In fact, sex change operations are often approved only if the individual claims he or she is correcting *for* heterosexuality. But this is not how I saw myself. Although my queerness had been a source of great anguish when I was a child, it had become an identity that I cherished as an adult.

I also thought about community. And, quite frankly, after living through childhood as an alien, I realized that even if I believed I would be personally happier as a male, I was not willing to lose or have to fight for (any more than I already do as a working-class butch) a lesbian community that would surely shun me. I enjoy being queer, and the lesbian community is my home. I would not change either.

Butch Breasts!

I was extremely lucky to find a surgeon who was comfortable in the language of butch-femme and transgender issues although we never spoke of my FTM deliberation. She put me at ease in our first visit, discussing relevant literature and acknowledging my partner as a well-known butch-femme advocate. We discussed my desired breast size—small, but not too small—sports bra size. She said I would be able to go without a bra in the summer and not bounce. I felt she acknowledged my butchness throughout the process, which helped to allay most of my fears. Still, I never came right out and said to her that I wanted small, tight, powerful breasts—butch breasts. Because I was still not completely at ease with my identity, there was a safety in the way we discussed butchness as being theory or interesting literature; we never discussed my butchness in relation to how I saw my breasts. I was still terrified, then, that I would go through this major surgery and wake up with cleavage!

I was transformed and thrilled with the results. So thrilled that about a month after the operation I sent my surgeon a Chicago Cubs cap and this note:

When I was a child, a neighbor lady we called Aunt Kay used to cut our hair. One day, when I was probably around eight years old, I went to get my hair cut with my Chicago Cubs cap on. I wanted Aunt Kay to cut my hair around the cap. I couldn't verbalize that I didn't want a "girl" haircut—I was a tomboy and wanted a cut that would look good with my cap on. Well, I didn't bring a tie in to show you how I wanted it to hang over my new breasts (although I thought about it), but you understood anyway. Thanks for my new "butch" breasts and for a great cut!

Implications for Health Providers

It is difficult for providers to consider the complexity of each of their patients, especially when providers have so little time with them. But the effort put into fully understanding the patient's needs and concerns is an essential component to the health care interaction. In the example of breast reduction (or enhancement) surgery a provider could engage the woman in a discussion about her gender perceptions—"What does being female mean to you? What do your breasts mean to you?"—opening the way for a greater discussion of the complexity of her decision.

Many health providers, including those currently serving lesbian clients, don't think about the complexity of gender and how it affects medical interactions and decisions. For example, medical procedures like Pap smears and mammograms may be uncomfortable for many butch women. Medical providers should discuss gender and sexual identity and gender and sexual roles in ways that leave open the possibility of fluidity. Providers who seek to change their rigid concepts of "heterosexual consistency" and who work to reject myths about homosexuality will find patients who are more open about their lives, more willing to be partners in their own health care, more interested in maintaining provider loyalty and more apt to refer new patients.

We must begin discussing gender, body image, gender identity and sexual orientation as the complex and interrelated issues
they are, within both the lesbian community and the medical
profession.

Speaking Out

The decision to be open not only about my breast reduction but
about the preliminary process of clarifying my gender identity was
not easy. The lesbian community is often very critical of issues
like cosmetic surgery and very judgmental about butchness. It is
also very complicated, as a professional, to discuss a personal
journey. Those who do may be viewed as less objective—less professional. But I have decided to write and speak about my experience for two reasons. First, I believe more women would
consider breast reduction as an option if they knew about it. I
know that I am not alone: In a recent issue of *The Advocate,* a
national gay and lesbian magazine, 34 percent of 2,525 lesbians
responding to a survey indicated they wished their breasts were
smaller.[2]

Second, I want to encourage lesbian health activists to discuss
gender identity when training health providers and advocating for
lesbian health concerns. Many lesbian and gay health educators
attempt to correct the heterosexual assumption of medical providers by simply stating that men and women can be either heterosexual, homosexual or bisexual; except for a little feminist
revision of gender and sexual roles, they leave the remaining assumptions and stereotypes alone. In doing that, they perpetuate
a societal myth about gender and gender identity that places
many of us outside of "normal." By not acknowledging and not
claiming fey men and butch women as a part of the gay and lesbian movement, we lie to the very people we are asking acceptance from—we deceive at the very time we should enlighten. We

need to learn that trying to hide parts of our community will come back to haunt us: As many families have had to discover, you can hide crazy Uncle Harry when the minister visits, but sooner or later dinner's served and Harry has got to eat.

It's 2:30 and My Neck Doesn't Hurt . . .

It has been several years since my surgery. The constant neckache I had before the surgery is gone. I can hardly remember what I looked like then, yet I remember vividly what I felt like. I often touch my breasts as I walk around my house, something I never used to do. The other day, I wore a new tie and rather than being constantly aware of its bulge over my chest, I almost forgot I had it on. I no longer feel like a freak. Now, I'm just a butch.

Notes

1. Donna Minkowitz, "On Trial: Gay? Straight? Boy? Girl? Sex? Rape?" *Out* (October 1995) 99–140.

2. Janet Lever, Ph.D., "Lesbian Sex Survey," *The Advocate* (August 22, 1995) 23–30. This survey is a convenience sample and is therefore not scientifically valid to describe anyone other than those who filled it out. Additionally, 86 percent of the respondents were white. I am including this information simply to point out that significant numbers of women who responded felt that their breasts were too large.

JANE A. PETRO, M.D.

Breast Surgery, the Surgeon's Perspective

I love to do breast surgery. There is nothing quite like it in the variety of procedures available to achieve a desired goal and in the variety of goals the patients bring to their surgeon. Breast surgery embodies a confluence of needs, desires and intentions that make each encounter unique, each procedure distinct and each result, we hope, satisfactory for all involved. Add to it that the breast is a politicized organ and an object of high emotions, and we have challenges from more than just the intellectual and objective perspectives usually associated with surgery and medicine.

To best tell the story of what breast surgery and, specifically, breast reduction surgery means to me, I also need to tell the story of how I came to be a plastic surgeon. It is a cautionary tale, intended to share how I became a surgeon and overcame my training. Training is patient care oriented; that is, the surgeon-in-training is busy doing things that provide care to hospitalized patients, but is not really taking "care" of the patients; she is taking care of the needs of the hospital and the attending physicians in regard to the patients. It is only later that doctors-in-training learn that when we listen, our patients can teach us everything. A resident does not learn to listen, only to do. So my first lesson was to listen and learn from the patients. This is the core of the meaning of medical practice: to listen and to learn while doing. To find out the expectations and hopes of the patients and, if possible, meet those wishes, fulfill their needs. But this happens later in the process of medical education, if at all.

Medical school (four long years of information overload) produces such complete incompetence that three to nine additional years of re-education are required to turn out a working physician. The initial education does not linger over meaning or the subtle context of values, nor does it recognize more than two genders or more than one kind of sexual relationship (heterosexual). Some schools do have curricula that teach "sexuality" and may address deviations from the heterosexual norm, but these courses—brief, elective or part of some larger issues—are not integrated with the general education. Issues of sexuality are rarely presented in a clinical context. In general, there is no time in the curriculum for more than dry "fact." Even during the regurgitation of these facts, the faculty often note how facts change. They emphasize how the understanding of a biological phenomenon changes, at times slowly, as an evolution of ideas, or at other times dramatically, as the impact of some radical new concept overtakes dogma. Thus we are taught to believe in facts, but not to trust them.

The breast, we learned during our first year, is a modified sweat gland. (Some of my male classmates cried at that thought.) The breast was not taught as a sexual object, but the undercurrent surrounding it—my classmates crying at the thought of a sweat gland, a textbook of anatomy using pinups of women to show surface anatomy, "dirty jokes" shared between male faculty and students, and the absence of education on sexuality, as if sex were not fit for medicine—mystified and colored the context of the teaching.

On one hand, the breast was an organ, subject to certain ills, on the other, it was taboo. When one of my classmates was about to get married, the physician doing his premarital exam commented to him, "When you get married, you can touch your wife's breasts." As if he had not or could not have before. Yet, this was the 1960s: Though we were all having sex, we were not talking about it. The breast, like sex, remained unconsidered or at least unmentioned in its rich context of meaning.

Residency, the training that follows medical school, differs primarily in that you get paid, rather than having to pay tuition. You get to practice medicine on the poor, on prisoners and on clinic patients. If you are liked or trusted, you get to practice on the private patients of your attendings, the "real" doctors who are there to teach and guide you. Supervision of residents varies from nonexistent to intense, depending on circumstance and level of competency. In recent years legislation mandating increased supervision has changed the structure of residency but not its most essential elements, the practice of medicine in a situation where it is really just that, practice. Residency is still not a time of contemplation. Meaning, values, the subtleties of action are not discussed, and there is not time for much more than technical competency. And so, the breast, no less than everything else, remained an anatomic structure to me, one to be enlarged, reduced, examined for disease, removed, recreated and admired when it met expectations, but rarely considered in its relationship to its owner, the patient. Because of sexual prudery, fatigue, inhibition, deep personal restraint or whatever, as a resident, I thought little about the breast except in a medical context.

As a chief resident, months, then weeks, away from being finished with the first stage of my training, general surgery, I had a wonderful time. In charge of all the junior residents, the chief is given a lot of responsibility, and, after four years of supervision, the freedom to operate nearly independently. At that time, in the mid-seventies, being a woman surgeon was still a relative rarity. I was the second female to complete the training in my program and had not had what I considered a hard time. Most of the male surgeons had been very nice, those who had not were not very influential, and the nurses had been my allies and support group.

At that time, a controversy regarding the best treatment for breast cancer was emerging. The traditional Halsteadian radical mastectomy, used for all stages of breast cancer for the previous fifty years, was being challenged by a few individuals who claimed that less radical surgery (a simple mastectomy in which the breast tissue was removed but not all the overlying skin or the underlying muscle) would be as effective as the radical procedure. Later they argued similarly for lumpectomy.

Unlike most of my colleagues, I never had liked the radical mastectomy, although I had not given any thought as to why not. The newer procedure, which included less surgical mutilation, seemed like a more desirable alternative. Later, in thinking about it, I could not help but recall the extreme reluctance with which surgeons recommended orchiectomy (the removal of testicles) as a treatment for metastatic prostate cancer, even as they were gladly and regularly amputating breasts for cancer and doing hysterectomy and oophorectomy (removal of the ovaries) to prevent cancer on their female patients. I even recall conversations that noted how little the breast, the uterus and the ovaries meant to their patients. Yet, in talking to the patients I met, that seemed not to be true. Women neglected lumps in their breasts for years, fearing cancer and mastectomy. And one young woman, after having her uterus and ovaries removed (almost casually, as part of her treatment for an ectopic pregnancy), was abandoned by her husband even before she got out of the recovery room, as if she were a cow that had lost its value. That patient, and her husband, had valued those organs.

When a nurse with whom I had become friends came to me

with a breast lump, I described to her the treatment options. She asked me to do a modified mastectomy, removing the breast and lymph nodes, but not the muscle, if the biopsy proved to be positive. I scheduled and did the procedure. On the day of surgery, a visiting professor, a surgeon from Yale, happened to glance in the room, noting a woman surgeon, a woman anesthesiologist and, of course, all women nurses, operating on this woman patient. He subsequently mentioned that the vision had inspired him to write an essay. Later, when I read the published essay, surprisingly it was not about surgery, or about women caring for women, but about Amazonian warriors mutilating themselves to more effectively use their bows and arrows to wage war on men. It was the first glimpse I had of how powerfully we (women) could threaten men.

Before that insight, though, something even more telling had occurred. When one of my attendings heard about the procedure, he brought charges of unethical conduct against me, accusing me of doing an inappropriate surgical procedure (simple instead of radical mastectomy) and of operating on an insured patient (we were supposed to care only for the uninsured, although that was not a written policy). It was his stated intention to use this episode to block my graduation, to prevent me from becoming certified and, therefore, to prevent me from both practicing as a general surgeon and continuing my training in plastic surgery. My privileges were suspended, and a hearing was held. It was a very scary time for me. After four years of work, I was afraid I would have to start all over again in a different field, assuming that anyone else would offer me a job.

Years before, during my internship, I had applied to obstetrics and gynecology for training and had been turned down by four programs, all citing nonacademic reasons: "We don't have a call room (sleeping quarters) for women," "We already have a woman (one out of eighteen)" or "We tried a woman once, and it didn't work out"—and the worst, "You would be disruptive" (I was known to be an abortion rights activist, and I belonged to NOW). Although surgery had initially been an alternative choice to obstetrics and gynecology, I was certain now it was what I wanted to do and, in retrospect, was happy I had not gotten into ob-gyn. The hearing was held, and fortunately both the patient and several colleagues testified on my behalf and the suspension was overturned. I was allowed to finish training in general surgery.

Following that year, I went into private practice in Gettysburg, Pennsylvania, with two wonderful men who were looking for temporary help so they could take a little time off. I needed work to fill in a gap before starting plastic surgery, and it was a perfect opportunity. Any questions I had about whether women could survive in surgery were answered by that experience. Except for the mayor, who didn't want a woman fixing his hernia, I heard of no other patients who balked at having a female surgeon. There may have been others, but I was busy, happy and, best of all, having fun.

At the time, it was common practice for women coming in for breast cancer diagnosis to have the biopsy done under general anesthesia; if the biopsy report indicated cancer was present, the mastectomy was done while the patient was still under anesthesia. (Biopsy reports could be given while the patient was still in surgery if the tissue was sectioned fresh, frozen and examined immediately, before being fully processed.) That seemed unusually cruel to me; a professor of pathology of mine who had also objected to this practice, referred to it as the surgeon's "Pavlovian response." He had a practice of making the surgeons wait for the final pathology report which generally came forty-eight hours later. That extra time allowed the patient to have a rational discussion of treatment with the surgeon. Was the cancer already metastasized? Was a mastectomy necessary? And, with philosophy changing, it gave the patient an opportunity to consider alternatives—radical versus modified mastectomy, lumpectomy and so on. I did something a bit different. I started doing some of the biopsies under local, rather than general, anesthesia and discussing treatment options with the patients in the operating room when the frozen section report came back.

When I re-entered training, as a plastic surgery resident, my first rotation assignment was in Erie, Pennsylvania, my hometown. The six months I spent there were particularly hard because one of the attendings wanted to make me quit. It never occurred to me that he would succeed, but the isolation and the stress gave me the chance to think about what I was doing and why. One of the most obvious things I saw was how badly women were being treated, not just myself, but also the patients. Women's breasts were being amputated, their uteri and ovaries were being yanked out, and no one was looking at what effect those acts had on the women themselves. Women were seen as objects to be cared for, without respect and without consideration for the emotional consequences. Male surgeons trivialized female concerns over castration ("you can't tell to look") and breast mutilation ("we are saving your life") and refused to consider the possibility that such paternalistic actions were not only unethical, but also irrational and not based on scientific objectivity. It began to be clear to me that these men were acting out their own psychopathology in the guise of medicine and that their power and control gave them autonomy while denying autonomy to their patients. I knew this was not something I was going to be able to change or control, except within my own practice through conversations with willing listeners, and by participating in medicine as an activist while encouraging my colleagues (nurses more often than doctors) and patients to do the same.

Over the years I practiced plastic surgery thinking about these issues, lecturing, learning and occasionally writing, but it was not until about the fifteenth year of my practice that the real meaning, the subtlety involved in breast surgery, became most obvious to me. The breast is the primary female sex characteristic. Breast development precedes the onset of menses and is a source of pleasure, and embarrassment, from preadolescence on. Breasts that are too large or too small may be objects of ridicule, emblems of sexuality and a focal point, both for boys and for girls. In adolescence about 10 percent of boys have breast development that is disturbing enough to seek medical advice. In most cases this is transitory and resolves within the first year of puberty. Occasionally a surgical referral is made, and, if the condition doesn't resolve, surgical correction may be done. That a boy is upset about breast development is not surprising, not considered pathological and is a covered benefit of most insurance policies. It never occurred to me, at the time of my own pubescence or until recently, that this normal body evolution could cause the same type of trauma in girls. Encounters with several patients illuminated these realities, enriching my views on the breast and on the process of transformations that breast surgery—whether enlargement, reduction or recreation—encompasses.

Marj Plumb's comments in her essay about her own breast reduction and conversations I have had with other women, "butch" and otherwise, make clear what should have been obvious all along: The emergence of breasts for some adolescent girls can be a betrayal of the body, a transformation that may be unwelcome, that inhibits "normal" activity, and, for butch women, a transformation that has the same deep emotional consequences as breast development does in male adolescents. Butch women (self-identified or not) coming to a physician to have their breasts reduced have different goals than do women with aesthetic concerns over breast size, whether large or small. Their desire reflects an urge to reduce not just the breast, but the femininity that the breast represents—to restore their "bra-free," topless, prepubertal body image. A reduction from a D to a C cup might be perceived as an unsatisfactory result by such a patient. Unless the physician has explored the patient's wishes in the matter, it would be difficult to guess that obliteration, not just reduction, might be the patient's real goal. This is a goal that needs to be actively sought, that cannot be anticipated. The patient must be extremely comfortable with her doctor to express the wish for a reduction to almost nothing. And the physician must be prepared for that possibility, open to the suggestion and willing to listen and to elicit the patient's true wishes.

In the novel *Stone Butch Blues,* the narrator describes her trip to the plastic surgeon in terms of a nightmare passage, the desire for total mastectomy making the procedure a covert and hostile encounter with medicine. Her breasts are amputated, and then she is kicked out of the hospital without even a prescription for painkillers. This experience was real, a cash transaction that took place without any caring or concern passing between the doctor and the patient. For the first time I realized the extent to which people will accept degradation to achieve their ideal image. But it embarrassed and humiliated me to think that any of my colleagues would subject their patients to such an experience. This reading made it possible for me to actively seek the patient's ultimate desire—to ask the question, "How small do you want to be?" and include a regression, "C, B or A?" allowing the patient the freedom to pick the extent of their reduction without fearing a judgmental comment or refusal if that desire amounted to a near total reduction of the breast.

The perception of the breast is different for different patients and not limited to butch/femme conceptions. For some, a large breast reduction may also be perceived as freedom from an excessively feminine ideal. As one patient recently told me, "I am having them reduced because I am ready to come out. Because I have large breasts, men automatically think of me as a heterosexual woman. I am comfortable with myself now. I don't need my breasts to hide behind anymore." This woman, though not butch, is reducing her breasts to claim her lesbian identity, desiring to maintain her breasts, but in a form that will permit comfort and a less matronly appearance.

In another variation of this process, I saw a patient years ago, an elderly woman who was dressed in black, used canes and moved with difficulty. When asked why she had waited until age eighty to seek consultation for her reduction, she said, "My husband, the bastard, wouldn't let me do it. I buried him this morning." When she left the hospital, it was without canes. Reduction for her was a passage to freedom, a separation from a condition that was not only burdensome, but a handicap as well.

In another example, a patient came in for reduction to relieve the shoulder and back pain attributed to her very large breasts. The major stipulation she put on the procedure, other than the reduction to a size C cup from her DDD status was that nipple sensation be preserved. As she was being discharged twenty-four hours after the surgery, she wondered whether it would be all right to have sex immediately. For this patient, the stipulation, "If it hurts, don't do it," provided the permission she needed. Her reduction, done for physical comfort was not associated with the symbolic gender and sexual identity experienced by other patients. Her breasts were an essential component of her sexual response.

Breast reduction is sought for many reasons, to reclaim gender identity, to proclaim sexual identity, to enhance well-being, to feel better about the body, to be able to wear different clothes or to be able to "go without a bra," each choice an individual one. Some patients willingly risk nipple loss, loss of sensation and loss of the ability to lactate in order to feel better. One of the common themes described by all large-breasted patients seeking reduction, regardless of sexual or gender identity, is the desire to escape the ridicule large breasts attract. Many men seeing a large-breasted woman, somehow feel free to acknowledge, shout, whistle or in some other way harass the woman as if the breasts were being carried, willingly proffered, for their enjoyment and comment. This type of sexual harassment can be escaped by dressing in ways that disguise the breasts, by avoiding public appearances, by ignoring the harasser or through surgical reduction. This last, while reducing the "target" of the harassment, does not eliminate, of course, the misconduct of others, but it does strengthen the targeted individual, freeing her from the "burden" of large breasts. This is not my interpretation, but the related experience of my patients.

For lesbians, these experiences are perhaps clearer, the harassment more readily interpreted as such. I do not believe, however, that the breast is less important or the decision for surgery, whether elective reduction or treatment for cancer, is less intense and difficult for lesbians, though the breast, in lesbian consciousness, is less loaded with the sexual connotations it carries for heterosexual women, is less objectified in lesbian romantic consciousness and less "shameful" in lesbian experience (witness the topless nudity at lesbian/feminist gatherings) and is used more often as a declaration of "woman" and less of sexual object.

Many of these thoughts are a direct outgrowth of the experiences I had during the past year caring for Marj, and for the others whose stories I related here. Marj, with her direct, incredible insight and lesbian experience provided me with a wonderful sounding board for these ideas and was a stimulus to the reflections that culminated in this essay. Being a lesbian who is a surgeon has not to my knowledge affected my professional actions. I don't think I practice medicine in such a different way from my female colleagues. But I hope that my gay consciousness has made me a more sensitive physician to all my gay patients. I know that the experience of being a gay person in a relentlessly heterosexual profession has made me more alert to and aware of the pain discrimination carries. And of course, the enriching conversations I have been privileged to have with my patients, gay and straight, have shaped my thinking about the practice of medicine.

Breast reduction carries a rich variety of interpretations, emotional associations and personal, physical, gender-related, sexual and social goals. As such, it becomes a procedure rife with meaning that must be examined. The patient's sexual identity, body goals and erotic goals all need to be confronted, considered and expressed to achieve what the patient, not what the doctor, wants. This makes breast reduction surgery one of the most interesting and challenging procedures in plastic surgery—one that has given me the most pleasure and provided the most satisfied patients of my career.

VAL ULSTAD, M.D.

The Next Step

I'm not exactly in the closet, but I have resisted becoming the poster child for the gay and lesbian medical student group. I love to teach and am usually very comfortable in the classroom, in front of a crowd. But right now, I'm very nervous.

The gay and lesbian medical student group has been very visible. The members have organized a symposium to raise awareness about lesbian and gay health, and they want me to kick it off. I direct the cardiovascular pathophysiology course in the medical school. The med students all take my class in the fall of their second year. They understand cardiology so they like cardiology . . . because they like cardiology, they tend to like me. I am one of the few female course directors in the medical school. I was a student in this same lecture hall sixteen years ago. I remember those days. My students tell me they trust me because I seem to remember what it is like to be a med student.

The students are, naturally, curious about their teachers. They have shown up today for my lecture—"What Are Lesbian Health Issues?"—because they are bright young student physicians who genuinely want to know how to be good health care providers, but they are also curious about me. As I start my lecture, I say, "If there are any of you who do not know—I am a lesbian." I hear the relief in their collective laugh . . . nobody leaves the room. I did not want to distance myself from the subject. My heart is still pounding.

I remind the students that lesbians have been women's health activists throughout history. Lesbian health issues are women's health issues. Lesbians have to contend with sexism as well as homophobia. I define homophobia. How will a lesbian get her health concerns addressed if she fears her health care provider? If a person hates herself because she is a lesbian, will she promote her own health and make wise choices? I proceed to give my lecture on the major health issues facing women today and point out how each issue poses a bigger potential threat to the lesbian patient. Being afraid to ask questions, being afraid to tell the truth, feeling bad that you didn't tell the truth, fearing rejection by your health care provider or having no access to preventative health care . . . these are lesbian health issues.

I finish the formal part of my lecture by sharing the shocking statistics released by the Gay and Lesbian Medical Association in "Anti-Gay Discrimination in Medicine: Results of a National Survey of Lesbian, Gay and Bisexual Physicians."[1] Sixty-seven percent of the 711 physicians and medical students who returned their surveys knew of instances where substandard medical care had been given to a patient based on his or her sexual orientation. My message is that discrimination happens frequently and that it is unethical and immoral. I am quite worked up at this point but decide that this is how I should seize this teachable moment. They are all still listening.

I'm feeling braver now, so I open the lecture up for questions. What will they ask me? Will they ask how lesbians have sex?

Instead, to my relief, they ask how to tell if someone is gay. I tell them about "gaydar." I say that even straight people can develop gaydar, but that the most reasonable thing is not to assume that everyone is straight! Consider the possibility that your patient may be a lesbian. Ask your patients: Who is important in your life? Are you sexually active? Is birth control an issue for you? Do you have sex with women, men or both? Be aware of "friends" or "roommates," and explore whether these may be significant others. A "partner" is not usually a business partner. Don't assume two women are sisters. Don't ask a female patient what her husband does. If you use questionnaires to gather intake information, use questions that are inclusive, and then read them before seeing the patient. I also remind the students that patients may lie to them—intentionally and unintentionally. Just by asking nondiscriminating questions, a health care provider may actually help someone come out, thus truly having a positive impact on the patient's health.

Resources for Health Care Providers

Gay and Lesbian Medical Association
459 Fulton Street, Suite 107
San Francisco, CA 94102
(415) 255-4547
email: gaylesmed@aol.com
http://www.glma.org
Physicians' organization: provides referrals for physicians and patients; holds two conferences a year—a lesbian-specific conference and a lesbian, gay, bisexual and trangendered conference; publishes a directory of gay and lesbian physicians.

Lavender Lamps
208 West 13th Street
New York, NY 10011
(212) 933-1158
Nurses' organization.

Lesbian, Gay, Bisexual and Transgendered People in Medicine
c/o AMSA
1890 Preston White Drive
Reston, VA 22091
(703) 620-6600
Medical students' organization.

National Lesbian and Gay Health Association
P.O. Box 65472
Washington, DC 20035
(202) 939-7880
Sponsors an annual conference on lesbian, gay and bisexual health issues; publishes a directory of lesbian, gay and bisexual health care providers.

They want to know about me. I tell them about my fear in medical school. I tell them about how little I knew about homosexuality then. I tell the story of meeting my partner in medical school, falling head over heels for her and hiding with her in the closet until we were both done with medical training many years later. When we got our first jobs, we came flying out of the closet —with a relief we still feel daily. We do not recommend waiting so long to come out and are amazed the relationship held up in our isolation and fear. They want to know more about our life. We have a wonderful life, and I'm proud to answer their questions. Fortunately, the questions don't get too personal.

My time is nearly up. We have really been discussing how to advocate for the health of our lesbian patients. Homophobia is a health hazard. Discrimination against gay and lesbian patients is common. Fear comes from ignorance. The medical school classroom may be one of the important places to change this. I suggest to the audience that if suddenly every lesbian or gay person in the world turned purple, everyone would realize that they respect or love someone gay or lesbian.

When it is over, they clap. I take a deep breath. I feel good—I was brave, I was not rejected. I guess I am a mentor, although I felt like a scared little kid. It would have made a huge difference for Kathy and me if one of our medical school professors had come out. Today I may have made it a little easier for these young health professionals to accept their gay and lesbian patients. It is so clear that coming out one person at a time is how the world will change. We need to let the world know who we are.

The gay and lesbian student group is thrilled by how many straight students attended. Afterwards they say, "I can't believe that so-and-so was here!" I think, Great—the worst homophobe was here, and I did not know it. I learn again the importance of being out there even when it is scary. I realize that these young physicians will touch thousands of lives. The gay and lesbian medical student group inspires me by their courage and visibility.

The curious straight students inspire me by their real desire to do the right thing.

The world changed that day for me. I am a little braver, a little more resolved to tell the world who I am. I faced my fear, and I am healthier for having done so.

Notes

1. B. Schatz and K. O'Hanlan, "Anti-Gay Discrimination in Medicine: Results of a National Survey of Lesbian, Gay and Bisexual Physicians," (San Francisco: The Gay and Lesbian Medical Association, 1994).

WENDY MORSETH

Waiting

"You should make an appointment with a surgeon for a breast biopsy."

Terror filled my chest, rolled up into my skull and washed through my body like a wave of cement.

Right breast, upper quadrant. There was a change since the last mammogram a year ago. A change, not indicative of cancer necessarily, not with the configuration of cancer, particularly, but something to pay attention to, to biopsy, to investigate surgically.

I buy new shoes, a hat. If I am going out, I want to go out in style. What a strange thing to think about at a time like this. It seems important.

I cradle my right breast in my hands at night. Comfort it, my hands, my soul. I wonder if I would have phantom erogenous feelings if my breast were gone. I cup my breast in my hands re-cording memory.

I think of my body becoming utilitarian.

Age? Forty-six.

Are you pregnant? No.

What form of birth control do you use? None, I'm a lesbian. That does not make my breast expendable, like tonsils.

I wonder if I would rather lose a finger, a few toes. No. I have mourned the loss of a tooth. There are no parts of my body I could lose without grieving. Would it be easier to have my right foot poked, squeezed in a vise, injected with dye, incised? There is no part of me that would not feel assaulted by this treatment. This is medicine.

I think of the possibility of chemotherapy. Losing my energy, my strength, my hair. I wonder which I would have the greater urge to throw off at the end of the day: my panty hose or my wig?

If I am dying, not in some inconceivable distant future, but imminently, just when I was about to . . . just when I was on the verge of . . . Everyone must think that, no matter when it comes. We work so hard at becoming ourselves, and then, suddenly, at one moment, we have become all we will ever be.

If I believed in a consciousness after death, that belief would not give me comfort, nor hope, nor reprieve. It would distract me from being in the present.

When I think I could have breast cancer, that I could lose a breast, or part of one, or that it is already too late even for a mastectomy, that cells have metastasized, I think of what I would regret: caring what others thought, ever once hesitating to abandon myself to pure joy.

The irony is that we are all dying, minute by minute, yet we behave as if we have forever. And when we are truly aware that we don't have forever, we come alive.

I wear my new hat and shoes, spread lots of huckleberry jam on my toast and say "hello" to everyone every day.

JULIE VAN ORDEN

Handling Your Tumor with Knowledge and Humor

I knew the instant I felt the lump that I had cancer. Most people, including my partner at the time and the surgeon who eventually biopsied the lump, felt I was overreacting. The surgeon said, "It will take me forty-five minutes to cut it out and tell you it's benign." Others offered statistics: "Eighty percent of breast lumps are not cancerous—it's probably nothing." So I dragged my heels making medical appointments. (Lesson One: *Never* discount your intuition. Make that appointment.)

Checkup time—finally! The gynecologist decided that my breast lump should be aspirated, which means the doctor pokes a needle into the lump to see if any fluid can be drawn from it. If there's fluid drawn, that usually means the lump is only a benign fluid-filled cyst. "It's solid," says the gynecologist. "It needs to come out, *now,* regardless of what it is." Transfer from kindly gynecologist to nasty surgeon. An episode of painful cutting (not enough anesthesia). A quick delivery of the excised material to the pathology lab (the surgeon decided he didn't like the way it looked). A phone call back to the operating room five to ten minutes later. "It's cancer," the doctor announced. Probably unable to cope with his own stupidity, he left the room abruptly without another word.

How could a doctor have treated a breast lump so lightly when breast cancer is practically epidemic, and then, after finding out it's cancer, deliver the bad news to the patient and waltz out without so much as a consoling word? (Lesson Two: If you, as a patient, *ever* get a reaction like this, get a new doctor—immediately! Ask for a consultation from your new doctor, not a second opinion. Insurance carriers may not pay for second opinions if they deem them not medically necessary.)

After the surgeon left the room (I watched in shock, not believing anyone could be so callous), I didn't know whether I was going to faint or throw up. I sincerely hoped I wouldn't faint and then throw up. I did neither. The scrub nurse (bless her heart as big as Texas) grabbed me and held on tight. I was then in shock at the compassion a nurse could feel for a total stranger. "This is not a death sentence," she said. "You have options." I heard, but I don't think I responded. She also promised to be with me during the ordeal to come. She kept her promise. Although not common practice, she managed to be elected the scrub nurse for the mastectomy and visited me in the hospital. She even called me or visited for the next couple of years to check on my progress. An extraordinary lady!

After the biopsy, I went looking for a new doctor, and I think I have never made a better decision. I found a kind, ruddy-cheeked man with sparkling eyes and an easy smile, who hugged me the minute he met me. (Lesson Three: Never allow yourself to be treated as if you don't matter. There are still surgeons out there who have a heart.)

My anesthesiologist was supposed to work miracles. He looked like Jesus Christ, which couldn't hurt. Never having been in the hospital before, I was scared stiff. He sensed this and told the nurses to give me something to relax me. Relaxed is an understatement. It gave me what I call retrograde amnesia. Apparently I was awake and alert on the way to the operating room. I even joked with my surgical team, saying that I was keeping all my friends abreast of the situation and that double-breasted jackets were no longer a Christmas gift option. They kidded me, saying I was the first "lie-down comic" they had known.

That was all told to me later—I had absolutely no recollection of it. The last thing I did remember was the nurse in the prep room asking me if I would like her to make me an origami pig. I said sure. The operation went very smoothly, and thanks to Jesus, the anesthesiologist, I woke up hungry and with no nausea. And not only was there an origami pig to greet me, but a swan, too. Well, I knew I was special then (those origami animals find a special spot on my Christmas tree every year).

I was surprised that I felt as little discomfort as I did during recovery. I was back playing tennis in nine days. The physical distress was the easy part. I was in the prime of my life, a dedicated athlete in the peak of health, and I was only thirty-four years old. The inevitable question came up: How could this have happened? Why me? I never used drugs, never smoked, drank lightly, wasn't overweight—I'm too young! Sure, I skipped a few meals, probably had too much fat in my diet, ate red meat and drank coffee, but, still, why?

My response to problem solving has always been to learn— read, study, ask questions, read some more—learn, learn, learn. I found I had two minor risk factors: An aunt on my mother's side had died of cancer, and I hadn't had a baby before I was thirty (not at all for that matter). Perhaps a combination of genetics and nature's "use it or lose it" mentality had nailed me.

Support from friends and family was overwhelming. The phone never stopped ringing. I finally gave up answering it and sat there smiling and/or crying while listening to all the wonderful

Early Detection of Breast Cancer

The American Cancer Society recommends that women follow these guidelines for early detection of breast cancer:

▼ Women age 20 and over should conduct a breast self-exam every month.

▼ Women age 20 to 39 should have a doctor examine their breasts every three years.

▼ Women age 40 and over should have a doctor examine their breasts every year.

▼ All women should have their first mammogram by age 40.

▼ Women age 40 to 49 should have a mammogram every one to two years.

▼ Women age 50 and over should have a mammogram every year.

messages. It was the swimming pool of illnesses (you don't know how many friends you have 'til you get one). But still, the depression came (algae in the swimming pool).

Depression—nothing I had ever heard about it prepared me for the depths to which I was about to sink. Understand that normally I am a very upbeat person, positive and confident. There was nothing positive here. The black pit is what I called it, and I was surprised to hear others describe it in a similar fashion, always using the color black. Total hopelessness and despair, a narrow, deep well with no light.

I would start by feeling a little blue. As decisions needed to be made and daily life maintained, I would start to feel overwhelmed. I would sink deeper into the pit. I would try to explain this to others, but they couldn't understand (you can't unless you've been there). They would try the "snap out of it" or "pull yourself up by the bootstraps" approach. Then I felt isolated, and that's when the walls would start to close in. Nothing would work. I couldn't make simple decisions. The effort of trying to force those decisions fatigued me so greatly I would finally sink to my knees wherever I happened to be at the time. I was totally and utterly defeated.

I would cry—not a sobbing, sweet-sorrow sort of crying, but screams of anguish and grief. All the emotions I had kept bottled up for everyone else's benefit (to appear strong and capable) were fully fermented and pressuring the cork. They were cries of betrayal and treason, humility and defeat, and total confusion. Even death looked like a better option in the face of this emotional torrent. Eyes swollen, throat raw, I would climb into bed and stay there until the feeling lessened. My personal savior was a triple shot mocha (bless you, Starbucks). If I could just drag myself out of bed and to the coffee shop, the combination of coffee and chocolate (I believe) chemically altered my depressed state enough so that I could begin to function and eventually get back to normal.

I found I couldn't lean on anyone or ask for the support I needed. I'd always been a very independent person, and I inherently knew I could wear my friends out with this depression stuff if I leaned on any one of them too hard. The only person I confided in was my new partner. She tried, I think, but eventually couldn't or wouldn't be supportive. She was too busy wallowing in guilt and self-loathing. She had left her husband of fifteen years and despised being gay. Her problems wound her tighter and tighter until she snapped one day and finally went for help. Too late for us though.

My parents had been nothing but wonderful to me, a true blessing, but I decided they didn't deserve to witness this anguish and pain. Mom would have done anything to help me, but I knew how hard the whole ordeal had been on her already. She suffered as only a mother can knowing I had cancer. As bad as I felt, I couldn't bring any more sorrow into her life. Even so, my parents did help, just by being as wonderful as they had always been, and although it wasn't a quick fix, in the long run I know it helped. I knew that if I had called, they would have come.

Support groups, therapy—people pushed me to get help. I couldn't do it. How could a therapist really care? Maybe I should have gone, I don't know, but for two and a half years I waged war with my mind. My emotions and my intellect were at odds.

Emotionally I was ruined, deep in depression. Intellectually, I couldn't understand my depression. My prognosis was good: nodes negative, only 10 percent chance of recurrence—7 percent if I took tamoxifen. I should have felt good. So what if I was a little lopsided.

I chose to take tamoxifen, an estrogen blocker. It is just one more weapon in a growing arsenal against breast cancer. My particular kind of cancer really liked the estrogen I produced—bonded with it you might say. Tamoxifen blocks or disguises the estrogen receptors on cells so that the estrogen can't recognize the receptors and attach itself to the cell, thus inhibiting growth. Unfortunately, the disguise works so well that the estrogen can't find the receptors in the rest of the body either. The result is quite often a chemically induced menopause. The side effects range from hot flashes, frequent urination and vaginal itching and dryness to nausea, dizziness and, if you're lucky, the cessation of menstruation (a side effect I was enthusiastically looking forward to but never had the satisfaction of experiencing).

Another side effect can be depression. Supposedly only a small number of women experience this, but, hey, my breast lump sneaked into the small-percentage category (remember, 80 percent are benign), so why not be one of the small percentage of tamoxifen users who get depressed? Anyway, robbing a woman's body of the effects of estrogen can really trash the psyche. My body and mind eventually adjusted to tamoxifen, but I'm sure it had magnified, if not caused, my depression.

A new and understanding partner helped tremendously. Just knowing I could have a loving hug when I needed it was a priceless asset. Here was the intimate support I knew would help and had needed since shortly after surgery. Is it weakness to depend so heavily on a lover to drag you from the depths of depression? If so, I'm weak, but I'm also happy and healthy again. The cancer was cut out and is gone, as far as I'm concerned. It was the residual depression that was the real enemy. It came far closer to killing me than the cancer ever did.

I know a little something about my own mind and body and how they interact. In college I took some pre-med courses and many psychology classes, including physiological psychology. Fascinating stuff! Everyone should know a little about the body and the mind. I mentioned that, early on, I couldn't intellectually understand my depression. Well, later, I did go back to my books and notes and devise a theory of what had happened to me. It was the first step in getting better, understanding what my brain was going through physiologically.

From the time you are born (maybe even before), the brain is busy developing neurological pathways to enable you to function normally without having to think about every movement. As a child, you struggled to take that first step, you teetered, maybe fell, balanced and tried again. Such an effort for such simple movement is inconceivable to most adults. By adulthood, the path from the brain to the legs has become a veritable superhighway with neurological impulses traveling at lightning speed.

Problem solving, coping and decision making undergo a similar neurological process, and again you have a number of pathways creating behavior and personality. These, I believe, are more complex and fragile, like a maze, but the more you work your way through the maze, the more adept you become at ending up in the right place. Consider emotional trauma to be like an earthquake to that maze. It can tumble structures that took years to build and can block the pathways with the resulting rubble. A simple decision-making process, like "What shall I wear today?" can become a frustrating ordeal in which you stare blankly at your closet and end up being overwhelmed and going back to bed. Better not to wear anything than suffer the agonizing task of rebuilding those stupid mazes and pathways. After all, it took more than thirty years to build them; how do you repair them in a matter of months? You don't. You take your time (if your diagnosis has given you this luxury) and you enlist help anywhere you can find it.

Read and learn about yourself, your body, your mind, your disease. Bernie Siegel, doctor and author, counsels, "Your disease can cure you." And knowledge is the weapon with which to fight your disease. You must first know that you have cancer. Usually and unfortunately, that is the only knowledge that can motivate you to learn. Once you're motivated you can learn about the disease, about being sick and about being healthy, emotionally and physically. Learn about Western medicine, Eastern medicine, nutrition, the healing power of the mind. Use your faith (if you have one) or a partner's love. Consider visualization. (Lesson Four: Don't close your mind to any possible ways of healing.)

I had always been taught to "look for the silver lining," and even in my experience with cancer and depression, I have found one or two. First, I feel fortunate to have been given, as they say, a second chance. I am a lot nicer to my body. It gets all sorts of minerals and vitamins and antioxidants. I have learned about the tremendous value of nutrition, and I feel better than I did before I was diagnosed. Second, I've lost my arrogance, but kept my confidence (Lesson Five: It can happen to me, and I can survive). I've accepted that I am indeed a mortal and no longer bulletproof. So many people are walking around without a clue. They don't treat themselves well and they don't take precautions. I can now take full advantage of those precautions. I've had the warning and consequently am watching myself and have others watching and monitoring with me.

One of the most horrible feelings I know is finding out death is growing in you when you had no idea. Invasion and betrayal. Eventually your body lets you know—a lump. You may sense something is wrong, but all too many times you find out too late. I feel confident that what I've learned about breast cancer is the most powerful weapon I have against it. You can't solve a problem that you don't know is there. And once you know it's there, you can't just lie back and hope it goes away. You have to take action.

WILLY WILKINSON

Remember the Place Where Your Soul Lives
Chronic Fatigue Immune Dysfunction Syndrome

Imagine, if you will, that your life does not consist of the usual things of everyday people. If you are basically able-bodied, maybe even take your health for granted, pretend for a moment that you don't go to sleep at night and get up and go to work, that your life is not a-buzz with people and things and activities. When you make plans with friends to get together, you're never really sure if you'll make it, because you don't know how you'll feel that day. When you do make it out to see your friends, they greet you and ask where you've been. Sometimes you tell them. Sometimes you don't.

Imagine, if you will, just for a moment, that it has come to your attention that there is something terribly wrong in your body. You feel it stalking you, pushing you down, making you tremble, bump into things, forget simple things like what you left the house for or the names of people you know. And why is it that, no matter how many hours you spend in bed, you can't seem to get up in the morning?

This is not a guided meditation. More like a harrowing flashback to the scariest, most deathly ill moment of your life. The time you ran a temperature of 104 degrees and you were so hot and tingly and delirious and drenched with sweat that you thought you were going to die. Remember how everything hurt all over? How brain-dead you felt?

Maybe you had some unfinished business at work that just had to be done, so you tried to get your brain and body to work anyway. Or maybe, no matter how much you tried, you simply could not do anything but lie in bed and sleep, get up once in a while to pee and then lie back down and stare up at the ceiling. You knew you should be taking vitamins and herbs and drinking lots of liquids. But even the thought of drinking water hurt, because of the huge, swollen glands in your fire-red throat.

Some days passed. The blaze in your body eventually burned out. You regained your senses. You felt kind of weak, but slowly you got back to the business of managing your life again. Do you remember a time like this? Was it that devastating flu that hit last winter? Or the mono that got you as a kid? Perhaps you have a different physical disability, and you are familiar with those slow days. Or maybe you're one of these incredibly healthy people who never gets sick.

Whatever your experience, try to imagine that you didn't get back up and go to work. The nasty episode did not conclude after a week. It went on and on and on. If you can picture that, then you have an idea of what it can be like to live with CFIDS.

Chronic fatigue immune dysfunction syndrome, a.k.a. CFIDS, is a debilitating autoimmune disorder that affects millions worldwide. Shrouded in controversy, dismissed as psychiatric—those ill with it are frivolously perceived as a "bunch of tired, rich white girls who don't want to work"—CFIDS is an illness steeped in social, political and economic issues. There are as many stories as there are bodies with CFIDS. What follows is a brief overview of CFIDS and the tale of my personal journey with it.

Because CFIDS is so difficult to diagnose, and because women appear to be the vast majority of those affected, skeptics in the medical profession have been quick to label it as depression. Yet significant physical symptoms from flulike illness to cognitive impairment, coupled with epidemiological data that indicate an escalating pandemic, have led some to refer to it as the AIDS of the 1990s. While controversy abounds as to its cause, another myth has flourished: Those with CFIDS are upper-middle-class white women. Yet talk to health professionals working in public hospitals and they will probably tell you that CFIDS is a disease of poor people of color.

Just what exactly is CFIDS? The Centers for Disease Control case definition of "chronic fatigue syndrome" (since renamed CFIDS by activists), first published in 1988, was designed to be deliberately restrictive in order to facilitate research and was not intended for the purposes of diagnosis or disability benefits. According to the case definition, basic criteria are prolonged or recurring severely debilitating fatigue that reduces activity level by at least 50 percent for six months or more, with other obvious causes of fatigue ruled out, such as cancer, bacterial infection, rheumatologic disorders or clinical depression.[1] Other criteria include eight or more of the following symptoms: low-grade fevers, sore throat, swollen or tender lymph nodes, headaches, general muscle weakness, muscular aches and pains, extreme fatigue following minimal exercise, joint pains, various nervous system complaints, sleep disturbance and abrupt onset of symptoms over a few hours or a few days.[2]

CFIDS is characterized by the following consistent features: sudden onset of flulike symptoms that never seem to go away, such extreme fatigue that the patient is unable to manage her daily activities or work, and unusual neurocognitive symptoms such as memory loss, disorientation, difficulty with speaking

What is Chronic Fatigue Immune Dysfunction Syndrome?

According to the Centers for Disease Control, a CFIDS diagnosis may be made when the following major criteria are met:

1. the new onset of persistent or relapsing, debilitating fatigue or easy fatigability in a person who has no previous history of similar symptoms;

2. activity level is reduced by at least 50 percent for at least six months; and

3. other conditions are excluded.

CFIDS symptoms may include mild fever, sore throat, painful lymph nodes, general muscle weakness, muscle pain, fatigue, headaches, severe joint pain, sleep disturbances, confusion, irritability, impaired vision and inability to concentrate.

and recall, and limited ability or inability to concentrate or comprehend.[3] Many factors distinguish CFIDS from depression, the most important of which is that most of the "depression" associated with CFIDS is *reactive* to the stress of such severe persisting symptoms. Further, the immune abnormalities associated with CFIDS are inconsistent with clinical depression.[4]

Whether its cause is viral, genetic or environmental, one thing is certain: The immune system is at the center of this illness, hence its renaming to acknowledge that fact. Immunologists theorize that the immune systems of people with CFIDS are in a constant state of "up-regulation," with cellular and chemical protectors set to attack. Normally, once a viral or bacterial intruder is destroyed, the system turns off. But with CFIDS, the turn-off signal never arrives, and the immune system continues to defend itself against a real or imagined enemy. Infection-fighting body chemicals such as interleukin and interferon cause the flulike symptoms of fever, fatigue and pain common to CFIDS.[5] This chronic immune activation has led researchers to conclude that CFIDS is, or is similar to, autoimmune disease.

Many people with CFIDS (PWCs), as well as virologists and physicians who treat PWCs, are hopeful that a virus or viruses to which this illness can be attributed will soon be isolated. There are others, like myself, who do not believe that CFIDS is caused by one entity. While the theory of environmental toxicity is a nebulous idea that is institutionally disputed, toxic exposure from pollutants in the environment and everyday products is a distinct possibility. Even while fifty thousand Gulf War veterans complained of a persistent CFIDS-like illness,[6] the Pentagon attributed these complaints to psychological factors, rather than chemical pollutants from burning oil fields and insecticides, inoculations for protection from germ warfare or the possible Iraqi use of chemical or biological weapons.[7]

Chemical pollutants, mercury amalgam dental fillings, parasites and the yeastlike fungus *Candida albicans* are considered possible culprits in this whole affair called CFIDS. While many people do not think about the threat posed by toxins in the environment, we are exposed to a constant barrage in our everyday life. Detergents, perfumes, cleaning products, building materials, pesticides, gasoline and adhesives are only some of the toxic products affecting our health on a daily basis. Surely there are other toxins and pollutants of which we are unaware.

While its cause is the subject of intense debate, CFIDS is considered a syndrome, or a collection of symptoms occurring together and characterizing a specific disease or condition that is not attributed to one entity, just as AIDS was initially considered a syndrome before HIV was isolated. In short, CFIDS is a "wastebasket term" for a condition that is not well understood.

Indeed diagnosis and treatment are difficult for such a complex malady. Diagnosis, by Western standards, is done by process of elimination, and treatment strategies are mostly symptom-focused. Yet while doctors of Western medicine focus on treating the myriad of symptoms associated with CFIDS, doctors of Chinese medicine, on the other hand, recognize this condition as a whole body that must be returned to balance. PWCs are treated for a "damp" and/or "heat" condition, or as my acupuncturist understands it, for *ngoh gum chu loi*, the deep flu. While acupuncturists recognize the imbalance of a "damp spleen" or a "cold liver," for example, few actually understand this condition as "a flu that never went away."

So is CFIDS contagious? A lot of people ask me this question, and their fears are understandable, especially since information about possible contagion was ambiguous in the early years of media attention on CFIDS. I had this same fear when I first read about the Incline Village outbreak back in the mid-eighties.[8] The CDC reports that CFIDS "does not appear to be transmissible from person to person" and there is no justification for isolation.[9] I have always contended that no, what goes on in my body will probably not go on in yours, unless you too are immune-compromised. While I have loved and lived with many women during the course of my illness, none have developed CFIDS. The real question, then, is: What events led to this state of compromised immunity?

When I got sick, like most, I was caught unprepared. All of a sudden my number came up, the lights went out, and everybody disappeared. I was pissed! And it hurt, oh it hurt.

There seem to be two kinds of people who get CFIDS: those whose health spirals downward after years of chronic health problems, sometimes since childhood; and those who, though once very energetic, ran and ran until their battery flickered. I would be the latter. Oh yeah. I was the jock, the activist, the one who bicycled across the United States. I talked fast, moved fast, had more energy than anyone I knew. And a naiveté and false sense of invincibility about my health.

At the time, I was an AIDS service provider in the Asian/Pacific Islander (API) community. I was out on the piss-stained streets talking to dope fiends and hookers about AIDS prevention. I was in the office, coordinating programs. I worked long hours, wore many hats. I was doing work that I loved, yet that took an enormous toll. For several years I was the only Asian community health outreach worker that I knew of on the West Coast, and one of two Asian dykes in the AIDS field in San Francisco. I was explaining the APIs to the outreach workers, the dope fiends and sex workers to the Asians, and the lesbians to everybody. As usual, I got shit from all directions for being of mixed heritage. The API community, especially those in health and social services, was particularly heavy-handed in that regard. Moreover, I was breaking up with my lover of six years. I was distracting myself running around with a lot of women. Gender identity issues—a recurring theme in my life—were coming up for me, but I couldn't deal. And I had questions about the work I was doing and my purpose in doing it that remained unanswered. I had a full plate. But it's not just the stress itself; it's how you handle it. And things had unraveled to the point where I wasn't.

At first I got sick repeatedly on weekends, then for a week at a time about once a month. Like a fool, I worked harder, over-trained and incurred more girlfriend drama. One day, after a good day's work, I went into the office bathroom to splash some water on my face, do my dishes and get ready to go home. As I leaned over the sink, the long fluorescent light fixture on the ceiling above me fell on my head, neck and back. My dishes crashed; I was dazed. And ooh, it hurt!

Well, sometimes, if you don't listen, the shit will hit you over the head. And yet, what did I do? There I was: a severe concussion, everything hurt, couldn't see or think "straight." People would talk to me, I'd watch their lips move, and I had no idea what they were saying. And the nagging fatigue and recurrent bouts of flu that had preceded the accident worsened. I would work all day and then come home and fall into bed until the next morning, and then drag myself out of bed and do it again. What a mess. I went on like this for two and a half months after the accident until my battery flickered out, and I had no choice but to stop. And when I finally lay down, when I finally stopped working, I began to realize how sick I really was. Because once

I lay down, I couldn't get up.

What do you do then? Your world as you know it has come to a screeching halt. Nowadays I watch people who are used to working long hours, juggling family responsibilities, with more commitments than they can handle and an impossible schedule. And when they get sick or injured or otherwise hit with sudden disability, they freak. Because that wasn't part of the plan. As if attending to our health is some extraneous burden. When our bodies tell us it's time to slow down, time to listen, it is always part of the plan.

So there I was, lying in bed staring up at the ceiling, scared, lonely, wondering if I was dying. It was absolutely terrifying. Friends disappeared, lovers left, colleagues had nothing to say, family didn't get it. I mean, I was needy, and who wants a needy friend? I got really skinny that summer because I was too sick to get up and fix myself something to eat.

I'd love to report that despite my circumstances, I got over all the loss and betrayal and displacement, and moved on smoothly into my new world, traveling in the Land of Illness. Not. It has taken a very long time to move through the anger and grief. The friends that never called back, the colleagues that turned their backs on me. The Asian/Pacific lesbian community that I had been so instrumental in bringing together, and that had been home to me for so many years, offered little support. I mean, I wasn't dying, not officially anyway. I just wasn't much fun anymore. I think part of the problem is that people have trouble fathoming the reality of CFIDS. They'd say, "You look great," and I'd be thrilled that I had managed to pull it off. They had no idea that I had spent several days in bed so that I could go out to this one event. And they'd say, "What have you been up to?" and because illness had so completely taken over my life, I'd tell them, for that was all the story I had. It took me a while to get that people didn't really want to know, and that I had to learn how not to talk about it. They'd say, "Well, you look fine to me," and

I'd wonder if it was a compliment or a way of discounting and disbelieving what did not meet the eye. This ambiguity of being sick as a dog while appearing to be healthy was a particular mindfuck, as I have gone through life misperceived around both my race and gender.

Struggling to dissolve my anger, I have wondered if perhaps people think that if you have a chronic condition you should just learn how to deal with it yourself. Particularly when you have the medical profession scratching their heads in bewilderment or denying its existence. And let's face it: People just don't want to deal with illness, immune disorder or otherwise. But then, I have to admit that I am no stranger to this able-bodied mentality myself.

Call it the invincibility of youth, or the big *fear* coursing through the veins of able-bodied people, but I was terrified of losing my physicality. And sure enough it happened. And as my life shifted focus to such basic needs as food and laundry, I quickly learned that the only people who could really be there for me, or even hear about it, had either been through a health crisis themselves or were close to someone who had. In my naiveté I thought my colleagues in the AIDS service community would understand. Not just understand—be there with support, referrals, resources. Show up at my house with food, or help me with basic chores as I had done for so many others. There were many lessons I had yet to learn.

When I came to AIDS work it was because I wanted to hit the streets and talk to regular old dope fiends about AIDS prevention. My attitude was not one of looking down on them, nor was it from shared experience, because I hadn't really been a part of that life. But I had struggled enough on the edge of survival to know about pain. Not that my pain was the same pain as that of the scruffy straight white dude I would encounter nodding on a park bench in the TL (San Fransisco's Tenderloin district).[10] Or the pregnant sister getting the shit beaten out of her by her old man. Or the immigrant massage-parlor worker desperate for English skills or a man to help her out of that trap. All I knew was that it didn't really matter. It was about moving through it. Finding inspiration to stay alive in the midst of slow death. Sneaking the condom on the trick, making the effort to use bleach even if you didn't have a reason. And in the midst of a suicide mission, who does?

So I gave them a reason. None of us followed anybody into the back alleys or wherever they did their business. We just gave them the tools. A one-ounce bottle of bleach. Lubricated condoms or Kiss-O-Mint. *Freshen your breath at the same time, honey.* We didn't care what they did, as long as they played it safe. When they couldn't find a reason like their children, or their lover, or their mother, or the simple joy of living, we gave them one. *Do it for me, babe. Stay alive, friend. I need you here.*

Yeah, CHOW (Community Health Outreach Worker) life is about touching souls. It's about stopping the spin for a minute to look someone dead in the eye and ask them to remember. Not their birth or their death or any of the crazy shit in between. Just remember. Who can find their soul in the midst of the madness? Who can even remember where it lives? The pulse of the street deafens, while yours quickens to the chase. Remember that there is something beyond this. In the quiet of your soul lies a place that wants to stay alive. *Use it every time for me, bruddah. Or don't share.*

When the shit hit the fan for me, however, *wasn't nobody there*. When I told an API disabled friend how my ethnic-specific AIDS agency dropped me faster than a burning pot, she said, "Then what was the work about for them?" I felt like a fallen family member who had brought shame upon them, so the only way they could deal with it was not to deal. When they ran into my ex-lover they—*whisper whisper*—asked her how I was doing. That was it. Not one phone call, not one get-well card. One day, in a fit of rage (okay, sick as a dog I was a bit off-balance), with my illegal termination notice in hand (three months after leaving on a worker's comp injury), I told my boss, "Even if I hated your guts I would've brought you food!" She said, "That's the difference between you and me." She was a numbers woman. She had never done my job.

And what about the men? There was this one brother, a gay Asian colleague with whom I had worked closely and who knew intimately of my work with folks on the street. When we ran into each other now and then at AIDS functions or memorials, he'd say, "Let's talk *drugs,* honey!" and we'd discuss complementary treatment options. He went on busily organizing and jetting around the country, and we lost touch. When I heard that he had become very ill, I went to see him. We talked; I massaged him. It was only then, at the last hour, when he was too sick to get up, that he understood what I had been going through. How sick I really was, how difficult it was to find resources and support. After he crossed over, he came to me and asked for forgiveness for not helping me in my time of need after I had helped so many.

The similarities between AIDS and CFIDS are numerous enough that it is not uncommon to hear the two spoken of in the same breath. Dr. Elaine DeFreitas has reported sightings of a retrovirus, which, though disputed at the CDC, has generated much excitement and speculation about a possible connection to HIV.[11] Other researchers have proposed a connection as well, given that there are so many common immune abnormalities;[12] in fact, many of the same drugs used in AIDS treatment are used to combat CFIDS. While PWCs do not exhibit the severe immune suppression found in PWAs (people with AIDS), some PWCs present some of the same opportunistic infections, such as candidiasis, parasites and wasting syndrome. Dr. Charles Lapp, who works with internationally recognized CFIDS authority Dr. Paul Cheney, states that the severe debilitation and psychoneurological symptoms indicate "impressive changes" in the immune system that are rarely seen except in CFIDS, AIDS and hematological malignancies.[13] Dr. Nancy Klimas and Dr. Jay Levy, both longtime CFIDS researchers, have described the overall picture as an acquired immunodeficiency syndrome that appears as a persistent viral infection, except that the natural killer cells are ineffective.[14]

Sound familiar? Dr. Mark Loveless, who has spent many years researching AIDS and CFIDS, states, "A CFS patient feels every day significantly the same as an AIDS patient feels two months before death."[15] This chilling commentary is substantiated by specific clinical data from research conducted at the Oregon Health Sciences University, as well as the general opinions of countless other medical experts.[16] Yet at least two factors separate CFIDS from AIDS.

When I first became ill, I lay in bed staring up at the ceiling for hours, that became days, that became weeks, that became months. I felt as if I were dying, but I knew from the epidemiological data that I probably would not. Besides, I had too much work to do before I signed out. In my anguish, I figured I had two things going for me: I'm not contagious, and I'm not gonna die from this. At that moment, that was all I had: those two facts that separated me from HIV/AIDS. Indeed they are significant. On the one hand, millions of young people (mostly men) are dying in their prime. Whole communities with very specific needs are calling out for prevention education and care services. On the other hand, millions of young people (mostly women) are so ill they cannot manage their daily lives but, except for incidents of suicide, are not dying. The cause of CFIDS is uncertain, and questions about a possible psychiatric link, as well as dispute over the nature of debilitating "fatigue," have resulted in pervasive disrespect, so prevention education and health services are next to nil. Significant numbers of lesbians are among those women affected. Consider this: The world has changed considerably since the

New York Times first reported on a "gay cancer" in 1981. What if we lesbians had been the ones to go? What kind of world would it be today?

People with CFIDS need well-funded support services. The CDC estimates that as many as 220 out of every 100,000 Americans have a CFIDS-like illness.[17] And yet, while a person with HIV has a plethora of HIV services in San Francisco, few resources are available to address the enormous health and social service needs of people with CFIDS. The hotline at the CFIDS Foundation in San Francisco, which was open only Mondays and Wednesdays between 1:00 and 3:00, lost its funding. I got on the waiting list of

■■

Living with Chronic Fatigue Immune Dysfunction Syndrome

RESOURCES

CFIDS Action Campaign for the U.S. (CACTUS)
P.O. Box 2578
Sebastapol, CA 95473
(707) 823-0725

CFIDS Association
P.O. Box 220398
Charlotte, NC 28222-0398
(704) 362-2343; (800) 44-CFIDS

CFIDS Foundation
965 Mission Street, Suite 425
San Francisco, CA 94103
(415) 882-9986

Chronic Fatigue Immune Dysfunction Syndrome Society
P.O. Box 230108
Portland, OR 97223
(503) 684-5261

SUGGESTED READING

50 Things You Should Know About the Chronic Fatigue Syndrome Epidemic by Neenyah Ostrom, New York: TNM, Inc., 1992.

The Doctor's Guide to Chronic Fatigue Syndrome: Understanding, Treating, and Living with CFIDS by David S. Bell, Reading, MA: Addison-Wesley, 1995.

Osler's Web: Inside the Labyrinth of the Chronic Fatigue Syndrome Epidemic by

Hillary Johnson, New York: Crown, 1996.

Recovering from Chronic Fatigue Sundrome: A Guide to Self-Empowerment by William Collinge, New York: The Body Press/Perigee Books, 1993.

Running on Empty: The Complete Guide to Chronic Fatigue Syndrome by Katrina Berne, Alameda, CA: Hunter House, 1995.

the "Fatigue Clinic" at the University of California at San Francisco. They say they hope to be able to see me in *two and a half years*. In the future, I hope that funding for the many creative, groundbreaking HIV/AIDS services increases, not decreases. And I hope that people with CFIDS will see the day when we can receive helpful information, quality, respectful health care and a hot meal delivered to our door when necessary.

Despite an astronomically rising incidence of infection, we are still the pariahs that PWAs were early in the AIDS pandemic. Ask any random college-educated person if they know what CFIDS stands for. How many people think this is just about being a little tired? Or that it's just a lot of unnecessary attention for yuppie women who don't want to work? Or that women of color don't get this? (I have been told by women in my lesbian community of color that we're all "cockroaches"—we can survive anything—and that only white girls or wannabe white girls get CFIDS.) We have far to go before this illness is acknowledged or understood in the general public, or communities rally around for our support.

Is it any wonder that stereotypes abound as to the race and class of women with CFIDS, when one is usually forced to trek far and wide through the health care system to be properly diagnosed and treated? Who has the resources to schlep from doctor to doctor, undergoing a battery of tests? And how much disrespect can one handle? Throughout the course of my illness, I have used so-called alternative therapies as well as Western medicine. There are many, many strategies too numerous to describe; the following briefly summarizes my experience.

In my search for appropriate care and treatment, I, too, was disregarded as "psycho" by at least four male doctors. One looked me up and down, then questioned my work and what business I had doing it: "What is this, Asian people with AIDS? You speak

Asian or something?" He then boldly *made up* something about
how I had been under psychiatric care for the past five years, which
he diligently wrote in a lengthy, decidedly unfavorable report. This
guy, who bore a striking resemblance to Ross Perot, was actually
hired by *my* lawyer for my worker's compensation case.

Even though I had health insurance, resources and connections, it was years before I found a decent doctor. The director of
a local women's clinic was nice enough to offer me a complimen-
tary visit with the clinic's medical director, but I found that she
was one more doctor I had to educate about CFIDS. While the
women's clinic was respectful, its treatment strategies were inadequate. Fortunately, after worker's compensation and state disability ran out, I was awarded Social Security disability benefits.
When I got that check, I sought care from an expensive doctor
knowledgeable in CFIDS and alternative treatments.

Thus the stereotype. Who can afford all that health care? Of
course, in this country you get health insurance only when you're
employed, not when you're sick and need it most. If you're
fortunate enough to receive federal benefits, you may have to
wait additional time before receiving health coverage; and then
the providers that accept it are, well, not always your first
choice.

As a Chinese person raised with an appreciation for acupuncture and herbs, I am more inclined toward Chinese medicine and
other holistic therapies such as chiropractic, bodywork and spiritual healing than Western medicine. These and other alternative
approaches, though an expense, have been my main approach to
treatment. Yet Western medicine surprised me. Two years into my
illness, I discovered that I had three parasites. Though most U.S.
labs are not equipped to detect parasites other than a few common ones like *Giardia* or *Cryptosporidium*, parasites are indeed
a problem in the United States. That downtown doctor had me
ship a stool sample to Great Smokies Diagnostic Labs in North
Carolina. They kicked back a full-color printout describing the

offending buggers (with pictures even) and the state of my digestive system. I may have harbored some or all of the parasites since the time I lived in Mexico in 1983. I killed the buggers with Western medicine, like a shotgun to the source, and my symptoms improved.

Other digestive disorders such as *Candida* overgrowth are common among people with immune system problems. Candidiasis, or chronic yeast infection, could be at the heart of chronic fatigue. That in part explains the overwhelming numbers of women affected, since the hormone progesterone stimulates yeast overgrowth.[18] Candida can affect all the body's systems, so getting it under control is imperative in combating CFIDS. In my experience, it has been very difficult to control, but changes in diet and the use of caprillic acid and Chinese herbs have been helpful. A number of books are available on the subject. For more information, I recommend *Candida: A Twentieth-Century Disease*, by Shirley Lorenzani.

Those who refuse to acknowledge these health issues claim that CFIDS is "all in our heads." So when was the last time you looked in your head? The most unique CFIDS story I have heard—and definitely the most bizarre—was of a woman I met in Chicago who spent five years with chronic sinus infections and debilitating fatigue. Her life slowed down considerably, and she was not the woman her friends had known previously. A doctor finally noticed a deviated septum in her nasal cavity. Apparently she had taken a spill on her bicycle, and a rock had gotten stuck in her nose. The doctor removed the rock, and she got better. When I met her she advised, "Have someone look up your nose." Wish it were that easy.

The part of your head you might be better off looking into is your mouth. If you have "silver" amalgam fillings, your teeth are filled with a metal substance that is 50 percent mercury. While the American Dental Association has insisted that amalgam fillings are safe (and cheapest), they warn dentists of the proper handling of the material. *Don't touch it*, they say. *Don't inhale the vapor. Clean up spills immediately. Store it in a tightly sealed container under water.*[19] Yes, it's the same stuff that's in thermometers. So what happens to the metal in your mouth? Your tongue touches it, you grind food on it. It breaks up, you swallow it. And you certainly breathe it. Yet mercury is not safe in any amount. It hangs out in your tissues and can affect all your vital organs. Some claim it is linked to countless diseases, including multiple sclerosis, lupus, Alzheimer's, arthritis and CFIDS. While amalgam fillings have been steeped in controversy since first introduced by New York City dental entrepreneurs in 1833, I believe the mercury in these fillings may be the most dangerous toxin that has sneaked into our daily lives. Dr. Hal A. Huggins, D.D.S., internationally known leader in the field of mercury toxicity and the treatment of autoimmune disorders, has developed specific guidelines for removal and replacement of amalgam fillings. Currently I am investigating the best treatment strategies for removal of the mercury from my mouth.[20]

Despite the debilitating symptoms, letdowns and health care headaches, the most difficult aspect of this illness has been challenging myself to change my life and the way I perceive it. Remember the cliché: crisis equals opportunity. Indeed "crisis" and "opportunity" are the same character in Chinese. And while I have resisted the work kicking and screaming, through all the pain I have emerged happier, clearer and more whole than ever.

I slowed down, smelled the flowers. Took responsibility for my life, including the illness that left me feeling so victimized. I lost the people that were not good for me. I changed my living situation, grew my hair. And the people that came into my life brought gifts beyond belief. The woman who, early on, asked me what in my life needed changing. The CFIDS buddies who call to discuss treatment, girlfriends, the blues. And most of all, just as soon as

I knew what I wanted and my hunger had dissipated, I found love like never before.

Years after doing CHOW work, I'd run into former clients. They'd say, "Hey, I got my kids back. I'm clean, got money in the bank. You saved my life, Willy." But sometimes the story was not so happy: "I'm strung out, Willy. My baby was born with health problems." Life or death, looking for a life line.

I have become my own CHOW. I have finally realized that no one can do it for me, just as no one could do it for any of my clients on the street. We just gave them the tools. It was up to them to follow through. No one could keep me alive when I was looking death in the face. This is all my journey.

Remember the woman in Chicago who had chronic fatigue for five years and then discovered she had a rock stuck in her nose? When I told her my story, she said, "You never get it all back, you never get it all back." So definitive, like a teacher of some law of nature that everyone's got all wrong. How could I expect that it would, that I would give of my heart and soul and it would come back to me? Maybe I'm the eternal optimist, but still I believe it does. You just have to know how to recognize it. It's there, and it's been there all along, like the spirit of living that resides in every one of us. Asking of us, no, demanding that we remember. Remember the place where your soul lives. The place where the pulse beats louder than anyone or anything else. You may have lost the address. You may have gotten lost on the path. Ran too many yellows. Got stuck in a jam. But you'll find your way. Because it comes back, it always does.

Notes

1. Andrea Rudner, "Chronic Fatigue Syndrome: Searching for the Answers," *Ms.*, May/June 1992, 33–36.

2. "Chronic Fatigue Syndrome: General Information, Possible Causes, Diagnosis and Treatment," Centers for Disease Control, May 1993.

3. Charles W. Lapp, M.D. "Chronic Fatigue Syndrome Is a *Real* Disease," *North Carolina Family Physician* (Winter, 1992) 6–11.

4. Ibid., 8.

5. "CFIDS Seen as Similar to Autoimmune Diseases such as Lupus, Rheumatoid Arthritis," *CFIDS Treatment News*, Winter 1992.

6. As reported on "News Unfiltered," *MTV*, January 15, 1996.

7. Associated Press, "A 'Gulf War Syndrome' Possible, Pentagon Told," *San Francisco Chronicle*, January 5, 1996.

8. Reports of a 1984 outbreak among two hundred residents of the small Lake Tahoe resort town launched modern-day concern about CFIDS.

9. CDC, "Chronic Fatigue Syndrome: General Information," 1.

10. Many "TL" residents are "hitting bottom" with drugs, prostitution and generally unsafe behavior.

11. Rudner, 34.

12. As documented in Hillary Johnson, *Osler's Web: Inside the Labyrinth of the Chronic Fatigue Syndrome Epidemic,* (New York: Crown, 1996). Researchers Paul Cheney (96, 142), Dan Peterson (96), Robert Gallo (150), Anthony Komaroff (655-6), Nancy Klimas (158-9), Michael Holmes (660-1), Jay Levy (484), Carol Jessop (484) and Alan Landay (484) are some of the CFIDS researchers who have drawn connections between CFIDS and AIDS.

13. Lapp, "Chronic Fatigue Syndrome Is a *Real* Disease," 9.

14. Ibid., 9.

15. Molly Holzschlag, "Congressional Testimony Smashes CFS Myths," *CFIDS Healthwatch*, Summer 1995, 1.

16. Ibid., 4.

17. Ibid., 1.

18. Shirley S. Lorenzani, *Candida: A Twentieth-Century Disease* (New Canaan, CT: Keats Publishing 1986) 31.

19. Hal A. Huggins, *It's All in Your Head* (Garden City Park, NY: Avery Publishing Group 1993) 36–37.

20. Ibid. See also Joyal Taylor, *The Complete Guide to Mercury Toxicity from Dental Fillings* (San Diego, CA: Scripps Publishing, 1988).

LIZA J. RANKOW

Thank You, But
A Love Letter to the Well-Intentioned

I know
you just had to tell me
about the article you read in a medical journal
or in *The Harvard Nutrition Newsletter*
Prevention Magazine   *Women's Day*   *The Advocate*
or the *National Enquirer*
while you were in line at the supermarket

or what you heard from your cousin who's a nurse
or your sister-in-law who's an internist
or from your neighbor   grocer   chiropractor   pharmacist
massage therapist   yoga teacher
or on the news   or on public television
or on Oprah   Donahue   Sally Jessie   Montel
or on late-night talk radio one time when you couldn't sleep

about someone

who had the exact same disease as me
or at least something involving the intestine
or maybe it was the stomach
heart   lung   uterus   liver   spleen   bone marrow   breast
or maybe it started with the same letter
or sounded kinda like it

but, anyway, it made you think of me
and you just had to give me the article
or cassette tape   book   address
toll-free phone number   person's name
for the medicine   special diet   herbal formula
vitamins   prayer treatment   algae   affirmations
support group   clinical trial   psychic
internationally known specialist
that made all the difference
for your child's classmate's mother's friend's aunt
or the woman on TV
or at the bridge game
synagogue   little league   group therapy

and you know if I would just
change my diet   attitude   job   residence   religion
exercise program   relationship   doctor   therapist
sexual orientation   meditation practice   name
or rest more   do more   eat more   fast more
not push so hard
seriously apply myself
it would make *all* the difference
and, really, you just want to see me feel better
once and for all.

I know
that you mean well
have my best interest at heart
are trying to help
I know that you love me   But
I have been living in this body
with this illness
for a very long time.
It has been my teacher and my tormentor
my guide   incentive   excuse   motivation   despair
inspiration   cross to bear
link to my family   punishment   reward   education
escape clause   enemy   friend   boundary   betrayer
responsibility
for a very long time.   The relationship is complex

and I have probably tried whatever you're suggesting
or at least something that sounds like it
or begins with the same letter
or comes from the same country
or was in the same magazine
at least once or twice
at some point during the twenty-three years
since my diagnosis.

So, please
just tell me that you care   ask me
if you want to know something   or want to help
ask before you assume what helpful looks like
or what I need   or what my lesson is
or anything about my karma
or what I can or cannot do   at any particular moment.
I have been a student of this illness
for a very long time

and I thank you for caring enough   for loving me
respecting me
enough to understand.

LIZA J. RANKOW

Long Time Cumming
Notes on Chronic Illness, Sexuality, Shame and Desire

At the age of twelve I began to miss a lot of school because of abdominal pain and diarrhea. The doctor called the condition colitis. When I was seventeen I came close to dying, and had a long hospitalization and the first of many intestinal surgeries. The diagnosis: Crohn's disease—an inflammation and ulceration of the large and small intestines that often runs in families. At eighteen, after several years of very promiscuous and only rarely sober heterosexuality, I came out as a lesbian. These are some historical facts. Yet there is a broader understanding necessary to this conversation. My father also had Crohn's disease, and my mother had debilitating migraines. The course of my illness was more severe than my father's and I took a perverse comfort in thinking I would die early. Staying alive—*wanting to live*—in the face of serious illness was a source of ambivalence to me.

I was raised in a subtext of shame and of silence about bodies and about sexuality. Outwardly my parents displayed an almost prideful adherence to liberal-intellectual, upwardly mobile, middle-class progressivism. They gave me books to learn about sex, but we never discussed the contents. There was an undercurrent of sexual innuendo and double entendre, and judgmental comments about my maturing body or my weight, but for the most part conversations about bodies did not take place outside the context of symptoms and illness. Daily, sometimes hourly updates on everyone's health status were the pulse I took to gauge the safety of my childhood world. At a fairly young age my body was defined by pain and incapacity rather than by celebration. The first time a lover told me that sex was *fun* and that bodies were made for pleasure, it stopped me in my tracks. I didn't have a framework in which to even conceive of that notion. But I desperately wanted to know what she knew. And I desperately feared that I never would.

I survived heterosex by going "unconscious," disassociating from my body. I survived the pain of illness in the same way. That well-learned pattern followed me into my sexual relationships with women and into my adult life. It allowed me to function in the era of 1970s militant lesbian feminist nonmonogamy. I was a standard-issue baby andro-dyke in Northampton, Massachusetts, long before its fifteen minutes of fame. We all wore the same "uniform" of jeans or khakis, flannel shirts, work boots and thrift-store suit vests. We all had the same half-inch-long do-it-yourself haircut. Sex was the "I do you, you do me, and nobody gets penetrated" variety. Lots of nonoppressive cuddling and kissing between protest marches, overthrowing the patriarchy and shifts at the food co-op. I didn't usually cum with my girlfriends, but since orgasm was a male-identified outcome-focused politically incorrect goal, it wasn't really a problem. We were into *process* and sameness. Only I wasn't the same. Every couple of years I would get really sick. I would get weak, run fevers, have diarrhea and debilitating pain. My weight would drop to a skeletal seventy pounds or less. In that pre-AIDS era young Amazons weren't prepared for one of their peers to be so blatantly and chronically ill.

I moved to the Catskill Mountains of New York and spent a year in a household among lesbians who lived with disability or illness. With these women I learned to accept the fluid continuum of ability, to honor and creatively adapt to the ebb and flow of symptoms. I gathered an appreciation of the myriad nuances of physical difference, as opposed to the simplistic dichotomy of able/disabled. In 1983 I moved again, this time to North Carolina. My family had relocated there, and my intermittent need for hospitalization and post-discharge care had brought me more and more frequently to Durham and Chapel Hill. I quickly sought out the local dykes and became involved in the community. But except for the occasional date, and the even more occasional "out-of-body" sexual encounter, I was basically celibate for many years. This was a celibacy by default, not consciously chosen. It was also a safe place to hide from the unwelcome changes in my body.

Years of illness, of exacerbations and remissions, of surgeries and medication, in time take their toll. Scarring, swelling, inflammation and infection have resulted in disfigurements that have gradually altered the topography of my body's most intimate places. This has been a source of unceasing despair, of shame beyond words. Here I was working diligently to recover from just the garden variety shame and body hatred so many women inherit from our family and cultural histories. As if that in itself wasn't enough of a task, the Universe gifted me with this extra "opportunity" for personal growth and emotional healing. And though it may be the gratitude that is born out of having no other choice, on some level I am thankful. Despite my daily wish for things to be different, *this* body has forced the issue, has called me to places within myself—of courage, honesty and emotional healing—to which I know I would not have otherwise gone. Actually, it has not been this body's disfigurement alone that has provided the impetus for healing, but also its erotic desires.

I had been out for twelve years as a generic lesbian. The party-line politics into which I had come out proclaimed butch and femme women an unenlightened historical footnote on the glorious path to the Matriarchy. And I bought it. I was a card-carrying, hetero-hating, radical-feminist-separatist, don't-fuck-with-me dyke. It takes an awful lot of energy to hate that much and be that angry all the time.

What Is Crohn's Disease?

▼ Crohn's Disease is an inflammatory disease that attacks the gastro-intestinal system.

▼ Inflammation may occur in the mouth, esophagus, stomach, small intestine, bowel or rectum.

▼ Symptoms include diarrhea, abdominal pain, rectal bleeding, fever, decreased appetite and weight loss.

▼ The disease can begin slowly or develop suddenly, and can produce a range of symptoms that affect the whole body.

Maybe it was that my physical and psychic energy had become a rare and precious commodity to me as a "sick girl," maybe it was the move south or maybe I just grew up a little, but over time my hard line softened. So "imagine my surprise" (to quote the songstress) when, through a decade of subtle shiftings, I came home to an innate erotic language I had never known existed. I felt like Dorothy leaving the black and white and gray of Kansas and waking up in the sparkling Technicolor of Oz. For the first time I felt a glimmer of hope that what that early girlfriend had said about sex being fun, and bodies knowing pleasure, might just turn out to be true after all.

I cannot address the topic of sexuality outside the context of my femme identity. My femme self is the pulse of my desire and the way I walk in the world. It is the passionate core that informs my work, my politics, my relationships and my sense of who I am as a woman who loves women. As a femme I have a different relationship to gender and to my body than I had before. In claiming my femme self I found home and healing in a cultural context that values and respects me in so many of the places that had previously carried shame. In the eyes of the butches in my life I find—for the first time—a mirror in which I can feel myself to be desirable. That mirror has been a bridge for me, nurturing my own feelings of worth, of self-esteem. But still there remains the shame carried around illness, around scarring and physical difference . . . and that shame creates a wedge of silence and separation.

Friends who have known me over time are aware that I have certain dietary and energy limitations that wax and wane, but the deeper conversations of what this illness means to me I have kept secret. Most people are shocked to learn I am not healthy. They have no place to reconcile this information with their experience of me in the world. "But you look so healthy," they'll often respond, as if that should settle the matter. It is offered as a compliment or a consolation: I may feel like hell, but at least it doesn't show; no one would have guessed. I have gotten good at passing. And when I am too sick to pass, generally I withdraw. It requires a thoughtful budgeting, precise calibration of stamina to symptoms. How much can I do? What will be the consequences? How much will I have to pay? How long will it take

Living with Chronic Illness

SUGGESTED READING

Chronic Illness and the Family: A Guide for Living Every Day by Dr. Lind Welsh and Marian Betancourt, Holbrook, MA: Adams Media Corporation, 1996.

Handling It: You and Your Long-Term Disease by Susan Molloy, Melbourne: Hill of Content, 1995.

Living with Chronic Illness: Days of Patience and Passion by Cheri Register,

New York: The Free Press, 1987.

Sick and Tired of Feeling Sick and Tired: Living with Invisible Chronic Illness by Paul J. Donoghue, Ph.D., and Mary E. Siegel, Ph.D., New York: W. W. Norton and Company, 1992.

We Are Not Alone: Learning to Live with Chronic Illness by Sefra Kobrin Pitzele, New York: Workman Publishing, 1986.

to recover? What is the trade? What is it worth to me? My body is the battleground over which these choices are made on a daily basis. And for all my careful planning, illness remains untidy and unpredictable.

I feel a profound sense of loss, of despair, accompanying each incremental change in my body's function or topography. In some chronic illnesses there is a progressive and cumulative deterioration, in some a rhythm of advance and retreat as symptoms flare and then remit. My particular path has been a combination: acute flare-ups of disease followed by recovery to whatever baseline becomes the new "normal" for me. Part of me grieves each loss, and part of me stubbornly hopes for a miracle. It is the dance on a razor's edge between giving up and keeping on.

Too often fear has marked the borders of my sexual life—fear of rejection, of inability, of pain or fatigue, fear of my own differences. Body seen as betrayer, enemy, Other: not to be trusted. My own flesh becomes unfamiliar and unrecognized. I find myself measuring my worth by the state of my symptoms, and enclosing myself in smaller and smaller boxes. And beneath the fear there is rage. Rage at the theft of something precious and unexplored, and at the polite silences that have allowed this damage to progress unchecked. I am resentful of the loss of freedom and the denial of pleasure. I struggle against the depth of my accumulated longing and the physical and emotional isolation, so much of it self-imposed. I am angry that nothing can be taken for granted—that every act, every choice, must be weighed against the strictures of disease. I am enraged at the wounding of this woman-body. My body.

Historically I have swallowed the rage, instead apologizing for my limitations, fears, needs, feelings of inadequacy. Apologizing for, and even hiding my body from lovers. Erasing the urgency of my anger and my longing. The habit of silence was learned early on in a family that subtly competed over who was sickest, and who was the highest functioner in the face of adversity. To suffer and still achieve was a sort of twisted virtue. To endure pain, a source of pride and artistry. Secrets were written deep in this body's tissues, encoded between cells, memories and emotion quietly festering as the burning in my belly. The strategies of internalizing feelings and denying needs that I so carefully developed for childhood survival have now become lethal. The physical costs are too great, the emotional price unacceptable. It is in everyday acts of breaking silence that I reclaim my body from the possession of shame; that I seek my power, my health and my wholeness.

I have constructed, through a combination of accident and intent, a professional life that is based on speaking out about queer sexuality, about honoring the full range of our diverse experience. I write, teach and consult on lesbian health issues. I talk at professional conferences, clinics, medical schools, state and federal agencies, using language I am not supposed to admit to knowing, to describe lives and desires that are not supposed to exist. I tell "secrets" for a living in order to carve out wider and wider margins of safety for the extended family of gender and sex outlaws I love and admire. They say we teach what we most need to learn. It is easier for me to believe in and passionately defend the beauty, the preciousness and the rights of my queer community than to believe in my own essential worth and my right to sexual pleasure. The perception of self as "damaged goods" is hard to shake, but I am learning to constantly push my edges. The more times I jump off the cliff, the stronger my wings grow.

As women living with illness or disability, as women living with shame based on injury, abuse or lies we were told about ourselves and our value, we are called by an internal will for survival to break the silence. There is within us a deep hungering for affirmation. The thing we fear is also our heart's longing: to be seen, to be recognized, to be known, and from that place of knowing, to be embraced. I am always amazed, when we begin to talk, at how many of us carry this isolation. How many of us leave our bodies (or parts of them) in order to have sex. How many of us don't have sex at all because that sacrifice is easier to endure than our shame. How often we are quelled by an unwritten hierarchy of suffering in which we assume we have no right to "complain."

I don't know exactly what stubbornness continues to will me back from the borders of surrender, but I am grateful for it. For me there is alchemy in the uncompromising urgency of desire. My need for the tender weight of a lover's body covering my own, the taste of her mouth, her flesh, her sweat; to welcome her into me and pour out my uncensored wet. *Shamelessly.* It is an act of courage, of celebration and survival, defying all the years of careful sabotage that told me I could never claim this for my own.

Ironically, the same body I had imagined to be the instrument of my separation has become the vehicle that draws me relentlessly to ever higher ground.

After this essay was drafted in February 1995, my father developed leukemia as a complication of the medication he was taking for Crohn's disease. He died exactly eight weeks from the day he was diagnosed. My father's death was the "trump card" that ended the family competition over who was the sickest and freed me from the race to the (big) finish line. And now, from this place of hard-won healing, I find I am grateful that I was not the winner of that race after all.

SALLY MIKULAS

Eyes
Graves' Disease

Prior to September 22, 1989, I was a very strong and physically fit person. I could lift a ninety-pound jack-hammer from the ground to shoulder level with one hand. I could shovel a cubic yard of sand (three-thousand pounds) over a four-foot wall in just over thirteen minutes. I was *fit*. But that day, in a freak accident, I broke my kneecap, the muscles in my upper leg and in my shin pulling it in half.

While I was still recovering from knee surgery and doing physical therapy, I started having other problems: a severe case of bronchitis that nearly became pneumonia, digestive disturbances, menstrual problems, increased fluid retention and even ear infections for the first time in my life. Eventually I developed tachycardia (elevated heart rate), a systolic heart murmur and severe edema (fluid retention). I nearly developed an ulcer and had trouble keeping food down. If the food did stay down, it ran through my body so fast it wasn't funny. I became very weak: I could hardly pick up a backpack blower and put it on, and once

I got it on, I could barely make it up stairs with the blower on my back. Some of my co-workers thought I'd suddenly turned lazy. One all but accused me of purposely taking sick leave so she'd have to take my place at a job she hated. I couldn't understand why I was so tired. One co-worker said I should go to bed earlier; another started telling people he thought I was on marijuana. I wasn't.

It was obvious something was wrong. I thought it was my smoking, so I quit. After two weeks with no cigarettes I didn't feel a bit better and finally went to the doctor. After two weeks of testing and scanning and X rays, I was told I had Graves' disease. I'd never heard of it.

Graves' disease is an autoimmune disorder that causes excessive production of thyroid hormone. My thyroid was more than triple the normal size and was overproducing a hormone that in turn told the rest of my endocrine glands to underproduce. All of my hormones were completely out of balance. The best course of action in a case that severe is to kill the function of the thyroid gland with radiation, wait until the hormone is depleted and then administer replacement hormones. It took about a year for the hormone to deplete and to find the right dosage of hormones.

I was on light work duty for three months; gradually my strength increased, and eventually I could do most of what I had done before, although I had a partial loss of range of motion in my knee and couldn't squat or kneel any longer.

In the spring of 1992, I began having trouble seeing my watch face in the dark. My eyes hurt if I so much as brushed my fingers across them lightly, and I noticed that liquid was collecting under the conjunctiva so that my eyes had what looked like little pouches of water on them. Weird!

At the time, my employment involved brush cutting, chain sawing and other tasks that put a lot of irritants into the air. Naturally, that made the problem worse. My eyes would water until I couldn't see where I was walking, but I was perceived as being too fussy. After all, everybody has to do his or her share. Nobody would believe that something was really the matter, that I wasn't shirking, wasn't making it up.

By July, I noticed in choral practice that I was seeing double for a split second every time I looked from my music to my choral director and back again. In August my family doctor sent me to an ophthalmologist, who diagnosed my problem as thyroid eye disease resultant from Graves' disease (or part of Graves' disease by some doctors' reckoning).

By March of 1993, I was unable to work. I could not control my eyes at all and had become a hazard to myself and to my co-workers. I walked into stationary objects and people because I couldn't see where they were, I couldn't shovel anything into a truck because I couldn't be sure where the bed of the truck was, couldn't work around open drains or ditches for fear of falling in, couldn't work around heavy equipment for fear of getting hit by it. I was utterly useless and completely exhausted from the exertion of trying. I had to admit to myself that I had to go on leave. It was a great relief not to have to get up at 5:00 A.M. to try to get my eyes to work well enough to get to work by 8:00.

The collecting of fluid and the watering of the eyes for no apparent reason is called chemosis. Other aspects of the disease are elevated pressure within the eyeball, blurry vision, double vision, severe headaches and photophobia (extreme light sensitivity). The double vision and the headaches made me the most ill, but the elevated pressure was of even more concern because pressure on the optic nerve can cause it to die. Contraction of the eye muscles, of which there are four for each eye, caused my double vision. My left eye was being pulled up and to the left, while my right eye was being pulled down and to the right. In May of 1994, my eyes were forty prism diopters off vertically and a minimum of fifteen prism diopters off horizontally.

I can only begin to tell you how sick I felt most of the time.

The pulling of the muscles in my head even resulted in sections of my skull being pulled out of place. Twice the ball was pulled out of the socket of my right shoulder. It was mind-boggling how much was affected by the tension in those little eye muscles. I had eye-strain headaches, muscular tension headaches and migraine headaches nearly every day. I learned biofeedback techniques, got deep tissue massages, went to a chiropractor regularly and did stretching exercises and visualization to combat the nausea and constant pain.

I had eight different pairs of glasses in a little more than a year. The last ones I got before the surgery in May 1994 had twenty-five diopters of vertical prism to help me see things a bit closer to reality. I still had fifteen diopters left to contend with, however. A couple of months before the surgery I woke up one day and realized I could no longer remember what reality looked like. It dawned on me that I'd even been dreaming in "wacko-vision" for quite some time. That was one of only a few times I was reduced to tears.

I became almost totally inactive because of the constant nausea and pain. I gained weight from lack of exercise even though I was on a very low-fat, low-cholesterol diet. People would offer me "help" like, "You should try hypnotism for weight loss. I don't have any will power either, and I lost eight pounds after going to see so-and-so." They didn't take my pain seriously but instead saw me as a glutton with no will power.

And those oh-so-irritating suggestions from well-meaning people. "You should take megadoses of vitamin A." But that wouldn't make the muscles stop contracting. "You should get a second opinion." I already had several of the best doctors, specialists all, west of the Mississippi. "Put an eyepatch over one eye, and you should be able to see okay." Not a chance, not for this kind of problem. "Why don't you have that new laser surgery?" Because it wouldn't fix this ailment. Over and over I would explain to people that this is a disease that must be allowed to run its course. It won't just undo, get better, go back to normal . . . ever. And it can't be stopped, but the damage can be repaired (unless the optic nerve dies). I began to find it very hard to keep a civil tongue when around those kindhearted but misguided souls who couldn't seem to understand, but I would manage to be polite . . . most of the time.

A dear, sweet fellow in the choral group I'm in was one of those diehard hopefuls. I explained about this disease over and over to this lovely man every Tuesday evening for what seemed an eternity to me. I wondered how many times I would have to tell him it was something that had to run its course before that fact would sink in. I pondered his apparent thickheadedness. Then one evening when he asked the same questions yet again, I lost control and yelled at him. "What have I told you about this disease? Will it just 'get better'? NO! What did the doctor say? The same old thing. *It's still the same disease! Don't you get it? I'm sick of the same questions all the time!"*

Wow! I don't know which of us was the more shocked at my sudden and extremely uncharacteristic outburst, but oddly enough, it turned out to have a positive result in the end. I apologized for yelling at him, and we sat down and had a good old-fashioned heart-to-heart, complete with hugs and a few tears. He admitted that he was thinking of himself in a way, that he cared about me, hated watching me hurt, wanted something to make me feel better, so he refused to stop hoping that some miracle cure could be found. He really didn't know, until I blew up at him, that his denial of my reality not only wasn't giving me hope, but was actually adding to my burden. Make no mistake, it isn't really that I'd recommend yelling at one's friends, but it certainly did help in this case.

On May 20, 1994, I had corrective surgery to elongate and re-locate the two most severely affected eye muscles. The surgery was a wonderful thing! It corrected my vision by thirty-eight prism diopters. I had been warned by the hospital staff that I'd probably feel quite sick after the surgery because the eyes are so sensitive, but when I woke up after the surgery, I felt a lot better than I had immediately prior to the procedure. *Aaaahh . . .* what a relief it was!

After the surgery I had to wait six weeks until they'd test me for a new prescription (I had a pair of pre-wacko glasses to use for the duration), and in those six weeks, I could tell that the disease had not run its course and that the muscles were still contracting. I had known that was a strong possibility, so I wasn't startled, just disappointed.

Americans with Disabilities Act of 1990

▼ The Americans with Disabilities Act of 1990 (ADA) grants civil rights protections to individuals with disabilities.

▼ It guarantees equal opportunity in employment, public accommodations, transportation, state and local government services and telecommunications.

For more information regarding the ADA, contact the Civil Rights Division, U.S. Department of Justice , P.O. Box 66118, Washington, DC 20035-0301, (202) 514-0301, (202) 514-0381-3 (TDD).

What did come as a shock after the surgery was that I couldn't write! I had to learn to write all over again. I knew what the letters should look like, but when I tried to form them they wouldn't look like the vision in my brain. So I bought a bunch of nice art pencils and crayons and colored in coloring books for hours a day for weeks to improve my hand-eye coordination. By the end of the summer I could write passably. Not great, but okay. To this day, though, if I'm extremely tired, I can't write.

Now, some days I can be at the computer for several hours, but other days I can only check the e-mail and stash it in folders. Once in a while I can't stand to look at the computer long enough to do that. Some days I still hide from the light most of the day in a darkened room.

I returned to work on August 7, 1995, under the Americans with Disabilities Act, which requires employers to make "reasonable accommodation" for a person's disability. I'm now an administrative specialist (that's a fancy name for a clerk) for the city of Seattle, and accommodation for my disability was quite simple: a desk away from bothersome light sources (doors, windows), an appropriate desk lamp with a twenty-five watt incandescent bulb and a new flat-screen nonflickering monitor for my computer.

Even though I knew I'd not be able to do the kind of work I'd done before, I still was rather concerned when I was told that I'd be working in city hall. I'd never worked in an office. I wasn't sure how I should dress and didn't have much in the way of "nice" fat-lady clothes. I was nervous about how my particular disability would be perceived now that it wasn't so visibly obvious, especially considering how I'd been treated before going on leave. I needn't have worried. People have been very understanding of my limitations.

I have significant permanent damage to my vision. I still have days when my eyes water all day and I feel as if I'm looking through a windshield on a rainy day with the wipers on the intermittent setting. I still experience considerable discomfort from light, especially sunlight. This is true both on sunny days and those with the thin "morning clouds" we hear so much about in the great Northwest. Now, I *love* rainy days. My eyes are most comfortable on days that most folks would describe as dreary, days on which there is not even a glimmer of hope that the sun will peek through. It really is true that "beauty is in the eye of the beholder," because I think those "dreary" days are beautiful indeed. They cause no pain, and I don't have to wear sunglasses or squint all the time, which gets old fast.

I still have a momentary lapse into double vision when shifting my gaze from one plane to another, but it's livable this way. I will always have to fight double vision and have to work at "keeping things singular." I know I may never drive a vehicle again, and I mourn the surrender of my commercial driver's license. Emotionally, that loss was one of the most difficult to accept as my reputation as a highly skilled driver was a major part of my identity. I began driving trucks on my aunt's place in rural Iowa at age fourteen, drove a school bus in Alaska, drove a taxi in the Seattle/King County area, and frequently drove trucks for the Seattle Engineering Department. Now I do not drive for fear of killing someone during a momentary lapse into double vision.

Some two years and three months after the surgery, there are still shifts in my condition, though they seem to come in spurts. That is, the situation will stabilize, and it seems for several months that the slow contracting of the eye muscles has ended. Then just when I let myself think that's the case, it will shift again. I'm certainly better off than I was when the disease was at its worst, and I doubt it will ever get that bad again. Yet I do sometimes wonder if it will ever truly be over.

ANNE WYATT

Surviving, Stepping and Living with Multiple Sclerosis

I treated myself badly for years, after years of being badly treated. I never expected to live past thirty, so I reacted rather than acted in my life. When nothing matters, anything is acceptable. I've averaged more than two jobs, two lovers and four homes per year since I turned eighteen. The average would be even higher if not for the stability of the past four years.

What has my story to do with lesbian health and health-related issues? After all, it is only my life, nothing very special, not political. I have to remind myself that the personal is political, and that I am a lesbian who faces and has faced a number of health issues. Even the way in which I dismiss my story—myself—and the reasons behind that are pertinent.

I am the oldest of five children born to a woman who became an elementary school teacher and to a man who became an elementary school principal. I mention their occupations because it is ironic to me that two such abusive people, one a diagnosed

Surviving,
Stepping and
Living with
Multiple
Sclerosis

■

123

sociopath, worked in nurturing professions. I'm sure there's some handy pop psychology to explain their choices. My own explanation is power and money. As a principal, my father had power over teachers (primarily female) and students (young, impressionable and easily terrorized). As a teacher, my mother earned money she desperately needed when she and my father divorced and she became a single parent supporting five children under the age of six. Not coincidentally, it gave her power over children in a structured setting.

My father regularly beat and raped my mother even when she was pregnant, which she almost always was during the five years they were together. I can't remember when he began beating me, but I do know he began sexually molesting me when I was two years old. Sexual abuse, including sodomy, continued until he and my mother separated when I was five. Someone asked me how I can be so sure of all this. I saw him beat my mother. I heard her being raped. I still have the scars from his beatings and sexual assaults on me. In a way, I'm glad he left evidence. It's easier to get past self-doubt that way. Self-loathing, well, that is an essential truth behind the facts of my life.

My parents' divorce might have been a relief except that my mother also was abusive. When I am rationalizing, I tell myself she was under a terrible strain. No wonder she snapped, what with five precocious and rambunctious children. Still, after all the therapy I've had and support groups I've been in, it is difficult for me to justify the way she expressed her frustration and rage. I struggle with the notion and probably always will, but I am (almost) certain I am not "a sociopath just like your father." I know (I think) it was not my fault that my mother and father married. I am (pretty) sure I was not responsible for my brothers and my sister even though I was the oldest. None of us deserved switches for Christmas or dog feces for dinner. How bad could children under ten in the 1960s be?

Early on, I vowed I would never have children. I didn't ever want to cause tears or screams of pain. The welts and scarring of my childhood would not be passed on by me. It did not occur to me that the damage caused by my childhood affected far more than my determination to avoid being a parent. The damage was there and is obvious to me now, but I had no way to make the connections then.

I first attempted suicide at fourteen. I started smoking and began drinking alcoholically when I was sixteen. I also became aware of, and rejected, my sexual preference at that time. I ran away from home at seventeen and was raped and attempted suicide again then. I barely managed to finish high school, and I weighed 180 pounds when I did graduate. At eighteen, I was stunned to be alive and desperate to get out of my mother's house. Despite my homophobia, I wanted to find other lesbians. I put myself on a 240-calories-a-day diet, lost fifty pounds quickly and joined the army, where all the lesbians were. But none of this came from anything but my own weirdness, right? Right.

So, I reached one of my milestones, age eighteen, and I wasn't dead. Still, although a survivor, I had no idea *how* to live. Maybe it is more accurate to say that, though I'd come from a horrible childhood, I wasn't through it. The lessons of my childhood— don't talk, don't trust, don't feel, don't cry—were lessons I carried with me into the army, into all my relationships, every facet of my life. The punishments of childhood *did* evolve, sort of, becoming crisis-of-the-day, crisis-of-the-week, crisis-of-the-month.

By the time I was twenty-one, I had been discharged from the army for latent homosexuality and had directly or indirectly attempted suicide three more times. I had learned to let someone hug me without obviously flinching, but I could not control my inward flinch or the flashbacks. I also drank too much. Booze was a legal anesthetic, very acceptable in the army and very acceptable in the lesbian community in 1975. The bars were the center of social experience.

After the army, I briefly attended a small private college. My

Surviving,
Stepping and
Living with
Multiple
Sclerosis

■

125

primary focus there was snorting speed and pretending a world-
liness that only a twenty-one-year-old among seventeen- and eigh-
teen-year-olds can get away with. Then a woman I had gotten to
know while playing softball my last summer in the army joined
me during my second semester at college. When she decided to
return to Washington state, I left college and went with her. I became a periodic drunk. That is, I went for long periods without
alcohol and even sometimes had alcohol without becoming
drunk. Mostly though, when I drank, I drank until I was drunk.

Being a survivor is both a weakness and a strength. That is,
one expects disaster, even courts it (weakness), but then has the
strength to get through it. By age twenty-five, I had held some
fourteen jobs in five states and abroad. I also had attended six
different colleges, accumulating an incredible number of unrelated credits. I had been involved with eleven women including the woman from Washington. I expected every relationship
to end, and each did. It took four years for me to sabotage the
relationship with the woman from Washington, but we split up,
just as I always knew we would. My timetable for my death was
messed up though. Since I'd missed ending up in a ditch by age
twenty-one, I was sure I'd be dead by the time I was thirty.

Although I suspected my inability to trust came from childhood, I didn't realize that my inability to focus was related to my
upbringing. In that respect, my life differs only in its details from
the lives of other survivors. The general outline is very much the
same: difficulties with authority, difficulty forming and keeping
relationships, sexual repression and/or promiscuity. It is a pattern
that exists and does damage in the lesbian community. I remember reading that a significant percentage of all women are survivors of sexual abuse.[1] So, if you're a lesbian, and you aren't a
survivor, chances are very good that you know someone who is.
There's a good chance you've even had lovers who were survivors. Please understand I am *not* saying sexual abuse causes lesbianism. I believe sexual preference is innate. I do think that the

aversion treatment of such abuse burns out any heterosexual tendencies in a lesbian survivor.

A friend of mine tells the following joke: *Q: How can you tell two lesbians are on their second date? A: There's a moving van in front of one of their houses.* She always gets a laugh with that one, a been-there-done-that kind of laugh. I believe we've been there and done that in part because so many of us are survivors. We reach for the promise of love without knowing what it is, how to give it or how to receive it. The result, at least in my experience, is numerous replays of the same poor relationship. The faces change, the details of disaster change, but disaster itself is inevitable and predictable.

The extensive use of anesthetics—alcohol or other drugs, codependence (why think about my life when I can worry about yours?), food, sex and so on—also is a predictable response of survivors. I think I'm a fairly typical example in that I didn't want to feel the pain of my upbringing. I really didn't want to know it was there. Alcohol, food and co-dependence were the bandages I used to block out thought, feeling and memory. Such anesthetics work, in the short term. Unfortunately, they keep you from addressing underlying problems, and they generate their own set of problems. In the long run, a person is worse off than before.

By the time I was twenty-five, in 1979, I had experienced a few

Living with Multiple Sclerosis

SUGGESTED READING

All of a Piece: A Life with Multiple Sclerosis by Barbara Webster, Baltimore: Johns Hopkins University Press, 1989.

Living Well with MS: A Guide for Patient, Caregiver, and Family by David L. Carroll and Jon Dudley Dorman, M.D., New York: HaperPerennial/HarperCollins, 1993.

Living with Multiple Sclerosis: A Handbook for Families by Dr. Robert Shuman and Dr. Janice Schwartz, New York: MacMillan, 1994.

Multiple Sclerosis Fact Book by R. Lechtenberg, Philadelphia: FA Davis Co., 1995.

Surviving,
Stepping and
Living with
Multiple
Sclerosis

■

127

transient episodes of what I now recognize as symptoms of multiple sclerosis. Burning in the soles of my feet, double vision, difficulty urinating, leg spasms—nothing so terrible or of long enough duration to make me think there was a real problem, much less that I should see a doctor. Besides, I had to find a job. I found work at a mill that paid $9.15 per hour. I was determined to settle down, and then everything was going to be fine. I bought a house.

In 1980, the recession hit, and the mill laid off many of its workers, including me. Fortunately it was 1980: The census kept me afloat. I was working the census and a part-time job at a fast food place that summer when I shattered my knee in a freak softball accident. The doctors had to rebuild the top of my tibia. I spent six days in the hospital, three months laid up at home and then several months rehabilitating. It was not clear I'd ever walk without some kind of aid. It *was* clear I'd never work in a mill again. More immediately, it was not clear how I was going to pay all the bills. It stretched my survivor instincts to find a solution. Fortunately, it was a crisis, so I was able to act.

CETA (Comprehensive Employment and Training Act) saved me. This government program paid tuition, books and fees plus a stipend for those enrolled in specific degree programs. I chose the practical nurse program. The community college P.N. course was the first focused program I had finished outside of high school and army training. It showed me I wasn't as stupid as I secretly believed.

It also showed me I wasn't prepared for either the politics of medicine or the dedication required of nurses. I switched my focus to journalism, got an A.A. degree and began work on a bachelor's degree at a university. Through all of this, I was working full-time, taking a full course load and maintaining involvement in student government. On paper, I looked like superwoman but inside I still felt like a failure.

In 1982 my maternal grandmother was diagnosed with non-Hodgkin's lymphoma. She had been my safe person throughout childhood, my touchstone of sanity, and I wanted to leave school and take care of her, but she insisted I stay in school. She was so proud I was there. I agreed to continue, but insisted on staying with her. I also kept the part-time newspaper job I had. The year my grandmother died, I was traveling 450 miles per week to take a full load of university classes and teach a class there, maintain my job weekends at the paper *and* care for my grandmother. In keeping with the attitude that I could never do enough, I also was involved in student politics, including working with the then Gay and Lesbian Alliance on campus.

Grandma died in April 1983. I began drinking every day, but otherwise went on as if nothing had happened. I was appointed director of Women in Transition for 1983–84 and elected to the Incidental Fee Committee, a group that holds hearings and decides funding for student organizations. I also continued my newspaper job. I was beginning summer term classes when I started to shatter. By end of term, I was so gone, all I *could* continue was the drinking.

It wasn't until September 15, 1983, that I admitted to myself that I had a problem with alcohol. I stopped drinking, joined a twelve-step group and decided to finish school. Sounds good, doesn't it? It was, in the long run, but long runs are for assessments. Actual living occurs in short moments. In those moments, I still wore a superwoman facade over a core of feeling worthless.

I earned a bachelor's degree in journalism and a certificate in women's studies in August 1984 and began law school shortly thereafter. In other words, I was so scared by the prospect of life outside the university that I chose an advanced degree program. My secondary motivation was a desire to feel complete. I still felt hollow. I still felt stupid. On the other hand, I was learning life skills in the twelve-step program.

In December 1984, I was able to give up all the part-time jobs I held because I got a terrific graduate teaching fellowship. My new job was part-time and my kind of work: crisis management

Surviving,
Stepping and
Living with
Multiple
Sclerosis

■

129

with a requirement of facile social skills. So, I was doing something that paid well, gave me status, took advantage of survivor skills and did not demand full-time focus. It was a success experience I needed. It lasted until 1989, some months after the multiple sclerosis diagnosis.

The diagnosis led to the breakup of a three-year relationship, four brief and abusive affairs, a basement apartment without heat or lights and a stint living in a van with two small dogs and two cats. At one point, I was living on $96 in monthly VA disability benefits plus $240 in welfare benefits. I became a regular tenant at rest areas and a consumer of the samples put out by grocery store departments.

I could have had a drink during that time. I surely wanted anesthesia when things got bad, but the years of twelve-stepping had taught me anesthesia wasn't the answer. It was incredibly annoying to face the facts, and yet facing them got me through. I went to meetings, volunteered for service work and focused on the Veteran's Administration as a target for the anger and frustration I felt. If the VA isn't an option for you, find something of similar monolithic proportion. A focus for feelings of rage and helplessness is important, and that focus shouldn't be you or another living being. Focusing on the VA allowed me to learn some key lessons.

First, survivors of a terrible childhood may not recognize support when it's offered. Second, substance abusers may equate supporter with sucker. Third, if the majority of those in a particular lesbian community are survivors and/or substance abusers, what kind of support can they offer others? Fourth, on-off rigid thinking is a hallmark of survivorship. In that light, what does one make of politically correct righteousness? I've been told directly that women don't hit women. If that's true, there's no battery between lesbians. I can testify that that just ain't so—women *do* hit women, and other women look away. Finally, I have learned that support for poverty and disability are dependent upon looking the part. Stay clean, sleep in a van and deal with a relatively invisible disability and your sisters may hiss at you for abusing a handicap sticker.

Oddly enough, I felt like a fraud when I first got the sticker. I mean, I wasn't handicapped. That's wheelchair stuff and physically obvious, like a severe case of cerebral palsy or something. Right? Wrong. I won't go into a detailed clinical description of multiple sclerosis, though it's tempting to try to avoid sharing feelings by doing so. I will say that MS is an unpredictable and progressive chronic disorder of the central nervous system. It doesn't usually shorten a person's life span. Is that good? Sometimes I think so. Sometimes I'm not so sure. Still, as my grandma used to say, it takes forty-three muscles to frown and only two muscles to smile. Since one of my principle MS symptoms is fatigue, smiling is a good way for me to conserve energy. I will admit that smiling sometimes is just a way to grit my teeth.

That's the deal, at least for me. Not courage, nothing fancy, but gritting my teeth and hanging in. If I'm about to fall, I try to roll with it so nothing but my ego gets hurt. I've learned not to turn around too fast and, definitely, never to close my eyes when bending over. I'm gradually losing sensation in my extremities. I can't feel a cat's fur with my fingertips, for example. Even so, I can feel the vibration of her purr with my palms and hear the sound of it. I can't walk more than fifty feet without an assistive device like a cane or crutch, but I have a scooter that can take me ten miles over fairly rough terrain that I would otherwise have to avoid.

Certainly, MS has meant loss, and more will come. I'm not thrilled about that. It scares the hell out of me, if I forget to live in and appreciate the moment. I grieve then and worry that my life is over, valueless and without purpose. I call such days Toosdays, as in "If I didn't have MS, I could do (*fill in the blank*) Too," or "What if I lose (*x* or *y* or *z*) Too?" I can wallow in *ifs* and *what ifs* with the best, but what a waste of time! I have a loving partner to love, stories, poems and plays to write, e-mail to send and receive, a house, a yard and animals to care for and appreciate. I'm over forty now, determined to live, and I finally have some idea how to do so.

Surviving,

Stepping and

Living with

Multiple

Sclerosis

■

131

Notes

1. One source, *Our Health, Our Lives*, estimates this number at one in five. While every study may say something different, they are all *estimates*.

HELENA BASKET

Bleeding Peaches

In January 1994, less than a month after my twenty-eighth birthday, I had a hysterectomy to remove benign fibroid tumors. I retained my ovaries and therefore a hormones-only menstrual cycle, but gave up my uterus and cervix. During this experience I encountered both good and bad elements of the American health care system. I also experienced misogyny, homophobia and ageism. Now, over a year later, I am profoundly grateful for my health. I do not regret the choice I made.

When I was in my mid-twenties I started to have unmanageably heavy periods. I could not fit tampons comfortably into my vagina and so wore menstrual pads. I bled through about one pad an hour for ten days to two weeks every month. I was exhausted. It was hard to adjust my life to this. I bled huge clots. They rolled out of my vagina like big soft fruits and went thud onto the floor of the bathtub as I showered. When visiting friends, rather than bleed all over their furniture, I chose the embarrassment of asking for a towel.

I had a half-hour commute to work, and on a bad day during my period, I would bleed through the two pads I had in my pants before I got to work and would have to turn around, go home and change. I kept a towel in my car and at work for "accidents." Once in an important meeting, I realized I was bleeding through my menstrual pad. Huge firm clots gave my cervix a pleasant twinge, dribbled out of me and rested inside my labia. They felt like skinned peaches in my vulva. When I felt a warm gush of blood, I finally gave up on the meeting and stood to go to the bathroom. My skirt was soaked with blood and so was the chair.

I started to have pain in my abdomen and was unable to urinate whenever I wanted to. The urination problem was wildly painful. I would have to go to the bathroom five or six times a night, disrupting my sleep, which added to my exhaustion. I would sit on the toilet, pee a tablespoonful and feel empty, but seemingly ten minutes later I would have to go again. When I couldn't urinate at all, I felt an awful pressure and pain, as if my bladder was working very hard to empty itself, but the sphincter had clamped shut.

One day a terrible pain overcame me and I lay stunned on the floor, unable even to speak. Eventually the pain passed, but the incident frightened me.

After several more months of intermittent urination problems, flooding periods and pain, my longtime lover, Denise, and several of our friends started to nag me about seeing a doctor. I was terrified of doctors and resisted. My experience with ob-gyns had been awful at best, from a moralistic doctor who informed my fundamentalist Christian mother of my request for birth control pills when I was seventeen, to a blindingly painful and cold-hearted clinic abortion when I was twenty.

However, when I finally agreed to see a doctor in August 1993, it turned out to be a good experience. I liked my internist, Dr. Limerick, right away. She spent a good hour with me, talking and listening, and then accepted another appointment to go over the same conversation with Denise. One of Dr. Limerick's first observations was that she thought the menstrual and urinary problems were related. I had a large fibroid tumor in my uterus, and she told me that I was so anemic I was lucky to be able to stand up and walk around.

She also told me in that first appointment that I would probably have to consider a hysterectomy. I was twenty-seven then, and although I had not made the decision to have children, I wanted the option. I was devastated. Dr. Limerick helped me to find a gynecologist. In the D.C. area my insurance coverage offered only four or five women gyncologists, so getting an appointment was hard. Most of them couldn't see me for six weeks or so. I didn't press it, because I was glad to have the time to think about all I had learned.

I finally got an appointment with a Maryland country doctor. Dr. Boxer was not gentle or sensitive, and when I told her I was a lesbian, she popped me into her "not sexually active" box and treated me as if I were a virgin. Dr. Boxer was not a good listener, and her exams were rough and impersonal.

I particularly feared pelvic exams. For years my cervix rested less than two knuckles' length in from the opening of my vagina. I couldn't even get a tampon in, much less fingers or a dildo. During a pelvic exam, gynecologists would shove in that speculum and crank it open which hurt like hell. Usually they ignored my cautions about how small my vagina was.

At Dr. Boxer's office, I had crossed out the listing for "husband" on the intake form and written, "partner, Denise Jones." I got some funny looks from the staff for that. Of course that's something that any longtime lesbian is used to, but I've never gotten comfortable with it and with how rude people can be. Then I had an intake interview with a crotchety old nurse who insisted on referring to my husband and my male doctor. I wondered if she was deaf. I kept correcting her: "My internist is a woman. My partner is a woman. No, I do not need birth control. No, there is no penis going into me, so of course I didn't know my uterus is in my vagina." Same old B.S.

During my first appointment Dr. Boxer wanted to start me on injections of Lupron, a drug that acts on the pituitary gland to stop production of hormones, inducing menopause. That would allow me to recover from the severe anemia I was suffering, and possibly reduce the size of the fibroid tumor. I said I wanted to go home and think about it; it was all happening too fast.

I began Lupron injections later that month, but, although Lupron stops most women's periods, mine became a permanent condition. The long weeks of periods merged, and beginning in September 1993, I bled profusely every day, week after week. The good Dr. Limerick's weekly blood tests showed that my blood counts had descended to less than half of the lowest number for a healthy woman.

Dr. Boxer kept saying, "Let's schedule the surgery for next week," but I was not ready. I wanted to give the Lupron a chance to shrink the tumor. I took massive doses of iron to counteract the anemia. I talked to Dr. Boxer about her staff's ignorance about lesbians, but she was unresponsive, blissfully ignorant and wishing to stay that way. Denise and Dr. Limerick agreed there was no reason to trust my body to a doctor I didn't trust.

I made an appointment with a young gynecologist that Dr. Limerick recommended, Dr. Bubbles. I convinced her staff to give me an immediate appointment by saying I was on a regimen of Lupron and needed my next injection right away. Dr. Bubbles was probably not more than thirty years old and full of reassuring language like "Cool!" and "Groovy." However, she startled me when she referred to my womb as "Mr. Uterus." I reacted snappishly, and she covered by saying that anything that gives women trouble is a man. Okay, nice save. I let it pass. I felt cautious about her but trusted Dr. Limerick's judgment.

During this time urination and menstrual flow problems were getting worse. I was frightened and asking both Dr. Limerick and Dr. Bubbles for help with my difficulty in urinating, but neither could offer an explanation or fix the problem.

Dr. Bubbles kept me on Lupron through the Thanksgiving holidays to try to shrink the tumor somewhat. My sonogram showed it to be eleven centimeters in diameter, at the upper rear of my uterus. I remained too anemic to be operated on.

One night, before Christmas, Denise and I were visiting at the home of friends. I really appreciated hanging out with this particular couple, because they were both completely comfortable with my condition. I knew I might have trouble urinating that night because I was drinking a lot of fluids and hadn't gone to the bathroom since early evening. But I was so used to this horrible routine that I was prepared to suffer the agony. I had learned that a hot shower, stretching and deep breathing would allow me to urinate eventually. And once I did, the pain would subside instantly. My doctors said this problem would go away after surgery, so I figured I could ride it out until then.

As the evening wore on, I tried to urinate several times with no success. Each time I would return from the bathroom pale and ghastly-looking.

Around ten o'clock I still hadn't peed and was starting to feel sweaty and faint from the pain. As Denise drove us home, I let myself feel the pain more. Groaning and gasping, I could only breathe shallowly. My stomach was distended, and the pain was awful. As soon as I got in the apartment, I ripped off my clothes and ran a hot shower. I shoveled through the medicine cabinet looking for a painkiller and then crouched in the shower, shivering and carrying on. Denise says I was screaming. I thought my bladder was going to burst, and I was too scared to know what to do. Denise said she was going to take me to the hospital, and I obediently picked up my head from the wet tiles and got out of the shower. I was in such bad shape that going to the hospital sounded good to me.

At the local hospital, Washington Adventist, the staff triaged me instantly and treated Denise like my spouse, which was a great relief for both of us. The nurse prepared me for my first catheter. It didn't hurt going in, but it was humiliating and uncomfortable. I told the nurse I sympathized with her, having such a gory job. She laughed and said the relief I would feel made it all worthwhile to her. She was right. In just a few minutes I felt the pressure subsiding. Over the course of an hour and a half I expelled more than a liter of urine. No wonder I had been in such pain, the nurses kept saying.

Before I was discharged, the emergency room doctor offered me the option of keeping the catheter in, but I declined because I was convinced this situation wouldn't happen again if I was very careful to urinate regularly.

Denise and I went home. We were worried that surgery had become an immediate threat, and we hadn't finished talking about it. We had to discuss fertility, having or not having children, the possibility of Denise agreeing to bear children, my sense of identity as a woman.

Ten days later, I went to Minnesota for a conference on multiculturalism in the workplace. This conference meant a lot to me. At my supervisor's insistence I told my conference room-mate, Dizzy, that there was a slight chance that I might become ill and have to go to the emergency room.

It was a good thing I had alerted Dizzy. During a morning lecture, I began to have urination problems, went back up to my hotel room and did the whole song and dance: hot shower, deep breathing, stretching. It didn't help. I called Denise in terror and disbelief that I would have to go to a strange hospital in a strange city with a woman I had only met the day before. Denise was very reassuring and suggested that I use the hotel's services for help. I called the front desk and asked them to page Dizzy. She appeared shortly, and all I said was, "It's happening. I don't want an ambulance." She took one look at me and turned into super-woman. She arranged for a cab, bundled me up and helped me downstairs. The cab was waiting. We drove to the hospital, miles away. I was moaning and crying, thrown into that fog of pain and fear I had experienced ten days earlier. Once again I was triaged right away. I knew what to expect this time and waited for the relief. Dizzy was wonderful, helping me to undress and holding my hand. The staff was also wonderful, gentle and reassuring and sympathetic. This time I kept the catheter in.

I called Dr. Bubbles once I was home, and she referred me to a urologist. Unfortunately he was a man. I resigned myself to this. My insurance company and Dr. Bubbles didn't seem to think my desire to keep my body away from men was worth consideration, and I was too tired and had too much pain and fear to fight.

Dr. Plumber and his crew examined my plumbing and deter-mined that my right ureter, the tube leading from my right kid-ney to my bladder, was partially blocked. He measured the fibroid tumor and observed that it was growing, despite the monthly Lupron injections. He cautioned me that if the tumor kept grow-ing at this rate, it was only a matter of a month until my right kidney was in serious trouble. He also commented that he could see the imprint of the tumor in my bladder wall.

As I sat up after the exam, thick, long clots started to pour out of my vagina and onto the exam table. Clots like raw meat spilled out onto the table, onto the towels they gave me and into the toilet once I made it there. Dr. Plumber and his staff were definitely concerned and didn't know what to do. Eventually the flow slowed, but not before I started to feel light-headed. When I was dressed and dry, Dr. Plumber sat me down to explain what *he* thought was the problem.

Had I been bleeding like this for a while? Yes, since Septem-ber 23, 1993, when I got the first Lupron shot. Did I wear pads all the time, or sometimes tampons? Pads only. Then Dr. Plumber leaned back and said, "You have a chronic urinary tract infection. Your vulva and your pads are harboring bacteria, which are very happy to have all that warmth and good stuff to eat, and you have been walking around with a bladder infection for months."

I was absolutely astonished. I couldn't believe it was something so simple, and I was furious that none of the other doctors had suggested this. Dr. Plumber gave me some antibiotics and urinary anesthetic to take, and I never had the problem again, thank God.

Because of the amount of blood I had lost at the urologist's office, Dr. Plumber suggested I go to the hospital for a possible blood transfusion. Denise picked me up and took me to nearby University Hospital, where I was hooked up to an IV and given a couple of drip-bags of saline and glucose.

Dr. Bubbles's associate, one of several male doctors that we had dealt with through the weeks, came in to give me a pelvic exam. He pulled on the gloves, and I said, "Don't even *think* about using a speculum." He roughly pushed his fingers inside me, and I did my usual arched-back-wiggly-butt dance of pain. Denise held my hand, and as I looked up at her I saw a look of rage on her face. She told me later that she had wanted to leap at him and scream, "Can't you see you're *hurting* her!"

After this experience, Denise and I were ready for surgery. I understood from my assortment of doctors that I had my choice of two surgical procedures: myomectomy, which would carve out the tumor and leave some semblance of a uterus, and hysterectomy, which would take out the whole apparatus. Myomectomy meant that I might still be able to conceive, but for the rest of my life my periods could likely be unpredictable and painful. The terrible periods were one reason I had gone for help in the first place. I wanted no more of that. Myomectomy also meant possible recurrence of tumors and future surgery. There was no guarantee that I would be able to conceive with all the scar tissue that would be in my uterus, and no guarantee that I would be able to carry a child full term if I did conceive.

As Denise and I talked about all this, I realized that it was unlikely I would ever want to have children. Therefore I was willing to exchange my fertility for long-term relief. Hysterectomy sounded like the right option. Now that I had decided, I wanted to get it over with. I called Dr. Bubbles and said, "Let's schedule a hysterectomy as soon as possible. I've had it."

Cheerful young Dr. Bubbles said, "You can't have a hysterectomy. You're too young to make that kind of decision, kiddo, and you're still fertile. I am definitely pro-choice, but you don't know what you'll feel in a few weeks much less a few years, and the medical review board would have my ass." I was profoundly enraged. How dare she question my stability, my decision-making processes, my right to make decisions about my own body?

I remained calm and observed to Dr. Bubbles that since Denise and I were lesbians, there were two uteruses involved, and if we later decided to have children, Denise could certainly be the bearer. Dr. Bubbles indicated that she thought I might change my mind about being a lesbian, too.

After all this, the pain, the months of agonizing conversations

Knowing the Facts About Hysterectomy

SUGGESTED READING

Coping with Hysterectomy by Susanne Morgan, New York: Dial Press, 1982.

Fibroid Tumors and Endometriosis: Self Help Book by Susan M. Lark, M.D., Berkeley: Celestial Arts, 1995.

Hysterectomy: Before and After by Winnifred B. Cutler, Ph.D., New York: HarperPerennial/HarperCollins, 1988.

Hysterectomy: Woman to Woman by Sue Ellen Barber, Wilsonville, OR: Book

Partners, 1996.

The Woman's Guide to Hysterectomy: Expectations and Options by Adelaide Haas and Susan L. Puretz, Berkeley: Celestial Arts, 1995.

You Don't Need a Hysterectomy: New and Effective Ways of Avoiding Major Surgery by Ivan K. Strausz, Reading, MA: Addison-Wesley Publishing Company, 1993.

with Denise and others I trusted, to be told that because of my age and gender I didn't know what was best for me was the last straw. I felt a calm confidence that I would have a hysterectomy, and it wouldn't be from Dr. Bubbles or Dr. Boxer. I knew I had only a month to find another doctor before my right kidney started to be really sick.

We asked among our lesbian friends to see if any of them could recommend a good woman gynecologist. We kicked ourselves for not thinking of that earlier. A friend recommended a lesbian doctor in Virginia. I called right away, and not only would Dr. Hero take my insurance, she also had an opening that afternoon. Providence.

Right away I knew Dr. Hero was the right choice. She was tall and graceful and gentle, like a character from a Madeleine L'Engle book. When it was time for the hated pelvic, she inserted one finger, well lubed, and waited until I relaxed a little. "I'm not going to hurt you," she said in her soft voice. And she didn't. She felt around so gently and pulled out so slowly that I was not uncomfortable at all. It was amazing. I felt so joyful to have found her. She interviewed me and afterward said she could see no reason for me not to have a hysterectomy, and she could do it in two weeks. To cover herself with the medical review board, she wrote Dr. Bubbles a letter describing her interview and her exam results, and that was the end of Dr. Bubbles.

I arranged to have six weeks off from work and for friends to come and keep me company after the operation, and started thinking about projects to keep myself occupied once I was home.

I was scheduled for surgery in the afternoon of January 11, 1994. The day before I rested and packed things like books, playing cards, stationery, "big-girl" underpants that came up to the waist and wouldn't irritate my incision, a Walkman, tapes, ChapStick and my security blanket, Quiltie. I wasn't nervous, thanks in part to a month of Xanax courtesy of Dr. Limerick.

When I got to the hospital with Denise, I had my last cigarette, and then the nurse came out to the waiting room and said it was time for me to prepare for surgery. I asked her if this was the last time I would see Denise, and she said yes. We had no privacy for our good-bye, so we just hugged very hard. Then I went through double doors into a very warm and quiet room, where a few other women, all looking very wan and anonymous in their gowns and puffy caps, waited. The nurse gave me my own set of these and asked me to change and put my things in a plastic bag, which she said she would take out to Denise. I had to give up my glasses, which made me anxious at first, because I can't see a thing without them. But I relaxed and just went with it. Then the nurse helped me up onto my little gurney and tucked warm, soft white blankets around me. I listened to the women on either side of me. One woman was about to have an abortion, and she was talking to her doctor in a way that made me understand that even now, minutes before her surgery, she wasn't sure this was the right thing to do. I empathized with her. The general atmosphere was of calm and kindness.

Nurses and doctors drifted in and out of my curtained nook, setting up things and getting me ready. A man came in and started to prepare my hand for an IV. I steeled myself, but all I felt was a tiny little poke. "Good job!" I gasped. He smiled and said he was the senior IV-putter-inner.

They started various drugs flowing into me, and then a gaunt, pale man who looked like a Halloween character came up, all dressed in blue, and introduced himself as the anesthesiologist. He patted my hand reassuringly and gave me a tiny amount of something in my IV, which further relaxed me. I now felt beatific.

I was rolled down the hall on my gurney to another waiting area, or holding area, I think they called it. This room bustled with people and beeping machines. The woman having the abortion was next to me, quiet now. More nurses and doctors fussed over me, but I was so woozy I don't remember what they did. Then someone said, "We're going to give you something to relax you now," and that's the last thing I remember.

My friend Elle had warned me that I would hurt *a lot* when I woke up, and that the first thing out of my mouth should be "painkillers." Denise had warned me that I'd feel cold and dry-mouthed and that it might sound as if people were screaming at me. Actually, I experienced none of these things. I vaguely remember a kind, dark face over me, saying, "You're fine, you're in recovery now." Then I remember being wheeled through more hallways, with Denise racing along beside me, her sweet concerned face and her long black hair over me. Her hand was on the gurney rail, and I knew I was safe and fine, as long as she was there.

When they got me to my room, I remember being gently lifted onto the bed. The nurse tucked me in, and Denise gave me Quiltie. I went to sleep.

Later, our friends Jacob and Jewel came by. I saw Jewel's face as if through a cloud of black fog, and I focused on Jacob's bright white shirt and pretty tie. I wanted to say, "Jacob, what a nice tie," because Jacob's bad taste in ties is a running joke with us, but all I could say was "Tie . . . " before going back to sleep. When I woke up, they were gone.

Denise slept on the floor by my bed. Every time I woke up, she was there. She touched me a lot, and her touch was like magic, as it always is. The nurses seemed to defer to her, and she was alert to every need I had.

The first time I felt pain was right after surgery. I woke up to the vision of a fairy-tale giant stirring my open abdomen with a big wooden spoon. It hurt a lot, but not the kind of desperate pain I had felt not being able to urinate.

Denise tells me that periodically I would wake up and say "ow" in a tiny voice, and she would reach over and push the button on the "pain box." The pain box was something like a remote control hooked up to my IV. I, or Denise, could push it every now and then and it would put some Demerol into my IV. It was lovely. I learned quickly that they gave me a minimum of painkillers, but if I asked for more I could have it. I took Percocet pills and used the pain box just as much as I could. In this way I didn't feel any pain at all. The nurses later told me that I took fewer painkillers than they would have given me on their own.

I felt so comfortable and relaxed. I had worried that it would be difficult for me to let people take care of me, but I didn't have that problem. I was perfectly happy to let Denise talk for me. She seemed to know what I needed without my saying a word. Mostly what I needed was to be petted and talked to. As I faded in and out, I heard the song "Pretty Pretty Pain Cave" from *Wayne's World* running through my head. In my lucid moments I thought that was pretty funny.

Very soon I was hungry. The food was less than satisfying. I wanted something substantial, or at least yummy, but all I got was Jell-O and broth. I slurped down the Jell-O and fell asleep.

Exploring was fun. First, I went to the bathroom in our room. Then I went back to my bed and fell asleep. Later, Denise held me up while I pottered inch by inch down the long carpeted hallway past the nurses' station. It didn't hurt, and I was enormously proud of myself. I felt my strength coming back every time I did a new thing. And then I went to sleep.

Two mornings after the surgery I sat up in bed, crossed my legs and read a magazine. Dr. Hero came in to say hello, expecting to see me asleep. But there I was, bright-eyed and filling out a questionnaire asking if I made my husband happy. Dr. Hero looked at my chart, asked me a few questions and then asked if I would like to go home. Yes, I wanted to. I was bored in the hospital, missed my cats and my apartment, and the comfort of silence and being alone.

Once I got home, I crawled into bed for about a week and

didn't get out except to pee. Denise nursed me and petted me and made sure I had everything I needed, which was mostly silence and rest. I was utterly content just to lie there for hours, gazing at the cats or the trees outside my window. For the first week or so Denise slept on the couch, because we were both worried that our customary sleeping habits might injure me.

At first I felt almost no pain, but as soon as the painkillers wore off I felt constant dull pain. I got used to it and allowed myself to groan and moan whenever I wanted to. My tummy swelled up quite a bit, and it was beautifully bruised in green, yellow and shades of purple. I delighted in pulling up my nightie to show our friends my incision. Not a few of them looked ill afterward.

Soon I started to get up and stretch. Boy, did that feel wonderful! I marched gingerly around, bending my legs at the knee and lifting them up as far as I could as I walked. When I was able to march around the whole apartment I knew I was getting a lot better. I stopped paying attention to my physical improvement after I was able to do two sit-ups in a row. But that took about three weeks, and it hurt a lot.

Within a week of being home, I was off serious drugs and taking only ibuprofen when I needed it. I was able to get up and down easily in about ten days, and in two weeks or so I went outside. After that I felt able to visit friends in their houses. I was extremely tired, though, and I remained so for almost a year. But all in all I think I had an amazing recovery.

I went back to work for a few hours each day at three weeks, and although there were times when all I wanted to do was put my head down on my desk and sleep, in general I was really glad to be out of the house and active, and I felt pretty good.

I masturbated about ten days after the surgery and came delightfully. I was very pleased, because that seemed to be a big concern of other women whose hysterectomy stories I had read. My doctor had also mentioned that my ability to reach orgasm might possibly be affected. In fact, that function seemed to improve. Denise and I were both very excited to try out my new vagina. We bought a little dildo, me-sized, and a harness.

It is now more than a year since my surgery. I marked the anniversary soberly. I continue to think I made the right decision, and I give myself lots of room to feel grief at my loss. I have felt no regrets. I know that I had a difficult choice to make, and my options were Bad and Worse. In exchange for the ability to have children, I have begun to understand that my life's gift is an independence that will allow me to develop deep emotional relationships, without giving myself to nurturing a child. I have a deep and calm sense that I have had children before, and will again.

To my utter delight, I have discovered a few interesting new capabilities of my uterus-less body. My scar, which is about five inches long and almost invisible in my pubic hair, seems to be directly connected to my clitoris. One of my cats likes to sleep on my lower belly, and when she kneads my scar I feel ripples of pleasure in my whole vulva. I have also discovered that when I massage my tummy I can feel my vagina. I can massage it until it starts to contract on its own, and this resembles a mild orgasm.

My sense of my body has changed. I feel redefined somehow as a woman, but I can't quite articulate what I mean by that. I have become very conscious of how reproduction-oriented my culture is, even among our gay friends. I tease my girlfriends sometimes, "You silly fertile woman!" I still ovulate, but of course, do not bleed or have cramps. I am starting to identify my period with the experience of sore breasts and hating all my clothes.

I feel freed by not having periods. Because I am not yet thirty I think of myself as a very young woman exploring uncharted waters. Denise is pretty stubbornly unwilling to consider bearing a child herself, and in the process of accepting that, I am slowly realizing just how much of my sense of life has had to do with my future reproductivity. I have a luxurious freedom to imagine all sorts of lives for myself.

Through this experience I have come to understand that just because a doctor is a woman doesn't mean that she is my kind of woman. I still avoid doctors in general, but I am glad to have found Drs. Limerick and Hero, and I will stay with them for the rest of my life if I can. I have learned there are some compromises I will not make, and a painful and intrusive gynecologist exam is one of them. Another I will not make again is giving control of my body to another person . . . unless it's Denise (and we have a password).

MADELYN ARNOLD

The Story of a Lesbian with AIDS

This is the story of a lesbian with AIDS struggling to get health care, as told to Marissa Martínez in 1995. The narrator worked as a medical technologist and phlebotomist at a hospital and a gay clinic until she retired. Her partner and caregiver, a cancer survivor, joins the narrator for part of the story.

Diagnosis

I worked in a hospital laboratory as a medical technologist. I would run around the hospital sticking people with needles and doing other procedures as well.

Back in the lab we had a very old-fashioned centrifuge, a little tiny thing that went round and round on the table; you had to stop it yourself. But if you were out of the room, it would just go merrily whizzing away.

Well, one day, something like that happened, and I heard what sounded like gravel in the machine and thought, "Oops! Broken tube." I turned off the centrifuge and opened it up, and sure enough it was full of blood and broken glass. I began taking the machine apart and washing the parts, and though I was trying to be very careful, I cut my hand.

Because of the accident, I had to fill out a form and have my blood drawn and tested as a safety procedure. Soon after that I developed a pneumonia and was in the hospital for a short time.

When I got back to work, someone in the lab said, "Have you taken a good look at your results?" I said, "No, what do you mean?"

That's when I realized there's no such thing as confidentiality. That's right. *Absolutely no such thing.* I sat down at the computer and looked at my ordinary values. I was surprised to see how sick I had been; I hadn't realized I had been that sick. When I got to the end of the results, I saw it said HIV. I go, "What! Who's doing an HIV test on me?" And it was positive. They confirmed it of course. Confirmed it by Western blot. I got up and walked around and immediately went to work like a robot. The same person came up to me after a while and said, "Why didn't you ask to take the rest of the day off or something?" And I said, "No, I'm okay." But about fifteen minutes later, I started freaking out, so I explained that I needed some time to think, and I spent the rest of the afternoon walking up and down the street hyperventilating.

The next day I asked who had authorized such a test on me, and it was pointed out that I had signed for it! And I had, admittedly, not read what I was signing because as far as I knew it was just a routine mistake in the lab, you know; I cut myself cleaning a centrifuge, big deal. That kind of thing happened all the time. I thought it was an accident report or something. I hadn't read it. I said, "Well, why didn't you tell me what the result was? I was right here in the hospital, in bed *X;* you knew, why didn't you tell me?"

And they became furious, especially the head of infectious diseases. He was absolutely beside himself. He asked, "How did you find out?" I said, "Well, I work with the damn computer!" And, you know, I was not strictly telling him the truth. The result was supposed to be kept from me until some schlemiel came to hold my hand and tell me. You know the procedure, a kind of counseling.

They said, "We tried and tried to get a hold of you." I said,

"Did you try looking in the hospital? You know, that's where I was!" He was just furious. We yelled at each other, and I knew I had lost all hope of cooperation with the system right then, because he was the only one who could grant it. Anyway, I wasn't about to let it be known that a co-worker had tipped me off. I would eventually have found it by myself, you see.

It certainly wasn't that piece of glass that did it, anyway. It had to have come from a previous exposure. I mean there had been several, actually hundreds, of times in twenty-some years, of exposures, needle sticks.

There were no "universal precautions" then. No. Probably wealthy hospitals had begun that, but it is extremely expensive to use universal precautions, extremely expensive, and for clinics and so forth it was death. As an example, in one clinic I had an ordinary tech exposure. I had to recap a needle, and when I capped it, it came right through the end of the plastic tube and into my finger. I said to the guy I had just drawn, "If you got any funny diseases, don't tell me, okay?" And he said, "Okay, lady. Okay." I thought, "Oh shit, I'm not going to think about this." But that was one of many, you know.

Doctors

It was this way. I have a doctor and, at the time, she was a resident and happened to be assigned to me. I went in to repeat the HIV test. I went in there without any particular expectation, even though I had been working at the gay clinic, and they had a very complex procedure of how to tell someone the results, either yea or nay. She and I talked a little bit. She wanted to get an idea of who I was with, if I was gay, straight or what, you know, and I was perfectly up front about that.

Then all of a sudden she went into lock mode. It was amazing: Her whole face froze, her body froze. It was like she was about to repeat some sort of pledge. And she went through this thing about what I was supposed to do for the rest of my life. I had never thought about safe sex, you know. And she was saying either it was none or it was protection. She recited this thing, and I got madder and madder and more hysterical. She was telling me that sex was over, that certain other things were over, too dangerous for me to do, that I couldn't do my own job. Afterwards, she shut her eyes for a few seconds because she obviously just hated it. I think it's because of that hatred that I'm so fond of her, but she was obligated to say those things.

I got a bunch of injections. I kept getting pneumonia, and they gave me injections to help immunize me. And we drew some blood for toxo; I had this enormously high toxoplasmosis level and was horrified. I said to her, half joking, "As long as I don't have neurological AIDS!" which is of course what I have, and she kind of smiled wanly. In the next few months I had about eight tests to make sure I really, really was HIV-positive.

I saw another doctor for a chest problem that I thought was developing into pneumonia. I told him I had HIV and I kept getting these chest infections. He acted like I was there to rob him or to sneak up behind him and bat him on the head or something; he was very weird, and it took me years to realize that he probably just hated queers, you know. I was not unused to that, but I had forgotten that's how people act. He was horrible. I would give him an answer to a question, and he would say, "I'll bet." He ended up saying, "I doubt that you are HIV-positive at all. I think this whole thing is a trick."

He just went on and on like that, but suffice it to say it was just terrible. Here's somebody saying I would get some benefit out of having HIV, although I was unable to think of what it would be.

Another doctor I saw was kind of a cuckoo, but at least she was honest. She asked me what lesbians do. Well, I wish I could have seen my own face, that's all I can say. I sort of stammered my way through the medical terms, what cunnilingus is and so forth: it seemed incredible to me that she had never encountered it, but I guess she hadn't.

She did me the favor of setting up a blood test with legal safeguards. She watched my blood being drawn and then took the blood herself to the Public Health Department. I was haunted by the idea that the doctor I had seen before thought this was a hoax. After that test, my HIV status was established.

Treatments

I knew more than the average physician about treatments, because the average physician didn't have an HIV patient, and I had worked at the gay clinic. They sent me to the head of infectious diseases because he "owned" all the HIV people so he could get money. The thing is he just sets my teeth on edge, and vice versa I dare say. Now, I never see him. I have been handed over to his assistant. Tuberculosis is the assistant's thing, and since I had once had TB, I ended up with him, but neither one of them ever wants to see me if he can avoid it.

I tried to get information about why I have so much pain. The infectious disease assistant told me he had never heard of HIV people having pain. So, I immediately believed him and decided I was imagining it. That's the way things were then, a couple of years ago.

Later, I looked for information in databases, because I had done library research before. What I kept finding was so hideous that I was always freaked out. It was all bad news. I did find some things about women, and they were very sick people indeed. They hadn't been diagnosed until they were nearly dead, you know, and they had so many things wrong with them. They were just terribly ill, terribly ill. I decided to stop looking things up. I'm not going to be my own doctor. You know the old saying: Anyone who is his own doctor has a fool for a patient. I decided not to be that kind of fool, so I stopped. I hadn't learned enough that was helpful anyway.

I was diagnosed with full-blown AIDS in 1991. I was given AZT, which was, at the time, much coveted; now we know that it doesn't do that good a job by itself. In fact, you really must have another antiviral to get anywhere with it. Many people have no real trouble with AZT, but I wasn't one of them. I was so miserable taking it that I decided to kill myself rather than go through that misery any longer. I literally had my knife at my throat when it occurred to me I could just stop taking the medicine. And three days later I stopped seeing green faces dripping from the ceiling, which I really had been seeing.

Infections

I have oral thrush, more or less constant vaginal thrush, and fungal infections in my skin and all kinds of stuff. And, oh yes, I have had attacks of shingles. That was lots of fun. Not just one, not just two, but approximately thirteen.

I have had TB. I may have had it as a child. It wouldn't be surprising, as my father had it. And his father died of it. It's possible I got it working in this one lab where the workmen established the lab hood's airflow backwards. This is the honest-to-God truth. That's one of the reasons I have histo [histoplasmosis] all over my chest. So I think I was already positive for TB, but I just hadn't shown it.

They gave me lots and lots of Isoniazid (INH) for the TB. I was supposed to take it for a year. I was within a month of that year when all of a sudden I started throwing up blood and was deathly ill. Unfortunately I tend to have less vitamin B6 than I should have and INH destroys B6 in your system. It was an honest mistake on their part because nobody could have known that I had that condition.

■

HIV/AIDS and Lesbian Risk

▼ Women who have sex with women may become infected with the HIV virus through a variety of means including intravenous drug use (IDU), sex with men, donor insemination, transfusion of blood products and occupational exposure.

▼ The Centers for Disease Control also believes that woman-to-woman sexual transmission of HIV is possible and has most likely already occured.

▼ The HIV virus can be found in vaginal fluid and menstrual blood and can be transmitted through small cuts on a woman's mouth or hands.

▼ Women are at particular risk when having sex with a woman who has her period or a yeast infection.

Love And Sex

(Partner joins)

Partner: We "met" online before we met in person. I was going through cancer treatment, and I didn't have anybody I could talk to about it who wouldn't freak out. So she talked about how she felt about being ill, and I talked about how I felt.

Madelyn: You never were treated as ill.

Partner: I never felt sick, but we talked a lot about it.

Madelyn: We happened to have these conditions, and nobody would listen to either one of us, but we did have each other.

Partner: I think it was '91 when we got involved. Well, it was a little bumpy getting started. Yeah, we kept trying to have sex and, you know, bring out the gloves, and she would go, "Oh no, no, no, no," [laughter]. We knew what barriers were but there was nobody around to tell us anything about using the gloves and to explain what a dental dam is.

Madelyn: A dental dam is this big [she indicates small size].

Partner: Nobody was using safe sex.

Madelyn: Well, they may have been, but they weren't talking.

Partner: We went to a safe-sex party, and we scared the bejesus out of everybody else who was there.

Madelyn: Because nobody else needed it. They just wanted to hear about it.

Partner: It was sort of a pilot safe-sex party, either the first or one of the first safe-sex parties. Well, we learned one thing at that

party. We'd pick up one thing and make up another thing, and
pretty soon we were the worldwide experts in safe sex between
women because virtually nobody else did it. People talked about
it, but it was real easy to tell who did it and who didn't do it,
because the ones who talked about safe sex but didn't do it would
suggest these really bizarre things that simply don't work. And
that was what we got: dental dams that are mint-flavored.

Madelyn: Right, why not try bubble gum?

Partner: Why don't you just chew on them, and have phone sex?

Madelyn: Yeah, we were sort of doing phone sex, I guess. The first
time we had sex was at my apartment.

Partner: I don't know, you mean where we actually succeeded?

Madelyn: Yes.

Partner: There were numerous aborted attempts.

Madelyn: Our first "success" was at my apartment. I had been
upset to start with because of all this gunk you were supposed
to put on. It just horrifies me that touching human flesh would
be dangerous, the idea that touching me might make someone
sick. This is where a little bit of knowledge is dangerous. Because
of my microbiology degree I know how small viruses are. I know
what they can get into. You can have a hangnail, and that's more
than enough to get millions of virions in. I mean, what if you'd
got a tear in the vinyl? Well, we somehow managed to get over
that.

We eventually had sex relatively frequently, and it was often
really, really good. We got fairly inventive. The interesting thing
is I had been cautious not to let her know I was into S/M—I had
been involved in it since I was twelve. For one thing it hadn't
become something you talked about in the general community
then. So, I just kept it to myself, because I still liked ordinary
sex too. And that's what most women would do. I got tired of
being called a pervert. But we eventually discovered we both
liked it, though it was kind of new to her. It was amazing: We
had two kinds of sexual expression that were terrific, and we

were beginning to use safe sex. I still feel it's like something you do with a turkey, wrapping up in Saran Wrap, but none of the other stuff works.

Partner: After she started taking methadone for her headaches, the sex thing didn't work anymore.

Madelyn: It certainly wasn't the way it was. I also got more and more pain as time went on. You were kind of sweet; you started drawing on me, remember?

Partner: She had different areas of her body that were incredibly painful, so I'd take a magic marker and draw circles around the parts I couldn't touch.

Madelyn: Especially at my spleen. And my legs and my arms began to hurt. I could ignore that for S/M without any particular difficulty, but it made ordinary sex very difficult.

It was really hard for me to make love to her. She could make love to me, but I had a real problem when it was one-sided. And this got worse and worse and worse. Now I have more areas with moderate to severe pain than I have pain-free areas. I think it was the headache that was the end of it though. When you have constant, severe headaches you don't feel like sex.

Advocate

Partner: When I'm an advocate I ask questions. I demand things; she's not very good at demanding things when she most needs them. She's in too much pain to do it for herself. Sometimes I just kind of plant myself there and yell at people. And they start running around.

Madelyn: I guess you really spooked them last week.

Partner: I just picked them up by the front of the shirt and shook them until their brains ran out.

She's been seeing the same group of doctors for quite a while. Most of them know who I am, and the ones who don't, get to know fairly quickly. One time, I thought she was in danger, and

I couldn't get the twit fill-in nurse to tell me whether she was there or not because I wasn't a relative. So I made her go get the clinic manager. And she was really nice to me. Really, really nice.

We have a durable power of attorney. I don't usually carry it in my back pocket, but I have it.

Madelyn: And it's part of my chart. But we need one that's accessible to you.

Partner: It doesn't help that much to put it in your chart because your chart is about four or five hundred pages.

Madelyn: When my doctor told me she had read every single page and typed out something for a referral, I thought, "Does she do this for every single patient?" I think I'd kill myself. Just the idea of somebody asking for one more document, you know, would be too much. But she does that sort of thing. She has never even groaned about one of the many million documents you end up asking a doctor to fill out. I don't even know what most of them are. There ought to be a better way of doing this. We are killing our doctors. No wonder they leave faster than they are going in.

Partner: Sometimes I live from crisis to crisis. Right now—we're still debating about this—I'm looking for a full-time job so I can get benefits for her. Her health insurance is making changes that make it harder and harder for her to get decent care. Last week was horrendous. They screwed up her prescriptions and she wouldn't have had methadone over the weekend; she would have gone into withdrawal because they didn't get the paperwork done.

Madelyn: And that's why I think we had such a profuse apology today.

Partner: Well, I may have affected them with my . . .

Madelyn: You may have [laughter].

Partner: You don't have to yell at them. They're real smart; they can figure out I'm going to slap them upside the head if they don't pay attention.

Madelyn: What did you say to them?

Partner: I just told them what they were going to do and when they were going to do it. The prescription was ready a half an hour later.

The Best and the Worst

Well, my best experience with medicine could have ended up as one of the worst except for the skill of a pediatric anesthesiologist.

They kept giving me injections to stop my vomiting, but they hadn't taken effect yet. Then they told me they were going to do a spinal tap. This would be my third spinal tap, so I told them, "I don't have a lumbar curve any more than I have a cervical curve, so when you try to get the needle in between you will not be able to and you will nick the bone. Please use a child's needle."

Well, they couldn't just listen to me, right. They had to use an adult needle, and after two tries, I said, "That's it. Go find somebody who can do this." They told me, "You want an anesthesiologist." I said, "Fine. Get me an anesthesiologist, a pediatric anesthesiologist." And they did.

This fellow they called was from South Africa, and we talked about South Africa as he was doing the procedure. He did not nick anything, and he used the smallest tip possible, so it took forever. I'm lying there, and he's sort of squatting, and it's *drip, drip, drip, drip,* and I know what he's going through: His knees and legs are getting cramped, he has to keep bacteria from falling into the tube, and he has to keep switching tubes.

I was really impressed with what he was doing, because he just kept right on talking about South Africa. I asked him if he'd ever gone to jail because of apartheid. He said, "Well, yes, and I discovered that I was not a hero." I thought that was the best line I had ever heard. "I discovered I was not a hero, and I got the devil out of there." He did an excellent job. He did a spectacular job when you consider how difficult a spinal tap is to do on me.

The other best times have been the times we have called and

said we are coming in because I need a shot, and they have ushered me through in less than five minutes, and I was out in ten.

Challenges

When I first found out I had HIV, I was pretty freaked out. I started drinking a lot more than I should have—a lot more than I was accustomed to drinking. I was actually rather on the thin side when I first learned I was HIV-positive, and to my surprise, within the first year, and even after I had stopped drinking, I gained weight at an outrageous rate. It didn't seem to have much to do with what I ate or even what I drank.

That's one of the reasons I don't want my former students to see me. The ones I see when I am out in public don't recognize me. I don't look anything like I used to look—anything. I look horrendous now, something I can't stand. I never look in a mirror—never.

AMBER HOLLIBAUGH

Lesbian Denial and Lesbian Leadership in the AIDS Epidemic

Bravery and Fear in the Construction of a Lesbian Geography of Risk

Wanted: Attractive feminine woman for romance, pleasure and possible long-term relationship; no HIV + 's need apply.

Looking for serious relationship with womyn-loving-womyn—no butches, druggies, drinkers or HIV's.

Lesbian looking for lesbian love, hot sex, good times, great partner . . . could be permanent! Femmes, fatties, HIV + 's, don't bother.

The above are examples of personal ads I found in lesbian publications from around the country—San Francisco, Los Angeles, New York, Illinois and Michigan—publications running the gamut from lesbian-separatist newspapers to sex-positive lesbian magazines like *On Our Backs*. And while the ads contain many different qualifiers and disqualifiers that are revealing about the lesbian community, they all share one terrifying disqualifier: no HIV-positive lesbians wanted here.

As the director of a lesbian AIDS project, I spend an incredible amount of my time disagreeing with lesbians who are still repeating the dyke mantra, "Real lesbians don't get AIDS," while listening to the growing number of lesbians who are HIV-positive or have AIDS and to their friends and lovers. Between these two groups of women is a third chorus of female voices full of panicky questions about risk, about whom to believe and how to think when they look at their own behaviors as lesbians. How can lesbians' risk for HIV/AIDS still be debatable thirteen years into the epidemic?

My Own History, Coming Home

I have been organizing around and writing about sexuality for fifteen or twenty years, and doing work around HIV for nearly ten. I have been a part of the large contingent of lesbians who, from the earliest days of the epidemic, began to do AIDS work and became AIDS activists. And, through those years, I have talked to lesbians about what compelled us to get involved. For some, it was the shared identity we felt with gay men that brought us forward early in the epidemic; for others, it was the dramatic increase in already devastating homophobia and gay bashing that occurred because of the government's misrepresentation of AIDS (or GRID—gay-related immune deficiency disease, as it was known then) as a gay disease. In that atmosphere of increased violence, "all gay people, both gay men and lesbians, looked alike." For many gay women and men of color, the devastation in their communities and the need for their engagement and activism were urgent and obvious to them. For many progressive lesbians, the communities most under siege were exactly the communities they were committed to working within (women in prisons, poor women, women of color, young women). And many of

Lesbian Denial
and Lesbian
Leadership in
the AIDS
Epidemic

■

161

us were losing friends every week, every month, more each year. Our reasons for getting involved were numerous, varied and passionate.

All those reasons applied to me—and one other I have seen clearly only in the last year or so, one about which I speak much less openly. I was deeply disillusioned and bitter at the horrific fights about sex that erupted so viciously in the feminist, lesbian-feminist and antipornography movements of the early 1980s, the fights that have now been called "the sex wars" in the feminist movement. I come from a poor-white-trash, working-class background, and I am a high-femme dyke passionately committed to butch and femme lives. The sexualities I defended in those bitter fights and the sexualities I wanted to continue to explore were drawn from all the ways women (and men) feel desire. But I was particularly driven to explore a woman-identified sexuality that was risky, smart, dangerous, often secretive and capable of encompassing great variation of erotic need. And I wanted sex to have a right to its own history without forcing some women to hide or reinterpret their past (or ongoing) desires through a constantly shifting lesbian ideology. I was also tired of trying to say that the political lesbian community was only the tip of the lesbian iceberg, with the vast majority of lesbians still an uncharted, vastly different set of groupings of desires, identities, contradictions and sexual dynamics. Many brave feminist women spoke against the right-wing drift of the sex wars and the porn fights, but we were a minority in a feminist and lesbian movement already beleaguered by Reaganomics, religious fundamentalism and the fight to maintain control of our own reproduction. Times were hard.

Finally, I wanted to return, go home again to the women I came from. I longed to build a *new* revolution, made up of lesbians who had mostly been left out of the current feminist explosion: working-class women; women in prisons, reform schools and juvenile halls; women locked in mental institutions for being too queer; women of color; women in the military and in the bars; women surviving in "straight" marriages and dead-end jobs who longed each day to touch another woman; women who were peep show girls, sex workers and carnival strippers; women who shot drugs and women in recovery from those drugs and the streets; women in trailers, small towns and cities across America; women who filled the floors of the factories, fast-food restaurants and auto plants of this country; women whose lives were centered in PTAs, shopping malls and teamsters' unions. These were the women I came from, and they were the women with whom I longed to build a movement. It was here, with these women, that I hoped for the possibility of a new political dialogue about sex and desire and power. They were also, I quickly realized, the women most immediately at risk for HIV.

The struggle against AIDS brought (and continues to bring) all my worlds together: Instead of being barely tolerated because of my sex politics and my sense of urgency about the meaning and power of erotic desires (Is that really political?) in the AIDS activist movement, I was welcomed. In those early years, when the government refused to take on the leadership of the battle against AIDS, we were forced to create a movement based on grassroots organizing, word of mouth and long-range goals. Each day we had to bite back our urgency and despair at how to get the messages out quickly enough. AIDS activism was a movement that understood the critical need to talk about the uncomfortable or ragged edges of our sexualities and desires and wasn't fooled by what we called ourselves—as though those identity words would explain what we did in bed (or who we did it with) or who we were on the streets or in our jobs.

My first paid job doing AIDS work was with the AIDS Discrimination Division of the New York City Human Rights Commission. The work was to intercede against the fear and stigma that had arisen so violently around HIV. Knowing where to look for those most vulnerable to HIV demanded a sharp understanding of class

Lesbian Denial
and Lesbian
Leadership in
the AIDS
Epidemic
■
163

and race in this country. As an educator and filmmaker organizing at a community level, I wanted to bring forward the voices and stories of the women (and men) who lived in long-overlooked communities, letting them and their stories finally stand center stage where they belong. In spite of the struggles over sexism and racism, and a refusal to understand or support women and men whose risks were different from those generally understood as gay, this was still work where everything remained to be done and anyone willing to confront those obstacles could join. And my heart was breaking from the deaths of those I loved. Life and death among my friends and in my communities, the urgency of people struggling to live with HIV, the need to integrate sex issues through the grid of race, class and gender, my love as a filmmaker for working-class people's stories—these pieces added up in ways that propelled me forward.

As I was doing the work, I began to confront my own history in a way I never had. At some time in my life (and into the present), I had engaged in every one of the behaviors that I knew put lesbians at risk. I heard my own personal and often secret, unspoken narrative in the stories and histories of the lesbians I met who had AIDS or who were at risk for HIV. I was a lesbian and I had been one for twenty-seven years. Through those years, I had engaged in every risky activity associated with AIDS, regardless of what I called myself at the time I was doing them. If that was true for me as a lesbian political organizer and activist, what was happening for the vast majority of lesbians, bisexual women, young lesbians, transgendered lesbians, lesbians who were "coming out," passing women and women-who-partnered-with-other-women? What about the hundreds and thousands of women who used none of these words as they loved and desired another woman? What was happening to them? And what about the huge unseen numbers who reside primarily outside the confines of our political networks, that vast geography of women building their lives against or with their desire for another woman beneath the "straight" female landscape of America?

Creating the Lesbian AIDS Project at Gay Men's Health Crisis in New York City has been a major part of that answer for me; it is my own history coming home. And because I see the issues of HIV for lesbians totally intertwined with the issues of sexuality, class, race, gender and erotic desires—issues I have been working on much of my political life—it has thrust me back into a level of organizing I haven't been involved in since the early civil rights and antiwar movements of the 1960s and 1970s. I went back to this work as an organizer committed to a politics of inclusion. Returning as a forty-six-year-old lesbian who has been doing this political work since I was seventeen allows the richness of my own life history to illuminate the gigantic map of our actual lesbian world, a map that needs to comprehend and chart the wildly disparate universes of queer female lives and communities in order to win our survival.

A Project for Women Who Partner with Women

The Lesbian AIDS Project (LAP) at Gay Men's Health Crisis (GMHC) in New York is only one of two such projects funded in the world. The other is at Lyon-Martin Women's Health Clinic in San Francisco. The Lesbian AIDS Project has two major missions: The first is to break the silence and denial about HIV in lesbian communities; the second is to demand that lesbians be counted as an essential component in the larger HIV/AIDS communities, as well as in the health, youth, people-of-color and women's organizations where we are in danger of struggling to survive with HIV.

In fulfilling these tasks, our job is to specifically identify lesbians' vulnerability to HIV and to identify the lack of services, visibility and inclusion for HIV-positive women who partner with women. The Lesbian AIDS Project is dedicated to enlarging our understanding of who is affected by the epidemic and

Lesbian Denial
and Lesbian
Leadership in
the AIDS
Epidemic

■

165

to educating about our risk for HIV among the distinct and varied lesbian and female bisexual communities to which lesbians belong.

We have not been seen or counted. The Lesbian AIDS Project is dramatically changing that. In our first year, we conducted a sex survey of women who have sex with women. We set up support groups for lesbians at GMHC and other sites, and beginning in the summer of 1993, internships for young lesbians at risk were available in our research and documentation project. We have created an information packet and the first lesbian HIV newsletter, "LAP Notes," and are working on a safer-sex brochure and kit. We have set up a lesbian mothers' HIV group, a lesbian couples' group and an HIV-positive lesbian substance users recovery group. We have also offered safer-sex workshops for HIV-positive lesbians and their partners, led by HIV-positive lesbians and their partners.

We are talking with other concerned groups in various communities to lobby for a lesbian prison discharge planner who will work with women to support their lives outside prison as lesbians living with HIV. In the winter of 1994, LAP began an HIV lesbian leadership training group and will be working inside GMHC to guarantee that our own house (its organization and services) are lesbian-specific or lesbian-sensitive. In 1994, we hired two more staff members to continue and deepen our community organizing and outreach efforts and to develop models and manuals that can be used to train the other communities about women who partner with women and HIV.

The Lesbian AIDS Project is about community, visibility and resource sharing. We do a great deal of work around general sexuality and lesbian health issues and are committed to guaranteeing that no lesbian will have to hide her identity or have others automatically assume she is heterosexual.

Doing this work has been incredible and has called on all my experience and intelligence. LAP is about making visible hidden women and communities, while protecting any woman's right not to identify if she doesn't choose to. Because of the complexities of our communities and of HIV work itself, the project remains constantly challenging and demanding.

Lesbian Denial
and Lesbian
Leadership in
the AIDS
Epidemic
■
167

Lesbian Leadership in the AIDS Movement

Lesbians have been leaders in the AIDS movement since its beginning. We have influenced and shaped the discussions, outreach programs, demonstrations, services and prevention drives since the first moments of this crisis. Working early on with gay men, we were often the first women to see how different communities were being affected by HIV and to use our political histories as organizers and health, feminist, civil rights and left-wing activists to inform the creation and responses of this new movement. In the broad leadership of so many and varied men and women fighting against HIV, the role of lesbians has been consistent and powerful.

While AIDS service organizations and government agencies in charge of the epidemic told us that "lesbians are not at risk for HIV," lesbians active in the AIDS movement, meeting in small groups to repair ourselves from the sexism or racism of this new movement, were talking about how many lesbians, how many women who sleep with other women, we were seeing who were HIV-positive. We would compare notes and shake our heads. It just didn't add up, and we would speak of it late into the night, trying to unravel the keys to our risk at the same time we remained completely invisible as a community at risk for AIDS.

Who Is the "We" in Our Sisterhood?

The lines of the map linking our communities of women who partner with women are very faint. The terrain through which most lesbians can openly travel is restricted. It is a geography rigorously determined by our backgrounds, our class and color, by rural landscape or city street, by whether we are politically active or spiritually inclined, by the narrow confines of age and health and physical ability, by the marks on the map that identify us as lesbians from the bars, the trade unions, the military, from gay studies programs or as art history majors, by how we each came out and with whom, by the shape of our desires and our willingness (or ability) to risk it all on our love for a woman, by our status as mothers or our decision not to have kids, by the nature of our dreams and aspirations, by our very ability to nurture and sustain hope for our futures.

As lesbians in this culture, we suffer from the same lack of power and resources common to all women. Within that oppression we must also navigate our health, sexuality and social existence in an environment committed to imagining that all women are heterosexual. In a universe without voice or presence, lesbians and our particular risks for HIV have remained submerged inside a "straight" female landscape, keeping us ignorant and uninformed about our own risks for HIV. We are a specific population of women with high numbers of HIV-positive members but no official recognition or accounting.

The "secret" of lesbian risk continues, and lesbian deaths increase. There is confusion among us, leaving the entire community angry and in doubt. Some lesbians deny all vulnerability to HIV, making the question of risky behaviors, from shooting drugs and sex with men to sex between women appear negligible or unrealistic and unknowable. This guarantees that lesbians who are HIV-positive or have AIDS will come up against a wall of silence and denial and be marked outside the status of "real" lesbians. Our histories as women engaged in these activities and behaviors work to disown us as an integral part of the larger lesbian landscape.

And it is here that race and class background become particularly vicious components of our risks and our understanding about HIV. For middle-class lesbians, the margins from birth can slip quickly away when (or if) it becomes known that we are sleeping with other women. For working-class women without any buffers, the picture is immediately fragile, yet our need for our communities of birth is accentuated if we are women of color, women whose first language is not English, or poor or working-class women who are responsible for and committed to the survival of our extended families. In this already contested setting, HIV/AIDS is often devastating, while our resources remain scarce. We are often forced to lie and hide our sexual desire for other women so that we can access the health care or social services we need. We also hide in order to guarantee the commitment and support of our biological families, our jobs, our neighborhoods, our children, our language and our access to valued cultural institutions. Medically, socially and economically, the less room we have to turn around, the more problematic our crisis becomes as we balance precariously between the women we desire and the help and support we need.

The process of "coming out," one of the most celebrated aspects of lesbian writing and storytelling, is often a high-risk activity. Think of it. This is often the time when confusion and silence about desire for another woman are the most terrifying to come to terms with. It is often a time of lots of sexual experimentation, often combined with drug use and drinking. It is a period when we feel between communities and identities, and it can often be a time of shame or isolation from former friends, our families and the authority figures in our lives. At whatever age, "coming out" is a highly charged and often dangerous path each of us walks. HIV magnifies that risk a thousand times over.

HIV makes a mockery of pretend unity and sisterhood. Though the women now infected with HIV cross all classes and races, they are predominantly lesbians of color or poor white women, usually struggling with long histories of shooting drugs or fucking men for the money to get those drugs. They are not the women

Lesbian Denial
and Lesbian
Leadership in
the AIDS
Epidemic

■

169

usually identified as those the feminist movement or lesbian movement most value and try to organize with to create a progressive political agenda. The HIV-positive lesbians who continue to come forward as leaders in the lesbian AIDS movement have histories and lives lived in neighborhoods most gay studies courses rarely describe, let alone use as the bases of understanding queer females' lives.

The question of HIV, of race and class, becomes a question of whose lesbian movement is this and whose leadership? Will lesbians who shoot drugs or who are in recovery be the women called upon to speak for our movement? Will categories that depend on the construction of "real" lesbians disappear and reveal instead the incredible numbers of women who hold another woman in their arms, regardless of what each woman calls herself or who else she may be fucking? Will histories of low-paying jobs, the revolving door of prisons, the military and bar life, and the sounds of kids playing while the lesbian consciousness-raising group convenes begin to be common and ordinary? Will the power of being butch or femme, the stories of life as a lesbian mom or a runaway teenage street dyke predominate? When will femmes with long nails and sharp-assed attitude be the voice heard leading gay pride day marches? Whose movement, whose voice, whose stories, whose hope for transformation and change? Whose? These are the questions I see in front of me every day.

Some Complications on Our Way to Understanding Lesbian HIV

The crisis for lesbians struggling to understand the impact of HIV in our communities is compounded by the general lack of decent, nonjudgmental information about lesbian sexuality. Because it remains unacceptable to love and desire other women sexually, we are also left with little substantial information about what we do in bed with each other, including what might put us at risk

Lesbian Denial
and Lesbian
Leadership in
the AIDS
Epidemic

■

171

sexually. Sexually transmitted diseases (STDs) of all kinds are little understood or discussed between women partners, and the fear and ignorance surrounding HIV compounds the already existing blank space silencing this discussion in our communities. And like all silences and prejudices, homophobia hurts us profoundly, leaving us unarmed and unprotected, as though forbidding the word *lesbian* in our existence can stop the act of our love. It doesn't, of course, it just leaves us vulnerable and uninformed. Our confusion about whether AIDS is really a lesbian issue reflects this oppression.

The denial about our risk for HIV is often supported by a circumscribed lesbian sexual border we have constructed, a border that refuses to acknowledge or accept that we sleep with each other in many, many different ways. We are butch/femme women, we are queer or androgynous, we are lesbian-feminist, we don't believe in labels; we practice S/M, we use our hands, our mouths, our bodies and sex toys to pleasure and please each other; and we may also sleep with men, whether we call that "bisexuality," "coming out," "economic necessity" or don't dare talk about it.

For a small, though growing, number of HIV-positive lesbians, the only (or primary) risk for HIV was their sexual relationship with a female partner who was HIV-positive when they became lovers. When these lesbian couples looked for good information about female-to-female transmission, they were rarely successful. And when they went to other lesbians to try to discuss it (if they dared), few other lesbians could help. Like all the other risks in our communities, female-to-female sexual transmission remains scientifically undocumented and unreliably researched. This lack of knowledge combines dangerously with continuing drug and alcohol use throughout our communities, which has always been an unrecognized crisis, a crisis compounded by our invisibility and our lack of political clout.

These activities and identities are components of our communities' sexual and social lives. While women who partner with other women have taken an extraordinary risk daring to love another woman, that has not guaranteed that our judgments against each other's erotic or drug choices won't be as cruel as the general culture's judgments against us. Our understanding of the reasons many of us shoot or snort drugs, drink till it harms us, experiment with substances that can kill us, are stories that we have not let surface enough inside our community, hoping that, by not telling aloud those pieces of our lives, we will not be hit any harder by social condemnation than we already are. It's as though we think that, by disavowing a set of activities (and the women we stereotype as doing them), we can protect ourselves from even more homophobia.

We also carry those historical silences into our sexual judgments as well, thinking that if we don't enjoy a particular sexual activity ourselves, no other lesbian could either. If another woman *wants* differently, she is in danger of having her credibility as a "real" lesbian questioned. Yet we are women who are sexual originators and social inventors, leaping across the sexual and emotional silences surrounding women's desires for other women, daring to touch and possess each other sexually, daring to claim our right to be sexual, to love and want another woman.

So Amber, What's Your Problem Anyway?

The Lesbian AIDS Project sex survey is very explicit and was created to try and determine how we are really having sex with each other, how often, in what combinations and with who else, and what we think of ourselves as we do it. This was not a survey primarily about relationships. The survey appeared in the 1992 *Lesbian and Gay Pride Guide,* of which sixty thousand copies were printed for the June Gay/Lesbian Pride March in New York. The guide is picked up and used as a resource book by a wide variety of lesbians, including women who don't necessarily hook into the gay bookstores and lesbian political organizations in New

York City. When the survey appeared, my answering machine was suddenly full of "anonymous" messages from "normal dykes" suggesting that what I really needed was to go "fuck a man." Sometimes the messages were from "regular" lesbians telling me how sick they considered some of the categories and activities included in the survey. Usually those messages ended with a free-swinging interpretation of what they imagined "I was into." These anonymous messages always hurt. It was clear to me how problematic the real world of female sexuality is for all of us and what an added minefield being a lesbian can be when it is thrown into the mix. Sex in our community remains our smoking gun, and the fight for whose hand is on the trigger counts.

Still, many women were thrilled by the survey; over sixteen hundred women filled them out and sent them back. The results of the survey were available from LAP in fall 1993. Women wrote their opinions in the margins and on Post-its stuck over the sections they loved or despised. Lesbians said, "Congratulations. I've waited a long time for someone to care enough about our survival to finally ask us what we do sexually." Women who answered used exclamation marks and red pens to write their ideas and express their opinions. "I didn't even know lesbians could do this!" "I love these questions. My girlfriend and I are going to try them all before we finish the survey." "Hot survey! Getting steamy just answering it." But other women wrote, " I didn't even know that lesbians could get AIDS."

In one of the surveys, I found a note attached. It said, "I am glad you're doing this survey for those lesbians that can use it, but my lover and I don't really have any use for these questions. *We are both women and because of that we understand each other's bodies and desires.* Maybe women that are more fucked up don't understand this, but for us it's really just natural. Thanks anyway (emphasis added)." In anthropology, this is called magical thinking, and this magical thinking is rife throughout the communities I have to speak with every day. It is the most central idea

Lesbian Denial
and Lesbian
Leadership in
the AIDS
Epidemic

■

173

I hear wherever I travel among lesbians: that, because we are women touching other women, we automatically understand and empathize so completely that we know intrinsically how to touch or caress each other, how much pressure to use when we suck or lick each other's bodies, how to stroke or fuck each other to climax. It is hard to imagine, then, how to begin discussing safer sex, negotiating with a lover, HIV and STD protection methods, talking openly about drugs or sex work or sex histories. In this

Safer Sex for Lesbians

Not all sexual activities involve the exchange of bodily fluids. Engage without risk in dry kissing, massage, body-to-body rubbing, masturbation and fantasy.

For oral sex, use a latex barrier such as a dental dam or condom split down the side:

▼ Plastic wrap is unofficially advocated as a barrier: While it is believed to prevent transmission of HIV, studies have not been conducted to prove this theory.

▼ Available at medical supply stores and sex shops, dental dams should be rinsed with water before use.

▼ Condoms should be clean, unexpired and stored in a cool, dry place.

▼ Apply a water-based lubricant to the barrier and place the lubricated side against your partner's vulva or anus. Hold it firmly in place using both hands. Discard barrier after each use.

For fisting or penetration with fingers, use latex gloves:

▼ Finger cots or condoms can also be used for penetration with fingers.

▼ Again, use water-based lubricants and discard barrier after each use.

Sex toys should be cleaned and disinfected between each use:

▼ Wash them with soap and water, then rinse and disinfect by boiling them for twenty minutes, or by soaking them in rubbing alcohol for ten minutes and rinsing with water, or by rinsing them three times in full-strength bleach, then in water.

▼ A latex glove or condom may also be used on toys. Check for breakage or slippage of the condom or glove and make sure entire surface of toy is covered. Discard barrier after each use.

context, magical thinking leads most women to assert that they don't think we can transmit sexual diseases to each other. And it leads to other dangerous and incorrect sexual notions, such as if STDs are transmitted between women partners, it's probably because of a "bisexual" woman. In this lesbian worldview, men are dirty, women who sleep with them are contaminated, and only real lesbians remain pure. Yeast infections are spread between us sexually, and high rates of STDs are increasingly prevalent among lesbians at risk of HIV infection,[1] and still this is rarely discussed. How can safer sex ever be a regular part of our lives when we are literally forced to risk our right to community in order to tell the truth about what we do and with whom we do it? The legacy of being women in this culture, of being denied decent, nonjudgmental information about our bodies and our desires, is multiplied for us as lesbian women.

HIV-Positive Lesbians and Young Lesbians Lead the Way

Still, in the face of this culturally imposed ignorance, I see women who love other women trying to carve out an erotic terrain of our own that claims and encourages all of us to explore and reckon with our desires for each other. That terrain comprises thousands of complex ways each of us feels desire and passion. Especially in younger lesbians I have seen a much more matter-of-fact acceptance of HIV risk for lesbians. These are women who have grown up sexually in the first decade of AIDS, and they are much less resistant to the idea of lesbian risk and HIV safety. And in lesbian communities already hard hit by HIV, the question of safer sex, regardless of presumed mode of transmission, is also different and more open. It is there, in working-class lesbian political and social organizations, that I see the most innovative and least judgmental struggle to integrate HIV knowledge into daily lesbian life. These are often communities of lesbians that have had the tragic example of numbers and the powerful voices of HIV-positive lesbians to reckon with and lead the discussion. For example, Bronx Lesbians United in Sisterhood (BLUeS), a membership group of one thousand, estimates that 10 percent of their members are HIV-positive. There, HIV is no stranger. In these communities HIV-positive lesbians are lovers, mothers, sisters, best friends.

Growing numbers of HIV-positive lesbians are speaking out more and more often. More than anything else, their bravery and their insistence on telling the truth of their own lives (and histories) have cracked the silence and denial in the larger lesbian communities. Like the role that HIV has played in other settings, AIDS transmission always exposes the gap between who we want to believe ourselves to be and what we really do in our regular lives. The leadership of lesbians who are infected or affected by HIV is a powerful and original model for the building of a new, more inclusive movement of women who partner with other women. It brings into one dialogue the lives of all of us throughout our evolution as lesbians. Often, these lesbians became activists and HIV workers when they were told their own antibody status. The work being done by them in AIDS organizations, women's outpatient health clinics, detox centers, youth programs for runaway lesbians, prisons, recovery programs and neighborhood organizations is rarely documented, but it is some of the most powerful lesbian activism happening. And it is building a new foundation and a different class base for a larger lesbian political movement.

Claiming the Power of Our Lives

Our right to be sexual with each other and to struggle with the issues of our daily lives, like our drug use and the sex we have with men, are all pieces of the lesbian puzzle. Whether or not the larger culture acknowledges us, we must recognize each other and our different struggles. The lesbian map is very large, our numbers are significant and we must pick up this fight to protect ourselves and each other while we fight to be seen and respected. We can't wait for other people to see what is right in front of our noses: We are an integral part of this world, not outside it—and so is a potentially life-threatening virus, HIV. Our community is not immune, and lesbianism is not a condom for AIDS. Like everyone else, we are vulnerable and must take the steps necessary to learn how to protect each other's lives. No one else will do it for us, and no one will do it as well. For millennia, we have been taking risks to love each other. Now we need to expand our understanding of who we are and what we do in order to understand the many ways we need to go forward. Our communities are fabulously sexual and inventive, our lives and histories varied and full of meaning. We can support each other in taking the steps each of us needs to be safe, erotic and powerful. And we can build a movement, starting here, that refuses to privilege rigid ideological categories over the truths of our lives and that bases its theories on a more complicated map of lesbian desire and lesbian voice.

Notes

1. Surveillance Branch, AIDS Office, San Francisco Department of Public Health, "HIV Seroprevalence and Risk Behaviors Among Lesbians and Bisexual Women. The 1993 San Francisco/Berkeley Women's Survey," (October, 1993).

Life's Cycle

CAROLYN PATIERNO

With Child

I write as my little girl sleeps. My partner and I had quite the experience bringing a child into our lives— an experience that took us from alternative insemination at home to fertility problems to our final destination of Nanjing, China, where we adopted our three-and-a-half-year-old daughter. That journey took nearly four years. Along the way, neither of us lost faith or gave up. We regularly reminded ourselves and each other that of all the struggles in our lives (not the least of which was the progression of HIV disease in two of our dearest friends) this was a positive, life-affirming and joyful one. Ironically, the most difficult part of the process was the frustration we suffered at the hands of insensitive health care providers.

Just after our second anniversary, we began the process. We chose alternative insemination from an anonymous donor. After researching sperm banks, we chose an extremely lesbian-supportive bank in San Francisco. The women at this bank were very knowledgeable, helpful, optimistic and personable. In addition, we had the full support of our loved ones, who joyfully anticipated the arrival of a child into our extended family. Our first attempts were spiritual and lovely. Eventually, however, the mechanical reality set in. We found that there's only so much romance that can be infused into a dry-ice kind of experience.

We tried to impregnate me during nine cycles before I decided to have a "fertility workup." At this point, issues related to lesbian health became a challenge. I needed to choose a new gynecologist because my employer had just switched insurance companies. Before doing so, I called the doctor to see if she had experience with lesbians choosing parenthood and, more importantly, if she was supportive of our choices. I was assured that she was both supportive and knowledgeable.

For reasons that I didn't understand at the time, but luckily did not question, I asked my partner to accompany me on my visit. It was a beautiful day as we walked from our home to this very fancy medical building adjacent to the hospital in our neighborhood. There was an air of confidence about the building that should have been comforting, but for some reason I was anxious. The doctor called me into her office and asked what she could do for me. I told her my story and said that I thought it was time to have a fertility workup. I sensed she was not comfortable. Her first question made it clear, however, that she was also ignorant.

She asked me why I was seeing her. I was taken aback because I thought I had just told her. I asked what she meant. She asked why I was seeing her and not the physician who was doing the insemination. Well, I thought, here we go. I explained that we were doing the inseminations at home and that my partner was inseminating me. She was aghast. "How does she know she's putting it in the right place?!" she exclaimed.

In most circumstances, I have a pretty quick, sharp wit. Yet, when given the perfect setup for the wisecrack of the millennium, I was dumbstruck. I could not think of a single thing to say. When I recovered, I asked her what she meant. I figured I had completely misunderstood the question. "This woman is a doctor! A gynecologist! Doesn't she know there is practically no chance we would deposit the specimen in the wrong place?" I thought to myself. Unfortunately, I had not misunderstood. So I assured her that my partner and I had an intimate understanding of female anatomy.

Her next statement was equally unfortunate. She said that if I had tried to get pregnant the "normal" way, that she would have checked my "husband's" sperm count. I said that alternative insemination was "normal" in my family and that I wanted to know what she would do in this circumstance. She said she would insist I use a local sperm bank and have a doctor perform the procedure. She said that, unfortunately, she didn't know of any lesbian doctors who did inseminations. I told her curtly I didn't necessarily need a lesbian doctor, that I needed a *knowledgeable* doctor who was supportive of lesbians getting pregnant and raising children—and that, apparently, she wasn't one of those doctors. I thanked her for her time and walked out.

I was so happy that my partner was in the waiting room! She saw I was furious and told me she had had a vision of my storming out of the office in tears. I wasn't in tears, but I did want to plaster this woman's name all over the neighborhood with the inscription LOUSY DOCTOR WHO DRESSES BADLY.

So, where to go from here? Reluctantly, I returned to a doctor that I had dropped four years earlier after her practice began to feel like a conveyor belt (I also didn't like her too-quick offer to prescribe Valium when all I wanted was a referral to a good therapist). In the interim, I had gone to a midwifery practice for my well-woman care, a practice of smart, capable, no-nonsense, inclusive and sensitive women I longed for throughout this process.

But, here I was back on the conveyor belt. The doctor was surprised when she realized I hadn't seen her in four years. She thought it had been six months. As she examined me, she asked, "So, why are you getting pregnant and not your partner? She's not into it?" Because I was in stirrups with a speculum inserted, I chose to concentrate on the first question and ignore the second. "No insurance," I stated matter-of-factly. "No insurance!? You have a full-time job! Isn't she covered?!" Probe, probe, probe. I explained that my agency's insurance company wouldn't cover domestic partners of the employees of firms with fewer than one hundred employees. "That's discrimination! That's not fair!" she responded. I told her she wasn't telling me anything I didn't know and that if she wanted to discuss it after my examination I would fill her in on the discrimination issues faced by queer folk like me and my partner. Needless to say, she wasn't all that interested.

She did, however, order a battery of tests including an endometrial biopsy. Another doctor in the practice was to perform this procedure of vacuuming a small piece of tissue from the uterus.

Support for Lesbian Parents

Lesbian and Gay Parenting Project
c/o Lyon-Martin Clinic
2480 Mission Street, Suite 214
San Francisco, CA 94110
(415) 525-7312

Lavender Families Resource Network
P.O. Box 21567
Seattle, WA 98111
(206) 325-2643

CenterKids
The Family Project
Lesbian/Gay Community Services
Center
208 West 13th Street
New York, NY 10011
(212) 620-7310

Love Makes a Family, Inc.
P.O. Box 11694
Portland, OR 97211
(503) 228-3892

National Gay and Lesbian Parents Coalition
P.O. Box 50360
Washington, DC 20004
(202) 583-8029

Custody Action for Lesbian Mothers
P.O. Box 281
Narbeth, PA 19072
(215) 667-7508

Lesbian Mothers' National Defense Fund
P.O. Box 21567
Seattle, WA 98111
(206) 325-2643

National Center for Lesbian Rights
1663 Mission Street, 5th Floor
San Francisco, CA 94103
(415) 621-0674

She handed me a graphically gruesome consent form and immediately left. I was undressed and alone in the examining room—left to contemplate the potential of a punctured uterus, hemorrhage, infection and sterility. A nurse came in, and I told her that because I was a health educator, I understood that most of these outcomes were unlikely but that the patient must be informed of the possibilities. I also told her that, despite my background, the consent form was upsetting (especially since the patient is informed that the procedure is painful). I suggested that in the future someone remain with the patient to explain the informed consent and to offer support and additional information, if necessary. She agreed with me wholeheartedly and said that she had been saying the same thing since she'd started working at the practice. She asked me to say something to the doctor when she returned.

But my suggestion was summarily dismissed with a "Thank you for your thoughts," and the procedure began. Unfortunately, the first attempt to get a sample was not successful, so the doctor made a second try. As she did, I blurted out that adoption was looking more and more attractive. Without skipping a beat, she said that adoption just "wasn't the same" and that she "couldn't really imagine adopting after having had her own kids." Here I was—a woman who may have had fertility problems severe enough to make conception impossible for all we knew at that point. For all she knew, *I* was adopted! I was dumbfounded. I was also in severe pain and in stirrups. I was so upset that all I could say was, "I disagree."

The next test was a hysterosalpingogram, in which dye is injected into the fallopian tubes and an X ray is taken to check for blockages. I was extremely nervous about this test. (Surprisingly, it was easier than the endometrial biopsy.) The radiologist seemed pretty benign as we got started. Then she asked the question that apparently was most intriguing to doctors, "Why are you trying to get pregnant and not your . . . your . . . your . . . " I was lying on a cold table with my insides shot full of dye. I decided that I just wasn't in the mood to give the lesbian educational minute. I think that of the two of us, she was the more uncomfortable. Yet, I just couldn't understand how a young woman—educated, living in a major city that is home to probably a million queer people—could not think of a single word to describe my relationship with the beautiful woman nervously waiting for me in the next room. She gave up and remained silent. After the test, I told her that "partner" would suffice or that she could have simply asked me how I refer to my relationship. She also wanted to know how we picked a donor. She was not completely comfortable, but I gave her credit for trying.

As it turned out, the credit was doled out too soon. I had paid the bill and was walking out the door with my partner when the doctor rushed into the waiting room. She called to me, got my attention and asked, "You've never had an abortion, right?" Wrong. She immediately knew that she'd blown it. She was horrified, and I knew it. But I couldn't muster up any compassion. Years of coming to terms with a decision made thirteen years earlier melted away at that moment. Suddenly I was my twenty-year-old self again: caught, exposed, regretful of my unintended pregnancy. My partner, like me, stood there stunned, unable to say anything. The doctor tried to fix what she had done by walking up to me directly and explaining a potential problem. But I was absolutely wooden.

It was the last straw. I didn't know what to do next. So I did what I should have done from the start: I called my midwives. It was like coming home. The midwife I spoke with was not surprised by my story. She believed I had been treated badly because, as a lesbian, I wasn't a "good risk"; the doctors knew I did not have a fresh and steady sperm supply and would, therefore, mess up their success rates. This theory may or may not have been on target (I had concluded that these doctors—women all—were just assholes) but what *was* true was that none of them understood anything about caring for lesbians. Therefore, I was willing to accept any kind of conspiracy theory from a health care provider who clearly cared about me as my whole self. The midwife told me she'd call back with a referral to a reproductive endocrinologist used by a lesbian patient who had recently delivered but had had a hard time conceiving. She called me back within twenty minutes with a name of a doctor, who turned out to be amazing.

A close friend accompanied me to this appointment, as my partner could not be there. The doctor sat and spoke with me for as long as I needed and then turned to my friend—who she knew was my friend and not my partner—and asked if she had any questions! I was so relieved, I was practically in tears. I went to an examining room where she noticed a basic problem after doing a simple breast examination. I felt weary with the memory of the difficult battery of tests I had already endured. We spoke briefly about forms I needed to fill out for the sperm bank. One asked for the marital status of the recipient. Knowing that I had a partner, the doctor explained that, for legal reasons, I had to indicate that I was "single." She was walking out the door as she told me this but noticed that I had tears in my eyes. She quickly came to me, put her hands on my shoulders, looked me straight in the eye and said, "The form is a legal matter. It's the pits. But it's the reality. In this practice, your family will be treated with the same respect afforded to every other family." And we were.

I soon, however, made a major decision to resign from my job, recreate my life and, therefore, postpone having a child until everything fell into place. But, life is a wonderful mystery, and miracles happen when you least expect them: My partner and I were given a golden opportunity to travel to China to adopt a three-year-old little girl. I revoked my resignation, saying to my boss, "I think we have a daughter. I need a job after all." And one year later, on May 13, 1996, in Nanjing, China, my partner and I were united with our sweet girl, Lily Jun. This, of course, is another story.

I don't regret our attempts at conception. I believe they were part of the journey that finally brought us to Lily Jun. It also made me a more strident advocate. I am more compelled to speak out on lesbian health concerns. I learned how easily a physician can render a patient powerless—even a strong-willed woman like myself, much less a woman with less confidence or experience. I also learned how easily a physician can make us feel cared for and comfortable, which makes the former that much more infuriating. There were also lessons learned about reproductive health in general, the business of infertility and the meaning of children in our lives. But, the overarching impact of this story was on myself as a lesbian seeking health care. I hope that we may all find the strength to express our needs clearly to health care providers that, too often, don't have a clue but do have the capacity to get one.

MARISSA C. MARTINEZ

Choosing Children

Kathleen and I sit nervously at our first meeting with the gay and lesbian parenting support group at the Seattle Children's Home Society. We recognize other couples from the community although we do not know everyone's name. The Zs arrive, the male couple who had recommended the group to us. The facilitator has everyone introduce themselves. My spirits fall as each couple talks about how long they have been involved in the adoption process: two years, five years. Some couples have had bad experiences with the adoption agencies. Our perspective changes, however, when the Zs announce they have been approved for placement of a two-year-old boy. He will be coming into their home in the next few weeks.

Before we leave the meeting, the facilitator asks Kathleen and me to do a home exercise. For the next week, we are each to compile a list of all the expectations we have for a child. She wants us to be honest about what we want and don't want, including physical characteristics, personality and gender. We are not to share our lists with each other for a week. At the end of that time, we are to compare them, noting the differences and using those as a starting point for discussion. "It is very important," the facilitator cautions, "that you both go into the process of having children with either the same expectations or at least a clear understanding of your differences."

At the end of the week, Kathleen and I compare our lists. They both have the same three items: that the child be sufficiently healthy to eventually be able to live independently from us, that the child be Hispanic or of mixed Hispanic heritage and that the child come to us as an infant. We have already learned from the support group that the likelihood of adopting a healthy infant, especially for a gay couple, is nearly none. Our chances are somewhat increased by our being a racially mixed couple and being interested in having a child of Hispanic heritage. But there are no guarantees. In fact, the facilitator has cautioned us that we need to voice our willingness to adopt a child of up to eight years or older.

Deciding Against Adoption

Soon after completing the exercise, I read a news report that a woman in Washington who had given up her son for adoption two years earlier has discovered that he will be placed with two men. She has announced she will fight the placement and has arranged to appear on a national talk show. I call Kathleen, and we verify that the gay couple is indeed the Zs. In contrast to the birth mother, they opt to stay out of the media spotlight in deference to the child. Kathleen and I add a fourth requirement to our list: We do not want our personal choice of wanting children to become a media event.

Instead we turn our efforts to natural birth methods.

■

Choosing the Fertility Clinic and Donor

Having decided that Kathleen will carry the child, we opt to go with a local fertility clinic that has a nondiscrimination policy on sexuality. Just to be safe, we decide she will go alone for the meeting with the fertility doctor.

She returns home with a prescription for multivitamins, brochures for three sperm banks and a "chemistry 101" ovulation kit. Choosing the sperm bank is easy: Only the one in California has Hispanic donors, two who are fully Mexican and two who are half Mexican, half Anglo. We order the full reports for all four.

To actively participate in the process, I will track Kathleen's ovulation cycle for the next couple of months, recording her temperature every morning. I also study the ovulation kit several times to make sure I will be ready for my part.

The donor profiles have come. Kathleen and I have different approaches to the information. Kathleen wants the short donor: She equates a short donor to a smaller baby at birth. I remind her that it doesn't matter how big they are grown up, it matters how big they were coming out—information we don't have. One sounds very similar to me: engineering major; large, extended Catholic family; medium complexion; dark eyes.

We call up our first order, Visa card ready. I joke with Kathleen that by using the credit card we even have buyer's insurance. Three days later, the clinic notifies us the sperm has arrived. Kathleen's cycles have been regular for the past three months. We are ready for our first chemistry experiment.

Two drops from this vial mixed with five drops from that one; wait two minutes. Add five drops from a third mixture, and wait another two minutes. Houston, we have fertility! Kathleen makes an appointment for the following morning.

■

Insemination Success

As with the adoption process, our excitement about the insemination is jolted by a news report that a lesbian couple seeking insemination at another local clinic has been denied service by a staff worker who claimed the services were for "infertile couples, not lesbians." Despite the nondiscrimination policy held by both clinics, Kathleen and I decide she should go alone for the insemination appointment. This is the only stage where Kathleen is willing to go alone. Once she is pregnant, we will both go to the ob-gyn appointments, and the medical staff will just have to deal with that.

We wait the requisite two weeks, then another. Kathleen is

■■

Alternative Insemination

RESOURCES

Chicago Women's Health Center
3435 North Sheffield
Chicago, IL 60657
(312) 935-6126

Feminist Women's Health Center
580 14th Street NW
Atlanta, GA 30318
(404) 874-7551

Fenway Community Health Center
Lesbian-Gay Family and Parenting
Services
7 Haviland Street
Boston, MA 02115

(617) 267-0900

Routh Street Women's Clinic
4228 North Central Expressway, Suite 201
Dallas, TX 75206
(214) 748-0498
(800) 880-0498

The Sperm Bank of California
Telegraph Hill Medical Plaza, Suite 2
3007 Telegraph Avenue
Oakland, CA 94609
(415) 444-2014

SUGGESTED READING

Challenging Conceptions: Planning a Family by Self-Insemination by Lisa Saffron, London: Cassell, 1994.

Having Your Baby by Donor Insemination by E. Noble, Boston: Houghton Mifflin Co., 1987.

Lesbians Choosing Motherhood: Legal Implications of Donor Insemination and Co-Parenting edited by Maria Gil de Lamadrid, San Francisco: National Center for Lesbian Rights, 1991.

now a week late. We pull out the "pee stick," a far easier test than the LH surge test[1]—just pee, wait and watch. The results are unclear. We try another one and get the same results. Later that afternoon, Kathleen has severe cramps and starts bleeding heavily. We suspect that an egg had been fertilized but that the embryo was not viable. I give Kathleen a back rub to ease her cramping. We'll try again next month.

Three months later, Kathleen and I have fallen into a regular routine: I test for LH surge on the fifteenth day; Kathleen calls the clinic for an insemination appointment; she spends the insemination day at home taking a break from the stress of work; two weeks later, we pee on the stick. Okay, Kathleen pees on the stick, and I time it. Each time the disappointing blank space tells us that Kathleen's period will start as usual in the next day or so, as it does. This month we have been more lackadaisical. I did not even test for the LH surge; I just guessed the day and then adjusted it to accommodate a planned trip to Portland. Usually, we both look on as Kathleen prepares the pregnancy test, and I time it. This month, I come upstairs to find Kathleen in the tub.

"The test is on the counter," she tells me. "It should be enough time." I peer into the window, expecting the usual flat white expanse where the positive result should appear. This time, it looks different. I focus hard on the space and see a clear, bright pink dot, the exact shade as the test dot. Oh, my gosh! I look up at Kathleen.

"Two! Two!" is all I can manage to verbalize as I dance around the bathroom. *We're pregnant! We're going to have a baby. Oh, my gosh! We're pregnant; we're going to have a baby. What are we thinking?!* This was only the first of many panics I would experience throughout Kathleen's pregnancy.

■

As part of the fertility treatment, the clinic provides an ultrasound to check that the embryo has indeed implanted itself on the wall of the uterus. On her last visit, Kathleen had seen two lesbian couples at the clinic for appointments, so we decide to both go see this new life growing inside her.

"There it is," the technician claims. With a few flicks, she has finally centered on a small white dot in the center of the screen. I'm willing to take her word for it—I certainly can't recognize anything on the screen. A minute later she hands me a photo. It is really just a zygote—a collection of cells. But it is our zygote. Kathleen is horrified when I take the photo to work and scan it into my computer to use as a wallpaper on my operating system desktop, but my work group sends me flowers and a card that said, "Congratulations on your bouncing baby zygote."

Choosing the Ob-Gyn

Kathleen and I sit in a small conference room with three other couples for a mandatory introductory class with the nurse practitioner from the obstetrics practice. No one sits on our side of the table. We read along in our packet of information about lists of birthing classes, other clinic-recommended resources and a list of the doctors in the practice. At the end of the scheduled time, when the nurse practitioner asks if there are any further questions, one of the men across the table leans over and asks "how we did it."

"Like this," I tell them, whipping out my Visa card. Their initial panic at possibly getting a demonstration fades into nervous laughter. Kathleen kicks me under the table. "Well, they deserve it; we didn't ask them how they did it," I try to convey with my look. I allay Kathleen's ire by explaining we used a fertility clinic and alternative insemination.

Afterwards, we stay to get the nurse practitioner's opinion on which doctor in the practice would be most compatible with our family. She makes two suggestions, but points out that for the appointments toward the end of the pregnancy, we will rotate through and meet all the doctors since we will see the on-call doctor for the birth itself. We decide to start with Dr. E, a woman. We'll go to Dr. R, a man, if that doesn't work out. I am fully prepared to go through every doctor in the practice if we have to. I hope we don't have to.

I volunteer to make the appointment with the obstetrician. I steel myself for the response on the phone. I would much rather do this in person, but my work schedule won't allow it.

"I need to make an appointment," I tell the woman who answers the phone.

"Can I get your name?" I dutifully tell her my name, but add that the appointment is for my partner. "Oh." I believe this is the required sound made by anyone presented with a lesbian or gay family for the first time. I am sure it must be somewhere in Miss Manners's handbook on etiquette. First time meeting a gay or lesbian couple? Nod politely and say, "How do you do?" First time meeting a lesbian or gay couple with children? Stare blankly and say, "Oh."

I give her Kathleen's name, and she proceeds to a list of questions, still stumbling once or twice over the word "partner." She asks several questions to identify when Kathleen got pregnant. I confirm that we already know she is pregnant since we were referred through the fertility clinic.

The doctor's visits are regular and uneventful. The nurses always acknowledge my participation in this process, taking me to the exam room while Kathleen heads for the bathroom to provide samples. Both doctors and nurses answer my questions along with Kathleen's. At one point, when Kathleen develops severe eczema from a combination of her raging hormones and stress at work, a nurse pulls me aside, out of Kathleen's hearing, and urges me to take on as much responsibility as I can to get Kathleen to rest more. "She needs to reduce her stress level," she warns. At that moment, I truly become a co-parent to the staff.

Midway through the pregnancy, Dr. E tells us she is pregnant and will start her own maternity leave soon! We switch to Dr. R after all.

The Birth

The "birthing bag" sits by the front door. I have included tapes of Kathleen's favorite artists, racquetball balls for giving back rubs, my power of attorney for Kathleen, the bottled water that Kathleen really likes, a pair of sweatpants for me and numerous other items I have deemed important but most likely will never extract from the bag. I put it in my car every day when I leave for work, take it out at night and put it in whichever car Kathleen and I take out in the evenings or on weekends. After finding ourselves at the hospital without it during two false alarms, I do not want to take any chances.

It is 7:12 A.M. Friday. We have made arrangements with Dr. R to induce the baby today since he will be on call. We are to arrive at the hospital at 7:30 to check in. A friend will pick up Kathleen's mother and meet us later at the hospital. Our friends from Portland, Jocelyn and Lynn, the baby's godmothers-to-be, will arrive later that night. I have the list of phone numbers for making calls after the baby arrives. I pull out of my parking space. After a quick drive around our block, I park the truck and run back into the house. I hop back in the truck with bag in hand. I am ready to become a parent.

By 8:00, Kathleen and I are in a birthing room. Kathleen has on her hospital bracelet tag. Dr. R comes in and explains the procedure to us. He'll apply a gel to induce labor. We'll wait for about an hour for observation, and then we can walk around downtown. His favorite spot is a nearby Pottery Barn. The nurse hooks up the fetal monitor. We are familiar with the machinery, not only from our birthing class but also from our previous visits. One line indicates the contractions; the number gives the baby's heart rate.

About twenty minutes into our observation period, I am fervently tracking the graph emitted by the monitor. "This is a big one," I comment. Kathleen is more forgiving at this early stage and simply nods, concentrating on the breathing we learned in birthing class. In my absorption, I fail to hear the urgent call on the P.A. system, "Dr. R, stat." Three nurses rush into our room. Kathleen is asked to turn over on her hands and knees on the bed. One nurse grabs the oxygen mask and puts it on Kathleen. Another nurse grabs my hand, drags me closer to the bed and presses my hand against the monitor on Kathleen's abdomen. "Hold this," she instructs. By the time Dr. R enters the room, the contraction has ended. We all stay in our designated positions through a couple more contractions before Kathleen can turn back over.

Kathleen has reacted very strongly to the gel. The contractions had piled on top of each other, and the baby's heartbeat dropped dangerously low in response. The doctor calls off the shopping trip. Kathleen must stay here and continue being monitored throughout the labor.

I lay out the contents of the bag and put on a tape for Kathleen. She does not want me to touch her, but her contractions are getting more intense, so we ask the nurse to help us with the hot tub. I try to stay focused on Kathleen, to read her mood, estimate where she is and what she may need. She is clearly uncomfortable and can't seem to fall into any rhythm. We are getting close to the cutoff time for having the epidural. Kathleen hesitates to say yes, and I know she is gauging whether my response is a judgment. I point out that it has already been five hours. "Take the drugs, and save your strength," I offer, not knowing what words she really needs to hear. We inform the nurse of our decision.

The anesthesiologist arrives and performs the procedure.

Kathleen is still uncomfortable, feeling the contractions hard on one side. He must come back and make adjustments. During the second round, I hear a baby cry down the hall; the other couple we saw when we arrived must have delivered. Dr. R comes in soon after to check on us. Yes, there was another delivery. It was her fifth, which made it shorter. He stays and chats. He was originally an engineering student but wanted to have a career in which he could interact with people more. Kathleen is much more relaxed now. Suddenly, it seems, we are all on a first-name basis.

I take advantage of the break to check on my mother-in-law and our friend in the waiting room. I give them a quick update on what is happening: Dr. R expects a few more hours, but the baby should come by dinner time. Jocelyn and Lynn should arrive at the same time as the baby. Yes, they have eaten lunch. I have to get back to Kathleen.

Six hours later, Kathleen is still not ready to push. She panics when the anesthesia creeps as high as her chest. She can no longer feel herself breathe. "I'm not breathing!" she informs me.

"You are breathing," I reply, working to keep the calm tone we were taught in birthing class. "You would not be able to talk if you weren't breathing." I am sure the logic will set her at ease.

"I'm not breathing!" she repeats. The nurse thankfully intervenes.

"Put your hand in front of your face." Kathleen complies. "Can you feel your breath on your hand?" Kathleen nods. "Good. Now whenever you feel like you aren't breathing, just put your hand up to your face and check." Kathleen nods, unwilling to put down her hand.

It is now almost 9 P.M. We have heard three more babies born, all from women who arrived after we did this morning. Even through the anesthesia, Kathleen's contractions grip her body as tightly, I am sure, as she grips my hand when they come. Dr. R comes in to check again and announces it is time to push. The baby is showing signs of fatigue as well. The doctor will help by pulling. He wants to try to avoid a C-section.

Kathleen is two hours into the pushing. The doctor has been crouched down, leveraged for pulling on the suction cup attached to the baby's skull. I have lost my entire vocabulary and know only one word: "push." Kathleen suddenly sits back on the bed, more relaxed than I have seen her all day.

"I'm done," she announces. "Put it back. I'm going home." The doctor's head pops up from between her legs. The nurse, preparing scales and vaccinations and other things that I recall do not relate to the word "push," whips around.

"I don't think we can put it back," I say. In birthing class, the instructor had related many scenarios to us about what might happen in the late stages of labor when the birth mother is exhausted. Your partner may cry, we were told. Your partner may scream at you. Your partner may say "I can't do this." I distinctly remember that "Put it back; I'm going home" was *not* on the list. "Push" does not seem a wise thing to say at this juncture. Again the nurse comes through. She has slipped over to the side of the bed.

"Kathleen. You're almost there. Can you sit up and try just one more?" Kathleen obliges, and I take the cue from the nurse. For the next half hour, we step through one push at a time.

At 11:40 P.M., with the combination of Kathleen's pushing, the doctor's pulling and the baby's deciding his time has come, Carlos Thomas pushes into the world, falling onto the small platform beneath Kathleen's hips. Startled at first by the deep blue tint of his skin, I try to remember the checklist Kathleen and I had made: arms, head, toes. I can't focus on anything except the mass of dark wet hair plastered against his head and his long limbs, limp from exhaustion. As he takes in air, the deep skin hue fades into a warmer, red-tinged complexion. This is Life.

"Marissa," I hear the doctor say. "We'll have you cut the cord."

"No, we won't," I reply. "You are doing a fine job without me, thank you very much."

I want to go immediately and tell everyone in the waiting room, but Kathleen won't let me go anywhere since the doctor is sewing up the vaginal opening, which has torn on the final push. The nurse cleans up Carlos and hands him back to us. Dr. R grabs the camera on the counter by the birthing bag and poses us for our first family photo.

Starting Over

Our experience with pediatricians has pretty well matched our experience with the ob-gyns. I made the initial phone call, explained our family situation and asked for a doctor who would view us both as parents.

Our only shaky moment so far came just prior to the finalization of the adoption. We had gone to the emergency room because Carlos had developed a case of croup. When the staff member at the desk asked for the parent information, she recorded Kathleen's name as the mother, but refused to take my name as the other legally responsible adult. I now carry with me a copy of Carlos's birth certificate for just such an emergency.[2] It has not come up since.

Kathleen and I consider ourselves very lucky that all three items on our list of expectations for a child have come to fruition in Carlos. Even the addendum of not becoming a media event has somewhat held, though Carlos has found himself included in several of my published pieces.

Kathleen and I have been thinking about trying for a second child. And whether we succeed or not, this time, I'm going to *all* her appointments.

Notes

1. Lutenizing hormone. This test indicates a hormone surge from the pituitary gland. This surge stimulates the ovaries to make an estrogen surge which, in turn, tells the follicle to ovulate. From the beginning of the LH surge to ovulation takes approximately twenty-four to thirty-six hours. A positive test result indicates that insemination should occur within twenty-four hours.

2. In Washington state, any two people can be the legal parents of a child. While Kathleen retains her rights as the birth mother, I had to officially adopt Carlos. His birth certificate shows both of us as parents.

My Life as a Volcano

Today is a perfect morning to start writing this piece on menopause. I feel haggard (a word I never felt like until recently). Today, ha, ha, I am a hag and not a crone. Last night was another sleepless one, a night of raging hot flashes, wide eyes, aching bones. I had one of those stirring premonitions of the impending situation before I went to bed, so I turned on the air conditioner. That turned out to be a mistake. Every half hour throughout the night, I awoke to the "aura" of an approaching heat wave which burst over me with cascades of boiling perspiration. As each surge subsided, the sweat chilled in the air conditioning, and my damp bedclothes became cold and clammy.

It seems like just the other day I was a sassy teenage butch in the fifties; but suddenly, we're in the nineties, and I'm in my *own* fifties, and the theme is menopause. In typical arrogant fifties butch fashion, I expected to breeze through menopause just as I'd breezed through menstruation. I was very healthy. My periods had always been regular and easy. I generally maintained a smooth temperament and optimistic outlook. I'd always eaten properly, supplemented my diet with vitamins and herbs, gotten plenty of regular exercise. I'd done everything right.

I wasn't affected by media hype around menopause, because when I was young there wasn't any. Menopause was known only as "the end of a woman's childbearing years," and since, as a dyke, I was not involved in childbearing, I knew that this couldn't possibly apply to me. Occasionally, at our frequent family gatherings, I'd witnessed a red-faced aunt fanning herself while her sisters joked about hot flashes, but I knew, as I grew older, that this wouldn't happen to me. After all, I drank herb teas and swallowed vitamin E and evening primrose oil and ginseng. I had a lot of information and made good use of it. What I didn't count on was the strength of my foremothers and the genetic heritage they passed on to me, the patterns and messages in my DNA.

Sometime during my forty-ninth year, I wake in the night to feel a line of fire creeping up from my midsection, over my chest, and into my face. *Aha!* I think. *This must be a hot flash.* I find that recognition somehow satisfying. The next night I have another, and another one the night after that. I really get into the experience, feel as though it's a rite of passage of sorts. Then the hot flashes stop. *That wasn't so bad,* I think smugly. That month my period, which I can usually predict down to the second, is two weeks late, and I bleed for fifteen days after that.

Three weeks later, I awaken again in the middle of the night, to the familiar heat rising up in my body and exploding in volcanic fury from my face and chest. *Here comes another hot flash,* I think with the satisfaction of familiarity. I have three more hot flashes that night and four the next night and four or five every night for the next three weeks. Having them starts to get *very* old. I do not start bleeding on time, and then I begin to experience sudden, intense heat rushes during the day, too. Nothing I do helps.

I call my mother on the telephone long distance. "Mom," I say when she answers, "what's our family heredity on hot flashes?"

"Terrible!" responds my mom. "Your grandmother had them until the day she died, and I still have two or three a week myself." Mom is seventy-three.

"Oh, great," I mumble. "Thanks, Mom. I love you."

The women I work with on my job follow me around, closing the windows I've opened as they get too cold, turning off the air conditioning when they can't stand it any longer. They are very patient with my needs. After six weeks of non-stop hot flashes, they subside, and I bleed heavily and with lots of cramps for the next two weeks.

I sit on the commode while blood and clots pour out of my body. Seems as though I am giving birth to an army of amazons, chunk by chunk, into the bowl. I wonder if I could pass out from the loss of blood this way, wonder if I have cancer or simply am experiencing one of the results of changing hormone levels. Who knows, maybe I'm even passing my fibroids. Maybe I'm passing my entire uterus.

I remember how my periods always used to be light, predictable, easy. Then sometime in my late thirties, my cycle shortened. I began to experience cramps that were *not* fun. My flow became erratic, sometimes very heavy or very light. Now I'm almost fifty, and lately, some really weird stuff has come out of my cunt from time to time.

I yank at the bed covers that are twisted around my body and between my legs. My eyes stare wide into the darkness of my bedroom. I throw my body over, straighten out, toss over again, seeking a cool place on the sheets, fighting the urge to hurl my body against the wall. I sigh, reach for the clock, look at it. The time is 2 A.M. Normally I sleep well, fall into a hard zonk as soon as I hit the mattress and barely stir until morning. Now I am slow to slumber, wake easily and cannot get back to sleep, sometimes cannot fall asleep at all. I am frustrated, exhausted, furious. I despair of ever being able to sleep through the night again; not that it would matter even if I could, since lately I am also up two, three, four times a night to pee.

I feel exhausted! I snap at friends, scream at children, cry easily. I fly off the handle with little provocation, wallow in dejection, experience the throes of PMS hell for the first time. Whenever I am enough in control, I warn everyone within range of an impending hormone attack. Fortunately, I am able to remind myself that nothing in my life has changed, that these ordinary events would not affect me so strongly were my hormones not swinging me around. Maybe the real problem is that I'm just *so* tired from not enough sleep. . . . I am thankful to the goddesses that these extremes don't happen very often and that the duration is brief.

My breasts are swollen, tender, burning. They haven't felt like this—like boils coming to a head—since they first started to bud. My sex organs feel like hot weights hanging from the bottom of my body—twenty-seven pound womb, thirty-four pound ovaries, fifty-six pound cunt. I do not like the way my body feels.

And where, oh where, has my libido gone? I've always liked sex, always been able to do it at a moment's notice. Now nothing could be farther from my thoughts. The idea of sex is an alien notion, and I really do not want to be touched in any way at all, not just sexually, but for *sure* not sexually. Except that sometimes, suddenly, unexpectedly, I might get an immediate, hard, horny feeling, usually at an entirely inappropriate moment; but if I *do* get turned on, even just a little, my cunt clenches, and it hurts. My general energy is good, but my parts are killing me. I do not like this at all.

My lover bemoans my lack of interest in sex. She is the only woman I know who went entirely through menopause and never missed a libidinal beat.

Friends tell funny stories about their own experiences of being somewhat out of step sexually with their lovers and assure me that this, too, shall pass.

The weird thing now is that my *scalp* hurts! Each hair feels like a hot wire penetrating my scalp, just the scalp, not the whole skull, not anywhere near the bone or brain. I used to love having my head rubbed, loved any kind of petting or stroking. Now I can't bear a touch at all on my head, my hair, my skin.

I look in the mirror. My parts hang, fold, bulge, shrink, crease, droop. Parts are wearing out, getting stiff, tiring more easily lately. My body is changing very quickly now, it seems. My cunt is pulling up, looking more like it did when I was a little girl, while my breasts have become wide and flat, like those of my old tantes. I'm losing hair all over, losing teeth, too, and my arches are falling. I look like a much older person than I feel like. Inside I'm still the same, the me I've always been. I don't feel very different inside at all—except when I reflect on this, I really do, too, at the same time that I don't.

I am having dizzy spells, episodes of muscle cramps and numbness, heart palpitations. Finally I see physicians. My body checks out just fine. I know what I'm experiencing is really a chain-re-action response within my organism to this change in activity of my endocrine system.

I wonder what I'd do if I had one of these spells that's so se-vere I couldn't keep on my feet while I'm in a store or on the street, and there's no place to sit down or even pass out. I imag-ine passers-by rushing to my rescue. What could I say? "Oh, thanks, I'm really perfectly all right, just having a menopausal episode—" Do you really think I could maintain my cool in the face of public embarrassment? I think about being embarrassed in public, remember a story my mother told me about the time she dropped a clot on the floor of the Louvre Museum, and I laugh to myself.

Sometimes it's difficult for me to know what is really happening, or why. I wonder, for instance, if my see-saw emotions are a sign of new dissatisfaction with my life, a symptom of midlife crisis, a result of changing hormone levels, or just a matter of not get-ting enough sleep. Is this unusually heavy bleeding a symptom of a serious medical problem or an indication of changing hor-mone levels? Are these leg cramps and spells of fatigue a sign of aging, a symptom of allergy or illness, or a reaction to changing hormone levels?

There's not very much information about menopause, and most of the best of what there is comes out of our own sharing of personal experiences. The little medical information we get is colored by the male members of the medical establishment. "Not much is known," a physician may say, "because women have only recently been living long enough to go through menopause." This is supposed to excuse the historic lack of interest in women's health.

Those of us older dykes who are now in or past our own meno-pausal years often had to buck the system for much of our lives in order to survive as lesbians in a hostile world. As women who often were also involved in early feminism, we try in our own ways to circumvent the male manner of defining the universe in their linear fashion. We also work to overcome the lack of attention paid to interrelatedness and the limited definitions of function and purpose. Lesbians have always been outside the mainstream, and we are usually the leading edge of small revolutions. We tend to be more aware of our social conditioning and want to break free from the dependency it encourages. We try not to listen to men who tell us how we should think and what we should feel—the doctors, the therapists, the advertising boys—in their attempts to control us and take our money and energy and

Making Decisions About Menopause

SUGGESTED READING

The Change: Women, Aging and the Menopause by Germaine Greer, New York: Fawcett Columbine, 1991.

The Complete Book of Menopause by Carol Landau, Michele G. Cyr and Anne W. Moulton, New York: G.P. Putnam, 1994.

Dr. Susan Love's Hormone Book: Making Informed Choices About Menopause by Susan M. Love, M.D., with Karen Lindsey, New York: Random House, 1997.

The Hormone Replacement Handbook: What Every Woman Should Know About the Benefits and Risks of Hormone Therapy by Paula Brisco and Karla Morales, People's Medical Society, 1996.

Making the Estrogen Decision by Gretchen Henkel, Los Angeles: Lowell House, 1992.

The Menopausal Sourcebook by Gretchen Henkel, Los Angeles: Lowell House, 1994.

Menopausal Years: The Wise Woman Way by Susun S. Weed, Woodstock, NY: Ash Tree Publishing, 1992.

Natural Menopause: The Complete Guide by Susan Perry and Kate O'Hanlan, M.D., Reading, MA: Addison-Wesley Publishing Company, Inc., 1997.

Off the Rag: Lesbians Writing on Menopause edited by Lee Lynch and Akia Woods, Norwich, VT: New Victoria, 1996.

Secrets of a Natural Menopause: A Positive Drug Free Approach by Edna Copeland Ryneveld, St. Paul, MN: Llewellyn Publications, 1996.

The Silent Passage by Gail Sheehy, New York: Pocket Books, 1995.

prove that they are smarter than we are. We lend our strength, and support each other in these efforts.

We dykes talk about our bodies. We talk about other women's bodies. We are familiar with women's bodies. We discuss the changes we are experiencing. Where older lesbians gather, we also usually make space to talk about menopause. We get and share information. We learn that much of what we are experiencing seems to be typical—or not. When we have the support of our sisters, we don't have to be bound by a need to be told how we are feeling. We consider information we get from the traditional medical doctor, but we also learn about different approaches to dealing with stress and difficult changes that may be associated with menopause. We discuss what "studies show." We try to be supportive of one another and respectful of individual choices. We try not to make judgements or do put-downs or trips on one another about being guilty or politically incorrect or functionally out of control around our choices, whether they be to do ERT (estrogen replacement therapy) or herbs or meditation or Prozac or nothing. We maintain our own integrity.

Okay. That's enough. I'm tired of working on this lousy essay. My dogs are barking at something in the field, and they won't shut up, and my temper and temperature are both rising hard and fast, and if I make one more typo I will hurl this machine through the window, and anyhow I really have to pee again. . . .

DEL MARTIN AND PHYLLIS LYON

Old Lesbians Come of Age

"We have had the unique opportunity to witness and observe the genesis of a new social move ment. This movement, which is still giving birth to itself, is one we would broadly define as a movement to empower older lesbians."

—Sharon M. Raphael and Mina K. Robinson Meyer,
"Old Lesbians Seizing the Moment, Changing Their World"
in *Lambda Gray: A Practical, Emotional and Spiritual Guide
for Gays and Lesbians Who Are Growing Older*

These women, who teach gerontology at California State University at Dominguez Hills, California, helped to provide the setting for the birth of a new generation of "old" lesbian activists. The occasion was the 1987 West Coast Celebration by and for Old Lesbians.

The organizers of the celebration established sixty years of age and over as "old." They defined conference goals: "To look at the

210

unique contributions to the process of aging already made by old lesbians; to act politically coming from our own daring and dreaming; to look at how ageism affects each of us; to dispel the illusion of inclusion; to find our common voices; to define our own turf."

Our attitude restructuring began at the registration desk when we picked up our identification badges on which our ages were prominently displayed. In the opening session, old lesbian activist Shevy Healey pointed out, "Such remarks as 'You're only as old as you feel,' 'You're in good shape for your age,' or 'That makes you look younger,' are not compliments, but are indications of ageism, of equating youth with beauty and desirability; old age with sickness, ugliness and powerlessness."

Barbara MacDonald, author with Cynthia Rich of *Look Me in the Eye: Old Women, Aging and Ageism,* provided the impetus for the celebration: "Our own panic about what's ahead is the linch-pin of ageism. We have become the old woman we have been taught to dread. But each plateau of life, whether it be forty or sixty or seventy, we find it isn't here yet. What we are experiencing is the cumulative deposit of the uncertainty of life. Illness, being confined to a wheelchair, or loss of sight or hearing are not inherent to old age, but rather inherent risks at any age."

The celebration had an indelible impact on the two of us and the 150 old lesbians (in their sixties to eighties) who experienced it. It raised our consciousness about ageism and gave us a new sense of being that signed, sealed and delivered us as committed Proud Old Lesbians.

By 1989, after the second such conference at California State University, San Francisco, the Old Lesbians Organizing Committee was formed as a national network. Later the word "Committee" was supplanted by "for Change." A manual on consciousness-raising about ageism was developed and published. Members provided ageism awareness sessions at the National Lesbian Conference in Atlanta in 1991, and again at the

Creating Change Conference of the National Lesbian and Gay and Lesbian Task Force in Durham, North Carolina, in 1993.

Over the years the two of us have worked in traditional politics as a route toward creating change. So when we learned by chance in a newspaper article that the White House Conference on Aging (WHCoA) was to be held in May 1995, we determined that a lesbian presence was necessary. State governors would be appointing delegates. That left us out. California's Governor Pete Wilson is no friend of our community. Then we found that each member of Congress had one appointment. We immediately contacted Congresswoman Nancy Pelosi and Senator Diane Feinstein whom we had known from the beginning of their political careers. We succeeded in attaining two of the coveted appointments.

Thus began a long and arduous *political* campaign to get sexual orientation and the specific needs of lesbians and gays on the WHCoA agenda. Space does not permit details of how it was accomplished. Suffice to say that with Nancy Moldenhauer, vice-president of the Older Women's League, a national organization, we were three "out" lesbians among 2,217 delegates. With the *primary* help of WHCoA volunteer Lisa Hamburger, vice-president of the National Association of Lesbian and Gay Gerontology, a half dozen other supporters and the National Gay and Lesbian Task Force, we succeeded.

For the first time in its thirty-five-year history WHCoA included lesbians and gays as one of the most underserved elder populations in America. This acknowledgment of lesbian and gay concerns was indicated in a number of conference documents. The 1996 Final Report of WHCoA included:

Resolution Forty-One as adopted: Encourage civic, social, ethnic, cultural and religious leaders to sensitize their communities and organizations to the subtlety of racial, age and *sexual orientation* discrimination and the social and financial costs of such practices.

Preamble: "We recognize the importance, value, and interdependence of people, regardless of age, sex, race, ethnicity, religion, culture, or *sexual orientation,* and seek to safeguard *all* persons from discrimination.

The following clauses appeared in various resolutions:

Support the Employment Non-Discrimination Act. Amend Title VII of the Civil Rights Restoration Act of 1991 to include lesbians and gays as protected classes.

Encourage district attorneys to prosecute cases in which sexual orientation discrimination is alleged.

Fund the establishment of new service programs when existing service agencies are not effectively serving the needs of senior gays and lesbians.

Include in-training programs that help educate police and other public safety personnel, social service professionals and district attorneys about statistics on hate crimes perpetuated against lesbians and gays, as well as specific racial minorities.

Address the unique needs of culturally diverse older persons, including minorities, ethnic groups, persons with disabilities, *alternative lifestyles* and communication barriers, for support services in affordable housing.

Permit appointment of unrelated persons as guardians when the proposed guardian has lived together with the proposed ward, or co-owned their primary residence, for more than five years just prior to guardianship and require the guardianship courts to recognize all legally executed advance directives regarding such matters among unrelated persons and domestic partners.

Amend current legislation (Older Americans Act, the Crime

Bill, AIDS funding, Social Security, etc.) to reflect attention to lesbian and gay aging caregivers.

To be effective, these WHCoA recommendations need to be enacted by Congress as amendments and/or additions to existing laws. WHCoA itself and the funding of senior programs comes under the Older Americans Act (OAA). Congress has not yet included lesbians and gays in the law. Citing these recommendations from an official government document, however, has its value to lesbian and gay service agencies in writing funding proposals.

Not only does the elder advocacy population need to be made aware of lesbian needs, but lesbian health advocates need to acknowledge and fight for the concerns of aging lesbians. Medicare needs to be introduced into the vocabulary of lesbian health advocates. For lesbians of eligible age, what Congress concludes in the current debate over the future of Medicare is crucial. Medicare has never provided full health coverage. Take the ability to see, hear and eat, for instance. Medicare beneficiaries must bear all costs for eye examinations and glasses (unless surgery is required), hearing tests and hearing aids, dentistry and dentures. Medicare deducts an annual premium from social security checks and requires a sizable deductible each year before coverage kicks in. Thereafter medical expenses are paid on an 80/20 percent basis. Medigap insurance, needed to cover these deductibles, becomes increasingly expensive as Medicare decreases what it will pay.

Old lesbians, like other women of our generation, worked for women's wages, few ever qualified for pensions, and our life savings have less value in today's inflated dollars. The high cost for these services can mean postponing or, for some, doing without these basic health needs.

Another issue that frightens those of us who grew up during the Great Depression are the Republican schemes to "privatize"

Social Security and Medicare. The assumption is that investing in the stock market will reap higher returns for these funds. It could also mean a disaster if Wall Street slumps into a "recession" or hits bottom as it did in 1929, when our families lost all their savings. The objective of Social Security and Medicare is to protect us, not to put us at risk.

Health Maintenance Organizations (HMOs), promoted by Congress under the guise of "saving" Medicare, scare us. These for-profit companies lure unwary old people into enrolling on a "no cost to you" basis. They never see a bill. Medicare pays the HMO on a specified monthly basis whether or not medical services are used. The more people signed up the more the HMO's income and the less the quality of health care. Old individuals are expendable. We have heard enough horror stories that HMO doctors are less inclined or forbidden to bother with complete examinations or

Entering Old Age

RESOURCES

Gay and Lesbian Association of Retiring Persons (GLARP)
P.O. Box 30808
Los Angeles, CA 90030-0808
(310) 966-1500
(310) 477-0707 fax

National Committee to Preserve Social Security and Medicare
2000 K Street NW, Suite 800, Department 71
Washington, DC 20006
(202) 822-9459
Senior Flash Hotline (800) 988-0180

Ten dollar membership includes Legislative Alert Service and *Secure Retirement* magazine.

Coalition of Older Lesbians (COOL)
1881 Morton Avenue
Los Angeles, CA 90026
(213) 913-3722 or (213) 993-4730

Gay and Lesbian Outreach to Elders (GLOE)
1853 Market Street
San Francisco, CA 94103
(415) 626-7000

Old Lesbians Organizing for Change (OLOC)
P.O. Box 980422
Houston, TX 77098

Senior Action in a Gay Environment (SAGE)
305 Seventh Avenue, 16th Floor
New York, NY 10001

expensive live-saving procedures on old patients. Further, most doctors have no or little training in geriatric medicine. We learned a long time ago, "You get what you pay for."

Social Security and Medicare beneficiaries who have paid into the system all their working lives have been called "greedy gee-zers." But the real culprits, as WHCoA pointed out, are those who are billing and bilking the system fraudulently. These charges have been substantiated by an audit conducted by the Department of Health and Human Services. According to Senator Susan M. Collins, R–Maine, chair of the Government Affairs Committee's subcommittee on investigations, Medicare is losing twenty-three billion dollars a year because of errors, waste and fraud.[1]

WHCoA delegates overwhelmingly opposed HMOs, block grants to the states, and changes in the Consumer Price Index to reduce cost of living adjustments. Instead of cutting services WHCoA has proposed that Medicare be expanded by adding Part C for medications, long-term care and in-home supplies. Long-term care would include home- and community-based services, not just institutional care—or as San Francisco delegates put it, "Shift from institutional bias in funding to home- and community-based services and *consumer-directed* personal assistance services."

Old lesbians who have been inventing their lives to date are now inventing their old age. We refute the lies that have made old women invisible. We reject the medical model of aging services, particularly the "one-size-fits-all" mentality of doctors who don't listen to clients and are oblivious to the fact that old bodies don't all respond the same way when they prescribe drugs. We believe that gerontology courses should be required for those in the medical professions.

We are also tired of the heterosexual presumption of service agencies. They should develop intake forms and outreach protocols sensitive to the language and labels used by alternative families, lesbians and gays. Caregiving agencies should be user-friendly.

We are concerned that forgetfulness has been so emphasized and attributed to old age by the media and other sources. "I must be getting senile," or "Maybe I'm coming down with Alzheimer's," are prevalent phrases as a result of such pessimism. Memory lapse can happen at any age. We just assume that being old we have so much more data in our memory bank it takes a little longer to pull it up.

Shevy Healy and Ruth Silver have traveled the country as ambassadors of Old Lesbians Organizing for Change (OLOC) in a twenty-six-foot fifth wheel, which hitches onto a three-quarter-ton truck. "The overriding common denominator in all the groups we've been to has been the universal seeking, really craving, of community. Old lesbians welcome a place to talk about their concerns with people who understand and respect them. While on the one hand they experience all the ridicule and injustices of

Entering Old Age

SUGGESTED READING

At Seventy by May Sarton, New York: W.W. Norton, 1984.

Fierce with Reality: An Anthology of Literature on Aging edited by Margaret Cruikshank, St. Cloud, MN: North Star Press, 1995.

Lesbian Passages edited by Marcy Adelman, Boston: Alyson Publications, 1996.

Look Me in the Eye: Old Women, Aging and Ageism by Barbara MacDonald with Cynthia Rich, Duluth, MN: Spinsters Ink, 1983.

Memory Board by Jane Rule, Tallahasee, FL: Naiad Press, 1987.

"Old Lesbians/Dykes" in *Sinister Wisdom,* Summer/Fall 1994, P.O. Box 3252, Berkeley, CA 94703.

OUT Word, Newsletter of the Lesbian and Gay Aging Issues Network of the American Society on Aging, 833 Market Street, Suite 511, San Francisco, CA 94103-1824.

Positively Gay: New Approaches to Gay and Lesbian Life edited by Betty Berzon, Berkeley, CA: Celestial Arts, 1992.

ageism, they have never felt so free, particularly when health is no problem. Some who have been in the closet all their lives . . . now want out, at least so far as being with other lesbians."[2]

We speak from the joy of that connectedness we have gained from OLOC. The gathering at the University of Minnesota in Minneapolis in 1996 was the best conference of all. (We've said that at least once in every decade of our activist lives.) But now, as we explore our own aging, reflect on our past, tie up loose ends and adjust to the slowing process of our aging bodies, that connection with one's peers is very important. Being with other old dykes, hearing their stories and observing their creativity beats any medicine that a doctor can prescribe.

That is why we are so concerned about our sisters who are still in the closet, becoming more isolated as their intimate social groups die off. Some tentative inroads in reaching into this closeted population have been made. Ruth Morales, social worker for San Francisco's Gay and Lesbian Outreach to Elders, has set up a program for the frail elderly, called the Lunch Bunch, at a gay-friendly senior center that has provided them a private dining room. Lesbians and gays who otherwise live in the confines of the heterosexual world because they fear coming out will reduce needed health care services, can at least "let their hair down" twice a month.

Well into our seventies we face another process—that of dying. The debates between the medical profession and old people about the right to death with dignity and the use of marijuana for medicinal purposes are of special interest.

Given the choice everyone would like to die peacefully while asleep; no one would want to be kept alive to linger in excruciating pain or in a vegetative state of consciousness. Many doctors claim to be healers and want no part in helping someone put an end to pain or a long-lasting comatose condition, even if the patient has personally requested or begged for such relief or release. We choose to oppose sanctimonious doctors who assume the right to deny these options to the terminally ill.

At the very least the medical profession and Medicare should humanize end-of-life care by applying lessons of hospice to other care settings. Ira Byock, president of the American Academy of Hospice and Palliative Medicine, points out that hospice has elevated pain relief to an art and "should be available in all clinical contexts, whether it is the cancer center, the general acute-care hospital, a nursing home or home-health agency."[3]

Throughout our years of advocacy for lesbians we have fought for the right of choice. That means one can choose whether or not to take advantage of the availability of certain rights. Personally, we want to have control over our lives as long as we can, to maintain our individual and collective independence. We hope to make connections not only with our peers but also with generations to follow in our common and diverse interests.

One final and pressing health care issue: *Please* deliver your arthritic lesbian sisters from "childproof" caps on medicine bottles.

Notes

1. "Senator Speaks Out Against Medicare Waste, Fraud," *San Francisco Chronicle,* June 27, 1997.

2. Shevy Healey, "Traveling with Ruth and Shevy," *Sinister Wisdom,* Summer/Fall 1994.

3. Leah Glashee, "Humanizing End-of-Life Care," *AARP Bulletin,* June 1997.

RIVKA MASON AND JAN THOMAS

Leah's Passing

Leah Moussaioff, Rivka's thirty-nine-year-old sister, died on June 6, 1995. She was diagnosed with breast cancer in October 1994 and was hospitalized four times for calcium poisoning caused by the cancer releasing her bones' calcium. During her last hospitalization, she suddenly removed the IV and said, "I want to go home." At that point a web of community came together to help her through a period when she was less and less able to speak of her own needs. The responsibility shifted to us, her loved ones, to arrive at the decisions we thought she would have wanted.

Rivka: I received a message from Leah's son Danny that his mother was going downhill fast—she might not make it through the night. I flew to Seattle immediately. Jan followed the next day.

As soon as I got to Leah's house, I peeked into her room and saw two women with shaved heads, Leah and Val, asleep on the bed. It shook me to see my sister so vulnerable. This really *was* happening! On some level it had been hard to comprehend until I was in her presence. Talking on the phone every week, I imagined her more alive in her being, but when I saw my sister's weathered body, I knew her time with us would be short.

Jan: Leah's house was full of people and activity. The spirit of lesbian community was clearly a powerful force supporting her in this journey. Although I had previously met only two of the women there, within a few days I felt I had known them all for years.

Val looked different from the way I had remembered her, as her hair was only a quarter-inch long. When Leah was considering treatment options, Val had told Leah that if Leah had chemotherapy she would shave her head in solidarity. Leah's calcium eventually went out of control, so she did a round of chemotherapy to bring the calcium level down. When Val came to the hospital afterwards, Leah asked if she remembered her promise. That's how Val came to shave her head: "I would have done *anything* to make Leah feel less alone in what she was going through—it was such a small thing."

Rivka: The focus of healing for a long time had been a special diet which we so hoped could restore Leah's health. Now Leah could no longer eat solid foods. As I viewed the remnants of efforts to feed her, scattered around the kitchen, I was reminded again of how hard Leah had been working to stay alive.

Being Leah's medicinal cook was my entry point—the way I could contribute concretely to her healing process. I took a handful of root vegetables and made a broth, hoping to get some nutrition in her to ground and strengthen her. When the broth was done, I put it in a large ceramic bowl to cool. Cradling the bowl in my hands, I moved toward the window that looks out from the kitchen onto her garden. As I raised the bowl to bless it, I prayed to the elements—the strength of the mountains, the healing rivers, the sacred sky and the powers of the winds—to come into the bowl, to cast healing magic into the broth, to nurture and heal her. My body shook as tears welled up; a few tears dripped into the bowl.

I put some broth into a glass with a straw and took it to Leah's room. I looked at her body, so thin from illness: high cheekbones sticking out of her drawn face, collarbones protruding from her shoulders, bony fingers drawn up close to her head. As if to convince myself, I thought, "This is my sister—this is Leah."

Alongside my sadness in knowing she was on her way out, I was full of love for her and happy to be in her presence.

"Sleeping" doesn't quite describe the place Leah was in; she was mostly in her own world, and when others interacted with her she would slowly open her eyes and acknowledge their presence. I said to her, "Leah, it's me, Rivka." She turned her head, looked at me and said, "Wow . . . Rivka . . . you're here." Her eyes had an otherworldly look to them. Then with a hint of a smile, she slipped back to that other place.

Jan: Women were mingling inside and outside the house. The phone rang constantly. Word was getting out that Leah had taken a fast dive downhill. In her living room, people were sweeping, clearing and rearranging things.

Sue came to say they were moving Leah's bed outside to the garden. Leah, just like Rivka, never passed up any opportunity to be out in the sun. She was conscious of being lifted. Any movement seemed to cause pain, so four women placed her on a chair and carried her—one holding up her head, the others supporting her on all sides. Holding court from bed in her garden temple, she looked like a high priestess. Here, no matter how many women were around her, there was enough space to accommodate and absorb all the energy coming from the people who loved her.

Rivka: Leah could no longer tell us what she needed, so a few of us gathered to discuss what was to be done. Keeping in mind everything we knew about Leah's intentions, we considered the options. Should we allow her body to take its natural course in letting go? Should we try again to intervene with Western medicine and keep her alive as long as possible? Would this cause pointless suffering?

Leah didn't want to die. She had worked hard to stay alive. Now her body was giving way, inviting her to accept the dying process. This was simply the truth of what was happening to her.

For Leah, being alive meant being able to get around and do the basic, simple things of life. She had no interest in lying in bed, unable to do anything for herself, without the realistic possibility of turning things around. With this in mind, we decided to intervene one last time with an IV flush to try to reduce her calcium level. We hoped this would restore her faculties enough for her to be part of the decision making for the choices we now faced.

Sunday morning after the IV drugs had taken effect, I was startled to find Leah sitting upright in a chair with her eyes open, asking for broth. No one could quite face asking her the questions that were hanging in the air: "What if this doesn't work and things don't turn around?" "Where do we go from here?" (Later I found out she had told Val she only wanted to go to the hospital if she broke a bone.) In her will she specifically said she didn't want to be kept alive by artificial measures, and she had stressed that she wanted to be pain-free and comfortable. This became our obsession—the focus of all our activities.

Ultimately, it became too much of an effort for Leah to suck liquids through a straw. How would she continue to get her pain pills? How could she receive fluids? What was the next step?

Monday morning Leah's hospice nurse, Margo, came by. We all felt relieved to be able to tell her what was going on and ask the hard questions. We thought Margo would suggest an IV as a way to get pain medication into Leah, but she helped us think it through further. Leah's inability to take in nourishment was a signal that her body had actively begun the process of shutting down. If we gave her an IV, her lungs would be more likely to fill up with fluid, worsening her breathing problems and increasing her suffering. An alternative was to make a paste of pain medication and water that could be absorbed directly through her gums, adding to the effect of the pain medication she was receiving through skin patches.

This was a wrenching moment and a definitive turning point. Leah was moving toward death. We made a collective decision not to interrupt this process. We felt that drawing things out and overriding what her body was trying to do was pointless and would only add to her suffering. We believed she would have wanted it this way.

Jan: Life continued to go on around Leah. At one point a friend appeared with a plunger to help unclog the pipes. Several other women sat talking, laughing and crying in a corner. Home-cooked food appeared, seemingly out of nowhere, brought over by friends. Meanwhile people did the laundry, talked with the many friends of hers who called or came by, sat quietly by her bedside, burned sage to clear the energy field in the house, made occasional calls to the hospice nurse, had deep talks with one another, ran errands, looked at pictures, cried, told stories about Leah and . . . waited.

Rivka: I was crying on and off throughout the day, but I kept feeling the need to let it all out in a bigger way. So I headed off to Lake Washington with Jan and my cousin Miriam, just as it began to rain. We dashed from the car and got under the protective canopy of a tree. Feeling the support of these two women by my side, within seconds I began wailing. My grief poured out of me just as a deafening crash of thunder resounded. I felt that the heavens were answering me. After this much-needed release, we headed home, as none of us wanted to be away very long.

Jan: Back at the house, the sounds of Leah's laborious breathing filled the room. We worried that she was suffering. Fai called Margo the nurse to tell her about the breathing change. It was a relief to hear Margo explain that because Leah was already losing awareness of her body's activities, it was probably harder for us to hear than for her to experience.

Attending a loved one who is dying can bring up primal

personal issues and feelings, times of illumination and moments of panic. Life feels tinged with depth and meaning.

Leah's Passing

■

225

Rivka: That evening the atmosphere of the house took on a new feeling, as meditative music and candlelight kept watch with us. The veils between the worlds felt thinner than usual. I placed two pictures of our mother, Rena Mae, by Leah's bed, lit by flickering candles, to bring her close by and help them to find each other.

Later I took off my jewelry pieces and slipped them, together with a few crystals and sacred objects, under her pillow to charge them with the energy. In another room Effie did emotional-body work with various members of the support family, helping us recenter ourselves so we could be more present to ourselves and to Leah.

Two of the women were able to see and sense energies not visible to the naked eye. "Oh, did you see that? The energy is spiraling out from her head . . . " "I see energy lines converging around her heart . . . " These observations added to our understanding of what was happening to Leah, beyond what we could see with our usual means of perception.

At one point we were amazed to see that Leah, although seemingly "unconscious," had clasped her hands in a prayer position over her heart. She remained that way for hours.

Jan: Around midnight Diana mentioned that in her native tradition something of the dying person is placed outside to help the spirits find her. So I went through Leah's house and chose a scarf and a particularly joyful picture of her. Outside the window where she lay, I draped the scarf across a rose bush and placed her picture in the center.

Tuesday morning we all milled around with varying degrees of sleep and non-sleep. Three women had shared the night-watch sprawled on mattresses by Leah's bed. Leah lay draped in a beautiful shawl, covered with flower petals and sacred objects. Although it was hard to believe, her heart was racing even faster than it had the day before. At one point we counted 160 heartbeats per minute. It was unsettling to hear her struggle for each breath.

When Margo came by to examine Leah, Leah's blood pressure was barely detectable. We all gathered in the kitchen to discuss what to expect next. Margo told us she was glad to see Leah's fingernails were turning blue, indicating she wasn't getting enough oxygen, because oxygen deprivation tends to produce euphoria. After hearing this we were relieved to be able to envision Leah going out peacefully.

I sensed Leah's breathing was shifting. Occasionally there were gaps, so I stayed close by. I very much hoped we could all surround Leah in love at the moment of her passing. A couple of big gaps in her breathing signaled to me that it was time to gather the women scattered throughout the house. First I found Rivka in the kitchen. Then I went to get Leia and Effie in the massage room. When I asked them if they wanted to come, they misunderstood me, asking, "Where are you going?"

"It's Leah who's going," I replied.

Seven of us gathered around her and took one another's hands. Her breath had become quite irregular. Val said, "We're all here with you," as she went around the circle and said each of our names. It couldn't have been more than twenty seconds later that Leah took her last breath. The sound of her breathing had filled the house for two days. But finally, all breath left her. She went in peace.

We stood silently for a time, crying, each present with her own experience of Leah's passing. Then Rivka and Miriam sang the Shma, a Hebrew prayer of blessing: *Listen Israel, the Source of all our being, that Source is One . . .* Chants and rounds followed. Loose petals from flowers throughout the house were collected and scattered across her body. More sacred objects were placed on her. One woman cradled her head and others caressed her hands and face.

At a certain point the circle opened up and we drifted off, each full in our own experience, as if a part of Leah's spirit had come into each of us. None of us would ever be quite the same again.

Leah had said that whatever happened after she died would be up to the people who were left. She had arranged for cremation but beyond that we were on our own. This gave us tremendous freedom. Spontaneously we evolved a creative collective response to her passing. First we circled to discuss plans for her memorial activities. "Let's open the circle to include Leah," someone suggested, so we reformed ourselves by her bed. As we made decisions, someone piped up, "I half expect her to sit up in bed and say, 'I don't know if I agree with that . . . '" We all chuckled at the thought. So much love filled the room. Miriam summed up the feeling of trust that had built among us over the course of the last few days: "This is a group of women I could climb Mount Everest with."

Rivka: Fai found out we could keep Leah's body with us for twenty-four hours. We were surprised to learn that if we wanted, we could take her to the crematorium ourselves. This appealed to us. Then Fai asked me, "Would you like to build a box for Leah?"

One of the many things that Leah and I had in common was carpentry. We had gone through carpentry school together in the early eighties, when I was first coming out. I felt grateful to have the opportunity to be close to Leah in this way: to be in her workroom, using her tools, making use of the recycled mahogany and channeling my feelings into useful action to honor her. I asked Irenia, also a carpenter, to help make the box. As we talked, laughed and shared stories of Leah, all that energy went into the making of the box—like the love of cooks pouring into a fine meal. It was finished in only an hour.

Throughout the evening and on into the night, friends and family decorated the "body box" using a wood-burning tool and colored markers. Flower pictures which had been taped to the ceiling over her bed were placed inside the box. In a visible, tangible way, loving energy would surround her and send her off.

Meanwhile, Leah's body remained inside the house, with candles burning nearby. We continued to speak to her and include her from time to time, as some of us believed that her spirit remained nearby for some time after the actual point of death.

Rivka and Jan: Preparations continued the next morning. While some women padded the box with soft, colorful cloths, others made a garden altar from the many flowers and other sacred objects in the house. A fire was lit in her outdoor firepit; people wrote messages to Leah and offered them to the fire. Her portable stereo, set under the body box, poured out some of her favorite tunes. Bowls of scented water were put by the altar.

Finally when all was ready, we gently carried her body outside to the garden and placed her underneath the same tree where she had lain in bed just three days ago. Surrounding her in a circle, we undressed her and began to wash and anoint her. The water we used to wash her soaked into the earth. We anointed her with salve she had made herself using herbs grown in her garden. No one said much.

Rivka found a dress in Leah's closet that Leah had bought in the Old City in Jerusalem as a teenager. She had loved it and worn it for years, so it seemed like the perfect thing to dress her in. After it was placed on her, we carried her to the box and set her inside. Then with several women on each side of her, the box was loaded into the flatbed of Leah's truck for her last ride.

Someone asked, "Do you think we need a lid?" (Yikes, a lid— it *might* be a little weird to drive around town with a body in a box and no lid!) Miraculously, an old wooden door found in Leah's garage fit her box as if it had been made for it. It was put on loosely so we could remove it and be with her body one last time at the funeral home.

Off we went, with two women leading the way on a motorcycle with flashing lights. The women in the back of the truck held hands across the top of the box as we traveled slowly through the arboretum and alongside Lake Washington, two of Leah's favorite places. Her Chinese herb pot, in which so many batches of healing herbs had been prepared, rode with us in front—it was to hold her ashes after the cremation.

Midway there, Rivka turned on the car radio and punched buttons for the stations Leah had liked. We found some great soft jazz and cranked up the sound so the women in the back could hear it. On a gloriously blue-skied day, after what seemed like a longer ride than it really was, we finally reached the funeral home.

With all of us standing around Leah in the viewing room just before we left her for the last time, Debra and Rivka said Mourners' Kaddish, which praises and reaffirms one's belief in Source and Spirit in the face of loss:

The great essence will flower in our lives and expand throughout the world. May we learn to let it shine through, so we can augment its glory.

Living True

■ ■ ■ ■ ■ ■ ■ ■

SABRINA SOJOURNER

Psychic Scars

Terri Jewell: dead. Single shot to the head. Apparent suicide. The news was more devastating than I could have imagined, startling for its unexpected nature. Two months prior to the suicide, I had spoken with Terri, who was also a writer. We talked about our lives, our work and how well things were going. We dreamed up a couple of projects for us to do together. She also shared her desire to move to Washington, D.C. We laughed and exclaimed. It was a wonderful conversation. We played phone tag in early November, and then she was gone. Terri Jewell: dead. Single shot to the head. Apparent suicide.

The news sent me to the edge of my sanity. I hate being in that place. But it was the place I had to stand to understand what had happened, to ask myself if I had missed something and if I was in danger. The edge of sanity is a place I have been pushed up against or fallen over more times than I care to admit. The last time I fell over, I didn't know if I would make it back, and when I started coming back, I didn't know if I would ever make it all the way back. Somehow I did, though it was a long, hard climb.

The edge is not a place I like to visit. I don't like examining the pain lying at and over the edge. I don't want to feel the waves of sadness washing over me. I hate the numbness—the blocking out of all feeling—with which I have to contend. More than the pain and more than the sadness, it is the place of numbness that terrifies me. When it comes, I am left to feel only terror. *It makes me fearful when I get to this place of no sensation / It is a void through which I slip upon meeting my despair / My old and pressing despair.*[1] I am unable to breathe, unable to think, unable to make a sound. I feel as if everything is crushing me, compressing me into dust and that a light breeze will blow me into oblivion.

Long before I started coming to terms with my own depression and tendency toward suicide, I was put in situations where I was the *sane* one dealing with another's depression, suicide attempts, erratic or manic behavior. It was surreal to suddenly have to manage my own depression—my own suicidal depression—and to discover the truth of my loneliness. I discovered I was a rock for a lot of people: the one upon whom others relied to pitch in; offer a hello, hug or smile; listen; cook or buy a meal—you get the picture. When I cracked, I discovered an ugly truth: Being Humpty Dumpty can be dangerous.

Falling, slipping, sliding—being—in depression is not a hard thing to do. Many of us go there as a result of severe change or trauma: loss of love, friendship, family; moving or having to leave a home or a job; illness or chronic condition; having been victimized by oppression, crime or domestic violence. The list is endless as to what can send us into a cocoon, needing time to grieve, rest and heal. When there are visible reasons for our depression, it is fairly easy to receive support. However, to experience severe depression connected only to the past is not acceptable. Everyone wants you to just "get over it." But no one is ever able to tell you how. How?

How do I get over the trauma of five years of being repeatedly raped by my father? How do I get over three years of an abusive marriage? The memories of those events are buried deep within the tissues of my body and even deeper in the ether of my soul. These memories often surface in pieces at unexpected moments triggered by a noise, odor, shadow, touch, voice inflection, word, color or something else of which I may be consciously unaware. It's hard talkin' 'bout pain

It's hard to talk about pain
The times places and spaces
Where life closes in on us and
Chokes us near to death
But life goes on and leaves us here
Tryin' ta talk 'bout pain[2]

During the rehashing of my past in the wake of Terri's suicide, a well-meaning friend told me I had to find a way to allow my child-hood wounds to heal. I was too stunned—and disappointed—to explain that they have healed. But, like any deep scar, there are times when they ache for no apparent reason or are touched in such a way I cannot deny their presence—that's what Terri's sui-cide had done. Being healed does not mean an old wound will never bother you again. Ask anyone with an old athletic injury. As I mulled over my friend's comment, I realized that this mis-conception—that once something from our emotional past is healed, it is gone—may be why many of us miss the pain of countless hurting people in our communities.

The truth is, how bothersome an old wound may be is deter-mined by the depth of the original injury. I have a scar on my left middle finger caused by a knife that severed not only the skin but an artery and a nerve as well. I had surgery to repair the artery and the nerve casing. Afterwards, I had to wear a cast for nearly two weeks, followed by other protective coverings and weeks of painful physical therapy. But sooner than had been predicted or anticipated, I was using my left hand and middle finger almost as well as I had before, though I had no feeling at the end of my finger.

But, for the more than ten years I have had the scar, there have been times when I or another would touch it in such a way that the pain would send me to the ground. Or I would grab hold of something, and it would feel awkward or wrong. I have accidentally hit that spot against the side of a table, desk or chair and had it vibrate as if I had hit my funny bone. At other times, the scar aches with a sharp throb that no amount of painkiller could affect. There are medical names for each of these phenomena, but there are no medical terms to describe their psychological equivalents.

I am not claiming to be unique when I say my psychic scars are as numerous as the scars on my body. What is interesting to me is that the statement no longer feels like a burden. I am a survivor of incest and spousal abuse. I am surviving racism, heterosexism, sexism, classism, religious intolerance and much more. I am also surviving my grief—like many of you, having lost too many people to HIV disease, cancer, murder, natural causes and suicide. And, I am examining the impact of years—many, many years—of suicidal depression.

I do not use the terms *survivor* and *surviving* lightly. Being a survivor is a statement of fact, implying the tragic events of one's past. Surviving is an act of defiance, implying appropriate resistance to tragic events of the present.

I was not meant to survive the horrors I lived through as a child, and that was where my nightmare started. As a child I did not have the words to describe what was being done to me. It did not help that I was asked to keep the activity secret. Part of me wanted to keep it secret because it felt too weird, too wrong, too nasty. Another part of me wanted to tell in order to understand all the feelings the secret evoked. The two parts started to fight inside me, and other parts emerged: one totally terrified of the consequences of telling; another craving attention and happy for whatever attention she could get; another wanting desperately to be a very good girl so that the bad things would not happen; still another trying to keep the others in line and make some order in my life; and yet another totally buried under the confusion of all the voices and just wanting to be a kid.

I did try to tell once. I told my mother, "Dad doesn't like me. He keeps doing things to me, things I don't like." The message was not heard. She didn't ask me to explain what I meant by "things I don't like." She assumed she understood what I meant and proceeded to explain him to me. The next thing I remember is getting a very severe stomachache and my mother wondering why I got sick and no one else. It would be years before I would remember taking a bunch of pills prior to the stomachache. In all likelihood, they were probably only aspirin, but I'll never know.

I survived what was not survivable, but I was severely traumatized. Before I understood that, I experienced the self-destructive acts of many friends, near-friends, acquaintances and myself. We were all living with unspoken secrets whose horrors haunted our waking hours as much as they stole our sleep and dreaming. I could not tell people that my father was a rapist and that I was his primary victim. I had moments in which the need to tell was so overwhelming that parts of me would pace like a trapped animal, drink until I was knocked out drunk, smoke pot until I was too silly to care, or eat until I was too sick to do much of anything. On the worst days, I would go through all of those tricks and more to keep myself from "spilling the (proverbial) beans." On the outside, I appeared to be "functioning within normal parameters." I was no more on the edge or out of control than anyone else. On the inside, I barely knew what day it was and was terrified of everything.

In 1980, I fell in love with a woman who lived in another state. We corresponded, spoke frequently on the phone and traveled several times between our respective homes. After six months, my son and I moved to her city and into her home.

The short of it is: It didn't work out. About six months after I moved there, she was diagnosed with cervical cancer and insisted I send my son to my mother's because it would be less stressful for her. She also moved me out of her bedroom. She had a hysterectomy and a few radiation treatments—all of which I saw her through. But by the anniversary of my arrival, I had moved out because she was having an affair with another woman. I was stunned and devastated. Though I had experienced betrayal before, this was the first time I had experienced such deep and damaging betrayal at the hands of a woman—or so I thought.

At the time, it was very hard for me to take care of myself. Not because I was incapable, but because from one day to the next I was unsure whether I cared what happened to me. In a way I had not before, I recognized that my anchor to life was my son. I had sent him away for someone who did not care about me. His not living with me was very painful, and I had a tremendous amount of guilt—always a bad combination. Talking to him only once a week was painful, but not talking to him at all was worse. I had not been in town long enough to be confident in whom I could call friend. That made my grief and loneliness worse. I remember thinking, "How did I get myself into a situation in which I was so completely alone? How could I have been so stupid as to change my whole life for another person? How could I have been so wrong about another's character?" There was never a good answer to those questions. The breakup was the beginning of a very slow, very painful slide into deep depression.

I forced myself to go out. I mistakenly thought the weirdness and disassociation I sometimes felt were just part of the overall weirdness I was experiencing about being alone. I made what I thought were friends. I struggled to make a living and occasionally genuinely experienced good times. I also experienced a lot of needless drama. Some of my own making, some made by others.

I got into therapy and made some important realizations, perhaps the most important of which was that the depth of the betrayal I experienced with this woman echoed the betrayal I had experienced with my mother. My mother's betrayal? She had not protected or rescued me from my father. True to form, though they had been divorced for nearly ten years, my mother initially was disbelieving when I told her about the incest.

This is the problem with psychic scars: Unless, through our depression, we inflict physical wounds on our bodies, there is nothing visible to the outside world to show what is incredibly visible to those of us who bear them. (My friend Bisha called her physical scars "warrior marks." She shared this view with Alice Walker, who subsequently used the phrase as the title of one of her books. A poem in the back of the book tells a piece of Bisha and Venus's story.) Most of us do not have recognizable visible marks, but many of us experience various stages of post-traumatic stress disorder for years, if not decades, before we ever reach any understanding of what is happening with us. About fifteen years ago, in a letter confronting my father about his abuse of me I wrote:

Sometimes, I think it would be easier on my friends and lovers if I were a recovering alcoholic or drug user, fighting a chronic or terminal illness—anything except an adult survivor of child abuse. I am chained and crippled by emotional bonds which cannot be seen. Even those which seem to be healing can be broken open by an interaction with any human being at any given time. It's a constant, exhausting vigilance I must keep. And, there is no one to help me. No one to help me help them understand what is not visibly evident to them and so painfully clear to me.

I struggle day after endless day to discover who I am. What is really me? And what is this garbage which weighs me down? They say to me, very sincerely, "Why don't you just forget it?"

There was a time in my life when I thought I had forgotten it, gotten over it. Now, I realize it was hiding behind a haze of drunken stupors, highs induced by marijuana, cocaine, hallucinogens or being in love. There were a number of covers I tried to pull over my head at different times to try and forget. And it never did any good. I woke up with hangovers or dry-mouth and still alone in my pain, the knowledge of what happened to me still gnawing in my stomach, and, so, I'd feed it, thinking that would help. (But) it never seems to care how much food I give it, whether it's the best or the worst. Junky or healthy. It's still not satisfied. It's still there—this gnawing in need of something. So, there would be another round of work, alcohol, dope, sex and food. There is always food. Always food. Always, always. It didn't matter what I did, how I did it, who I did it with or where![3]

One of the last times I tried to commit suicide, I was still living in the Midwest. I had come out of a bar, gotten into my car and driven out into the country. I was several miles outside of town when I realized I was searching for the right tree to speed into. I pulled immediately off the road and just sat there, terrified to move a muscle. Though it was not the first time I had tried to commit suicide, it was the first time I had not seen my attempt coming. All I could do was sit there and feel my terror. I wanted to get home, but was afraid to drive. I wanted to call, but I didn't know who. Besides, I was in the middle of nowhere. Just to get to a phone I had to drive eight miles.

I don't remember how I finally got myself home. I only remember waking up to a phone call, reminding me that I was supposed to go camping. I was afraid to get out of bed so I begged off. One of the inviters called. As we talked, something inside me understood that she knew I was in trouble. She got all the equipment I needed together, came over, packed me and placed me in her car. Over the course of the next few days, she and I spent a lot of time in a boat fishing, sharing and being quiet together. She made sure I got up and got busy every morning, that I didn't drink too much and that I got hugs throughout the day. By the end of our time together, I knew I had to ask my friends for help.

Telling resulted in the loss of most of my lesbian friends. When it took "longer than expected" for me to "snap out of it," I lost all of my lesbian friends. The friend who was with me on the fishing trip hung in there as long as she could, but she was not well herself. Three months after our fishing trip, she was hospitalized for trying to kill herself. We never saw each other again. The people who saw me through my depression were a white gay man, who had had his own bouts with suicide, and two heterosexual women—one black, the other white. (I mention their race and sexual orientation because we are such a divided society, it is significant when we find our way across differences to meet deeply pertinent human needs.) They called, visited, shopped for and held me through the toughest time of my life. Not a day went by that I did not have some kind of contact with all three of them. I even got to the point where I could call them and ask for what I needed or share that I was okay that day. They provided me with human contact, groceries, a hand to hold and protection when I ventured outside my apartment. I was in therapy and on antidepressants, both of which were very helpful and useful, but ultimately, they were the people who helped me save my life.

It took a while, but I figured out I had to be and experience where I was in order to move to a different space. In other words, I had to be in the depression. I had to feel and release the despair. I had to release the screams that had been locked inside me since the first time my father raped me and the layers of screams that were added with every subsequent attack. The beatings I experienced at the hands of first my father and then my ex-husband had their own layers of screams. The betrayal I experienced repeatedly at the hands of my mother was dispersed throughout the layers of pain, anger and outrage. I had to scream. I had to cry and wail. I had to rant and pace and sob. I did not have a choice. If I wanted to feel different, I had to purge myself emotionally of the pain that had been holding me prisoner for longer than my awareness of that pain.

I also had to embrace parts of me I had rejected, particularly my-femme-self. I had rejected the femme-pretty-sexy-vamp-woman within, holding her responsible for the rapes, beatings and assaults. There are two ironies to that statement. One, as a feminist, I had always been infuriated whenever "society blamed the victim." Two, intellectually, I had long stated my belief that I was not responsible for what had happened to me. However, it was not until I started loving my-femme-self that I truly forgave myself. Because I had to work during this time, I was lucky enough to get a job that did not demand much of me. It kept my mind fully occupied, but required nothing more from me than the time I put in each day. After work, I would go home. The worst days, the ride home was like descending into a slow hell. By the time I reached home, I was in tears, and all I could do was cry until I fell asleep. On good days, I would look out the window of the bus and take interest in what was occurring along the route home. I could even manage to cook something for dinner. On bad to moderate days, I would arrive home to zone out in front of the television, hide in an inordinate amount of sleep or eat myself beyond numb. Sometimes I would get so upset about how much I was eating that I would throw up the food. Other times, I would just eat more. For over a year, reading wasn't possible because my mind was too jumbled. Fearful I would lose my intellectual muscle, I started doing crossword puzzles. Their randomness matched my intellectual health. Most importantly, it relieved another fear.

I cannot describe to you the moment at which I knew I was finally okay—not better, but okay. I only remember waking up one morning not dreading the day ahead. The feeling caught me so off guard, I cried. Sometime after that, I woke up looking forward to the day. Again, I cried. Feeling good for the first time did not last long, but neither did it stay away long. Relatively soon, I was able to string more good days together than bad. Slowly, I started reclaiming my life. I was able to keep my apartment clean and take a walk around the block and go into a grocery store without experiencing a panic attack. I began to take more interest in how I presented myself to the world and spent time figuring out what outward images matched my more solid inward images.

I had reached bottom. As I learned to navigate my way across it, naming, identifying and relieving fears became a key activity. Through therapy, it was a process I had been doing for years. During this bout with depression, it became my means of building the ladder that would enable me to climb back into life. I reclaimed my spirituality and asked for the guidance of my ancestors, inviting them to be part of my healing process. My spirituality became the framework on which to hang the rungs of my named fears. Ritual—the means of embedding into one's unconsciousness that which we wish to manifest—became as important as breathing. I relearned the ritual of everyday life. Everything—from making coffee every morning for myself to listening to National Public Radio, writing in my journal, cleaning my home, watering my plants, listening to birds, talking to my son every week, fixing my hair, buying earrings and taking meals with friends—grounded me and gave me a sense of belonging.

Being rooted in the everyday made the examination of the more terrifying fears—the fears that sent me in search of a tree—easier. While I made many important discoveries, there were six that proved to be crucial.

One: *Keeping the unspeakable secret protects no one.* Secrecy made me a slave to the pain, shame and assorted crazy feelings connected to the incest. I lied about my family and about my activities to protect the secret and hide the pain/shame. As important as it was to name for myself what my father had done to me, it was equally important for me to take opportunities to let other women—especially women of color—know they were not alone in their struggle with pain.

Though I had participated in many discussions, support groups and friendship circles involving black and other women of color, I was thirty-two years old before I met another woman of color who admitted to being molested. In our communities the level of secrecy about abuse is incredibly intense and has direct connections to internalized racism and sexual cultural taboos. The pathology of internalized racism sometimes causes us to view our imperfections through a white-eyed lens. This can result in our turning an unseeing eye to issues such as violence within our families because, we fear, to admit that such things happen is to

Surviving and Healing from Sexual Abuse

RESOURCES

Survivors of Incest Anonymous (SIA)
P.O. Box 21817
Baltimore, MD 21222-6817
(410) 282-3400

SUGGESTED READING

The Courage to Heal: A Guide for Women Survivors of Child Sexual Abuse by Ellen Bass and Laura Davis, New York: HarperCollins, 1988.

Crossing the Boundary: Black Women Survive Incest by Melba Wilson, Seattle: Seal Press, 1994.

Daybreak: Meditations for Women Survivors of Sexual Abuse by Maureen Brady, New York: Hazelden/ HarperCollins, 1991.

The Mother I Carry: A Memoir of Healing from Emotional Abuse by Louise M. Wisechild, Seattle: Seal, 1993.

Secret Survivors: Uncovering Incest and Its Aftereffects in Women by Sue E. Blume, New York: Ballantine, 1991.

The Sexual Healing Journey: A Guide for Survivors of Sexual Abuse by Wendy Maltz, New York: HarperPerennial/ HarperCollins, 1991.

She Who Was Lost Is Remembered: Healing from Incest Through Creativity edited by Louise M. Wisechild, Seattle: Seal, 1991.

Strong at the Broken Places: Overcoming the Trauma of Childhood Abuse by Lynda T. Sanford, New York: Avon, 1992.

admit that we are the animals, creatures, monsters—fill in the blank—white society says we are.

The ostrich approach to serious problems only causes them to get worse. On the other hand, being the "bean spiller" also has its repercussions. Yet, isolation and fear of discovery can sap one's energy. I intimately know the consequences of all three scenarios and many more. There are times when I look back on my life and am truly amazed that I am still alive. That sentiment goes beyond the knowledge of the times I actually tried to commit suicide. It extends, through hindsight, to all the self-destructive behavior of which I was often less aware.

A willingness to learn to be open is what aided me along the way. Being open includes "coming out" as a femme, a feminist, a single mother of a boy-child, a writer, a spiritualist and much more. It has meant taking all of me and my celebration of life through every door I pass. It has also meant learning to appreciate my ability to spontaneously make a glass of lemonade whenever life hands me lemons.

Two: *I already know the worst thing I could possibly know about what happened between my father and me.* My father repeatedly raped me between the ages of nine and fourteen. There can be nothing worse. That I only remember fragments of most of the incidents does not detract from the horror or the believability of what happened. Most importantly, I do not need to remember every detail to be sure that it happened. I know it happened and I believe myself. I affirm the memories held in my senses as equal to the ones held by my intellect. While it would be helpful for my family to acknowledge the truth, it is much more important that I no longer deny the truth.

Three: *I am responsible for how I respond to oppression, not for the existence of racism, sexism, heterosexism and other forms of oppression.* My disappearance or death would not make oppression go away. That was a very important message to grasp because even well-intentioned people want to believe that if (people of color, women, Jews, old people, gay people) would just shut up about (oppression), it would go away. That message can and does seep into our psyches—our bones. So we weigh a situation and decide not to "push" because someone might not understand and assume we are deliberately trying to make them feel bad. We even become good at making excuses and understanding that they didn't mean it the way it sounded. However, someone not intending to step on your foot does not make it hurt any less when they do.

The truth is, none of us like it brought to our attention that something in which we have participated has produced the perception of bigotry. After all, we are good people acting with the best of intentions. But sometimes our best intentions can result in awful, unintended mistakes. When our best intentions result in someone getting excluded or being insulted, we need to *be* our best by rising to the occasion, sincerely apologizing for insulting another and learning from the moment. That is especially important when we are interacting with people we consider to be friends or with whom we want to develop a friendship.

Four: *Talking about pain, acknowledging its presence and naming its poisons are a means of relieving it—not reliving it.* Releasing pain's energy into the world gives me power, energizes me and allows healing. Holding pain inside gives it power over me. It shackles my mind, heart and soul. Mostly, it immobilizes me, prevents connection and lulls me senseless. It sounds strange to say that part of what I had to learn was to live with my despair. Yet, nothing could be more true. I had to sit with it, embrace it and feel my way through it. I had to warm it so that it would speak to me, and then I had to listen to what it had to say. I had to learn to let others hold me while I held my despair. I was able to do it first with my therapist and then with my friends. Most of what the despair had to say was nonverbal. I, literally, cried for days on end. I screamed, wailed, moaned and whimpered. I raged a lot, more than I ever thought possible or knew I held inside. It was joyous and discouraging. It was cleansing and mortifying. It was healing and terrifying. Sometimes I felt very different emotions in the same moment. I feel very fortunate to have come through it whole because there were times when I just did not know how I was going to be come morning. By engaging my despair, I found life: the energy and will to live, strategies to get through hard days and the knowledge (instead of baseless or vague hope) that they would pass.

Five: *I fully embraced my identity and stopped fighting other people's battles inside me.* I live at the intersection of race, class, gender, sexual orientation, regionalism and more. My identity is a weave of many experiences and sensibilities, not a set of boxes or compartments. From this place I was able to embrace being all of who I am, especially my-femme-self. Accepting femme as a core thread in the weave of my identity was an unexpected source of freedom. Being femme is not a role: I am not acting out somebody else's script. Being femme is not an adherence to somebody else's definition of femininity and beauty. Until recently, women of color were not part of that definition. Making peace with my-femme-self, I discovered that the *disowning* of her was acting out somebody else's script and living by somebody else's definition of what it was to be a lesbian. Through embracing her, I realized how much oppression I had faced within the lesbian community because I was femme.

One incident that best summarizes all the issues happened just before I left the Midwest. I had been asked to emcee an evening of activities for a local lesbian conference. I had originally been told that there would be a "lesbian fashion show." I was very excited about the idea because another woman and myself had begun to share with each other some of the tension we felt as each of us came more out as femmes. At some point, the agenda changed and the evening was a play interwoven with a talent show. The play was about a "typical" woman complete with "fuck-me-pumps" making a transformation to "dyke." The situation became quite awkward since it could be said I was dressed as a "typical" woman complete with "fuck-me-pumps" and could have—by their standards—passed.

Being true to my-femme-self was never about "passing." In fact, I believe the whole concept of femmes passing is based on the internalized homophobic fear that being straight is preferable to being lesbian—NOT! By embracing, loving and appreciating my-femme-self, I learned to let any discomfort remain with others. I no longer take on others' attitudes, just as I no longer take on other types of oppression aimed at me. I embrace all aspects of my perspective, personality and soul. I no longer live anybody's script except my own. I give myself the freedom to respond, or not respond, without defense to others' well-meaning, but intrusive questions.

Somewhere along the way I had abandoned my-femme-self (unsuccessfully) to the ravages of life. In a way, denying her was a way of not identifying with the "pretty" or "sexy" woman who "gets herself into trouble with men." In recovering her, I embraced important aspects of my perspective, personality and soul.

I cannot say enough about the importance of embracing one's identity. I have found incredible personal power and joy through doing so. The more comfortable I am with being an artist-writer-mother-of-a-male-child-feminist-African-American-Cherokee-femme-lesbian-and-more, the harder it is for me to fall into another's bias-trap. I recognize offensive, oppressive and bigoted behavior and when I am the subject of a zap—a funny remark that can also be quite hurtful—and most of the time I am able to respond in a manner that gets my point across without my joining the offender in the quagmire they created.

Six: *I learned to trust myself, and I learned that trusting others is not about giving something—usually some form of my power—over to them.* It is more about trusting myself to be able to recover if they disappoint me. Being able to face being disappointed by others is part of interacting with people. Even good people who love and care about us a lot will disappoint us from time to time. No one is perfect, including myself. For those of us who have been abused, trust is a major issue. Our therapists usually work with us on learning to trust (believe in) others. The nuance that gets missed is the need to retune our instincts so that we can again believe in what we *feel* to be true about a person or a situation, and react/respond appropriately from a place of strength. The process of repeated abuse and the secrecy that usually surrounds it contorts our ability to trust inwardly perhaps more than our ability to trust outwardly. Part of the abuse tug-of-war is clinging to the false belief that "this time" the situation will be different—even as our guts are screaming to us to take flight, or sirens are going off inside our head telling us to take shelter.

Learning to trust myself meant learning to listen to myself long enough to discern the difference between the alarm bells of potential danger and the fears of my inner child. Reacquainting myself with my instincts and trusting my recovery, I was able to cut off and get out of abusive relationships faster and eventually almost completely sidestep them. In trusting myself, I found I made better choices regarding the development of friendships, collegial relationships and physically intimate relationships. I also learned that every disappointment is not life-threatening, that I must face and come to terms with abandonment issues and how to be my own best friend.

I still have bad days, but not as many in a row, and sometimes the darkness does not even last a day. When the bad days happen, the first thing I do is *not* panic. I flow with the day and give myself the opportunity to uncover what the gloom is hiding. For this last exercise, I miss having a therapist, but my last two attempts at working with a white therapist left a sour taste in my mouth. However, if you are a person of color seeking a therapist, do not allow the lack of therapists of color to be the reason you do not pursue therapy. There are good white therapists who are able to work well cross-culturally; I have had several. Go to your first appointment with a list of questions to determine if this is a woman (or man) with whom you can work.

I have not had thoughts of suicide in a very long time. However, every time I hear about the suicide of a lesbian—especially if she is in my age group—I find myself doubting my wellness. When those thoughts arise, I can quickly determine if they are a signal that something is wrong or that I'm tired, or are nothing more than an old tape finding its way to the fore. I know I do not want to take myself out. I do not want to have to come back and do the work I have already done plus deal with having killed myself in a prior life.

I know the worst truly is behind me and it can only continue to get better. Part of being better also means finding a way to cope with having my scars unexpectedly hit or touched. Every time someone close to me dies, the scars are touched and the loss is echoed throughout my body and psyche. When they take themselves out, or another with them, it is the kind of pain that sends me to my knees.

In the past four years, I have lost two women friends to suicide and two to a murder-suicide. The gift I take from the four of them is the knowledge that the journey is not over. I will continue to be faced with reminders of how hard, lonely and difficult the world is even as I celebrate and embrace being healed. It is navigating the nuance that enables me to stay here. Like the Wizard in Ursula Le Guin's Earthsea Trilogy, I cannot live without my shadow. If I try to run away from it—suicide, sexual abuse and pain—it will follow me. The harder I try to run away, the more intense its pursuit feels. Only when I stop, turn and embrace the shadows do I fully embrace myself. When I stand, walk, run and play with them, I am powerful, for I am whole.

To my friends gone by their own hand:

> *I heard you*
> *I heard your pain*

A thundering echo of my own cry
I ached for us both
knowing
>   *I am luckier*
For I have you as a guide
>   *to signal the way through*
>   *heart hungry hours*[4]

Notes

1. From the poem, "No Texture," *Psychic Scars . . . and Other Mad Thoughts,* a self-published book of poems and narratives by Sabrina Sojourner, 1995.

2. Epigram from the poem "For Janet Collins," in *Psychic Scars . . . and Other Mad Thoughts.*

3. Sabrina Sojourner, *Finding My Way Home* (unpublished).

4. From the poem "For Janet Collins," in *Psychic Scars . . . and Other Mad Thoughts.*

SUSAN KRAJAC

A Sense of Well-Being

You are nine years old when the heartburn begins. In school you are a good reader but have difficulty with comprehension. Your grades are average. You are mostly meek, yet, starved for attention, you imitate the teacher behind her back for your classmates. You have frequent, mysterious stomach ailments that allow you to miss school and stay home with your mother, who smokes in her bathrobe and watches game shows all morning. Your three older brothers alternate between tormenting and ignoring you. Your father is mostly drunk; your shoes are always in his way.

As a teenager you turn to Newports, drugs and Pabst Blue Ribbon. In high school you win medals in track and field, but you graduate near the bottom of your class. After becoming frightened of the prospect of lifelong factory work and hangovers, you are admitted to college on probation. You meet people who expand your drug repertoire. The stress of academia makes you miserable—you wish you would be hit by a bus on your way to speech

*class. You are secretly in love with your girlfriends, consumed by
your desires. It takes you five and a half years to graduate.*

*Mysterious aches and pains plague you; you are always tired,
you sleep on the job. You sleep with the first woman who shows
an interest in you, even though she is unkempt, drunk and controlling. Goals are elusive clouds; you are forever beginning projects
and promises of a more productive life. You leap, and you land on
square one: You play a game of hopeless hopscotch. You drink lots
of Scotch. When drugs and alcohol no longer remove pain, you
sober up, but things don't really change. Your only excitement is
riding your bicycle. You feel stagnant, angry and mentally slow.
You wonder if you are destined to a life of mediocrity.*

When my psychotherapist, Roseanne, recommended I see a
psychiatrist for depression, I told her my fear of intoxicating my
body with drugs. I had been sober for nearly four years; taking
chemicals for my problems wasn't an option. Also, I was suspi-
cious of the patriarchal tendency to deem women "mad" and then
silence us with medications, operations and asylums: I had read
The Yellow Wallpaper. I knew about the removal of wombs to cure
hysteria. I had read *Woman on the Edge of Time* and watched
Thorazine and Valium come and go. I wasn't going to join the
annals of "zombified" women by taking a pill. I was sure antidepressants simply masked the psyche. She nodded her head; I
thought it was settled.

Instead I took the test that made Minnesota famous: the Minnesota Multiphasic Personality Inventory. The mass murderer
Jeffrey Dahmer and I took the MMPI the same week, only
Dahmer's results had been enlarged on a giant posterboard for a
courtroom of people to see. The results are rendered in a line
graph. "You're in a room with one hundred people," Roseanne
said slowly, explaining the measure of my depression, "eighty-five
of them have never felt the level of depression that you experience." Suddenly I, too, felt the judgmental glare of a large,
courtroomlike audience.

You are sitting in a class in Lind Hall when you hear the shots. Two, powerful gunshots—or is it the echo of slamming doors? You look around at the students, animated in their discussion. No one else seems to notice. You feel the blood drain from your face when you hear another; the shotgun maniac is getting closer. You try to catch someone's eye, perhaps you mouth, "Did you hear that?" The students are oblivious to the outside world; their innocence out-wits them. The rest of the building seems strangely quiet. You stare at the door, waiting for the killer, perhaps a disgruntled janitor or an angry student, to emerge.

Roseanne's grim prognosis made me feel special: I had feelings more intense than almost everyone else at that party of one hundred people. I envisioned a swaying crowd laughing in a large kitchen; everyone held champagne glasses. I sat alone watching from the dining room, legs crossed, head bent. No wonder I found parties uncomfortable. I now believed those partygoers were truly happy; they never had to feel my level of anguish. My vision ended with the prospect that someday I, too, might be floating on a higher plane. I was determined to enter the kitchen.

Two women from Minnesota designed this nationally re-nowned tool—the MMPI. The hundreds of questions have little significance independently, but one's total scores are compared with those of people known to be depressive, sociopathic or normal before they took the test, some mysterious group of people in asylums, jails and graduate schools who provided a basis for the scores. One's self-esteem, hostility levels and passive-aggressive tendencies are gleaned from true-false questions like: "I like tall women" or "I read all the editorials in the newspaper."

My lover is five feet, eleven inches. I have a degree in news and editorial journalism. Which came first, the idiosyncrasy or the disease. Did one beget the other?

You and your lover are watching a movie on the VCR. You lack the ability to become absorbed in the drama. You must be constantly aware that movies are not real. You wonder how that scene

*was filmed, how long it took the actor to remember her lines,
whether or not the two in the love scene actually like each other,
or if one of them has coffee breath. You notice inconsistencies in
the hair from one split-second shot to the next. You annoy your
lover when you try to talk during the movie's climax. You have
become bored, and you are unable to concentrate on the plot.*

A person with my scale of depression, according to one analysis, tends to use bodily complaints to avoid emotional situations,
and to use these complaints as a way of manipulating others. We
may whine, complain and make others miserable. We tend to be
defeatist, solicit help from others and then sabotage this help. We
may "shop" for physicians and/or counselors. In the seven years
I've lived in Minneapolis I have had four therapists, just as many
chiropractors and two dentists. I've also had six hair stylists. I
haven't had the luxury of being choosy with medical doctors, half
the time being without insurance, but I can boast of having my
own general practitioner, gynecologist, proctologist, ophthalmologist, dermatologist and, now, psychiatrist.

*You walk over to the food co-op on lunch break. Your lover will
be there today, cutting blocks of cheese. You walk into the back
room: no sign of cheese activity, no lover. "Did she call?" you ask
casually, terror welling up inside. There was no word from her. She
is more than an hour late. "I'm worried about my girlfriend," you
tell the cashier weakly. "I'll never see her again," you worry pri-
vately. You are vacant, drained. Your lover has been in a fatal car
accident. She always calls when she's late. You buy an apple, a
bagel, even though you are no longer hungry, and walk back to
work, thinking: "It has really happened this time; I can feel it." A
call minutes after you return. She was having lunch with a friend;
just got to the co-op. You tell yourself again not to get carried away.
How many accidents has she been in during the last two years?
How many times has she died? Hundreds.*

Again Roseanne recommended medication. She explained that
depression is a physical illness, like being diabetic. Antidepressants

are to depression as insulin is to diabetes. I didn't buy it. I requested more time in therapy before resorting to medication. Roseanne agreed, but by the end of the hour had convinced me that the depression would sabotage therapy, that antidepressants adjusted awry hormone levels, that I wouldn't be able to tell day-to-day that I was on medication—but over time would see an overall improvement. If one is not depressed, she said, antidepressants don't do a thing.

I agreed to see a psychiatrist. I quietly surrendered my endless elusive campaigns to uncover the mysterious problem that kept me fatigued and confused. Since getting sober I had tried so many things to feel better: eliminating caffeine and dairy products, yoga, vegetarianism, lifting weights, biking, creative visualization and, finally, turning full circle, steady doses of cappuccino. Like many depressives, I didn't realize depression is an illness. I was tested for B12 deficiency, mercury poisoning, Epstein-Barr virus, anemia and mononucleosis. I was thirty-one years old, and I wondered when "life" would really begin. I had exhausted my options. I made an appointment with the dreaded psychiatrist. My insurance decreed which clinic I could patronize: There were no female doctors on staff.

You wonder if your lover really loves you—doesn't she know how terrible you feel? How can she love you when you feel so mean, ugly and empty? She tells you, "I love you," casually in the car. You feel and say nothing. You no longer trust her love. But it is you who has lost the capability to love. She asks if you love her. "Yes, of course," you answer automatically, looking out of the window. Your love is cognitive; your feelings, numb.

I was angry, anxious, hopeless and slept better during the day than at night. I wasn't getting along with my co-workers, I lost faith in my friends, I was irritated by my lover. It occurred to me that I was the problem. I called my friend June, who two years past had spoken plaintively about her despondency and had calmly planned her death. I had been unsympathetic, having heard her litany before. I urged her to give her life over to the needy rather than destroy it—I told her to join Mother Teresa. A stay in the hospital and medication had saved her. "June," I cried into the phone, "what have antidepressants done for you?"

"Enabled me to cope," she said. "They allowed me the freedom to deal with the problems, instead of being so consumed, so focused in the depression." I had already seen how medication had contoured her shapeless existence. She was able to work again. She took science courses at the university. An avid bowler, she had even bowled a perfect score.

You are in a glitzy, downtown shopping plaza riding up the giant-sized escalator when you see the photography shop you want back on the first floor. The steep stairs are moving too fast, and your balance wavers as you step off. You are holding your breath as you make your way to the down escalator. All you can see are the first two stairs before they disappear into a precipitous drop. You are too terrified to step on. You feign you've forgotten something and move out of the stream of people. You look unsuccessfully for a safe, confined, slow elevator. You are forced to enter a skyway that leads to another building. Finally, there's an escalator: gentle slope, high walls on either side, moves slowly—you risk it. Out on the street you must walk a block back to the plaza, the photography shop. You glance at the escalator vowing you will never ride that monster again.

Dr. Shure, a slight man with a moist handshake, rarely looked me in the eye. I wondered what medications he was prescribing for himself. He had reviewed my case from Roseanne's file and determined I was suffering from double depression: "a sort of chronic low-grade depression topped by situational depression." In other words, I had probably been depressed all my life, plus I had an acute depression sitting on top of it. He prescribed Prozac because of its reputation for having minimal side effects. He warned only of a possible headache or stomach cramps. Dr. Shure emphasized the importance of combining the medication with "talk therapy." I asked about the controversial problems associated with the drug—suicide and violent thoughts or behaviors. He dismissed them as bad press and said that those cases had been refuted. It was as I had suspected; of course he would defend his profession's tools. The double-speak was absurd: Prozac will lessen social anxiety, he said, yet it may also produce social anxiety. The drug would take up to three weeks to enter my system. "And then you can expect a sense of well-being," he added gently.

You are driving down the freeway following an old station wagon. It has a second back seat that faces the rear. A woman and bearded man face you. He is pointing a pistol at you—or is it a soda bottle? You switch lanes. Before you can pass the car, it moves in front of you again. Clearly you see a gun. Clearly he is going to shoot you. The road splits. You quickly change lanes, away from the station wagon, away from your destination.

The depressed body responds with inappropriate hormone surges to outside signals, like daylight and stress; the prolonged consequence of this biological turmoil results in psychological problems. Depression constitutes a change in brain state. Different neurological areas are stimulated and repressed under the duress of depression. Self-reproach reigns. Dark thoughts of violence and negativity emerge.

I took my pulse and blood pressure using the drugstore computerized setup while I waited for my prescription to be filled. The high-tech "nurse" reported my pulse to be seventy-two, faster than my usual rate. I was to take twenty milligrams of Prozac, just one little green and white capsule, every morning. A half hour after taking the pill I could tell I was "on something," and it reminded me of the beginning of an LSD trip. I was fascinated by brilliant red lava leaping down a Hawaiian volcano on the television. I didn't think I was supposed to feel high, but I certainly didn't plan on informing the doctor. My head buzzed and tingled as I ran my hand through my hair. Out in the world I was stunned by the attractiveness of passersby. I spoke with a rare fluency.

The next several nights I lay awake. I could not dismiss my heaving heart. I squirmed under the covers and feared every lapse between beats, certain of a nearing attack. I had read that when the heart goes into fibrillation, it means the electrical activity of the heart has been disrupted. The article described the ineffective heart as looking like a sack of worms. I could not erase the image of all those red worms wriggling out of my heart. Finally, my heart teeming with worms, I telephoned the psychiatric nurse. She asked me to take my pulse. Upon discovering it was ninety-six I began to shake with fear. If my rate were 120 or more, the nurse said, then she would worry. She asked if I had any violent thoughts, if I was suicidal, if I had a rash, tremors, vomiting or diarrhea: She was obviously reading a list of possible side effects, a list that frightened me even more.[1] She directed me to avoid aerobic activity and said the side effects would lessen with time. That night, somewhat comforted that my blaring heart wouldn't convulse, I was able to sleep.

The initial troubling side effects of blurred vision, dry mouth and rapid heartbeat eventually diminished and were replaced by the wondrous ability to concentrate. I was astounded one evening to find myself completely absorbed in an ordinary television production. My thoughts were strangely uncluttered. I was pleased and excited by this development. My sleep pattern had also changed: I gave in fully to sleep after a lifetime of lying watchful in the dark.

Two things had been given to me rather quickly: concentration and sleep. I yearned to recover the part of the heart that didn't act simply as an organ. My heart may have just as well been my colon or my liver. It had forgotten excitement, love. I longed for the return of simple affections. My heart had been absent for some time, but messages of its return began to emerge. Hearts appeared in my plants—their heart-shaped leaves. I watched hearts materialize in the way steam evaporated from the window. I saw images of hearts stamped into pipes and other utilitarian objects scattered throughout the building at work. I hoped these floating hearts would somehow awaken mine. One night I fell asleep in front of the fireplace. I awoke with a strange heat in my chest cavity; my heart had caught fire. I desperately tried to retain the flame, but by morning it was extinguished.

Your muscles begin to unthaw. You notice an odd sensation in your stomach. Your breathing is relaxed, your stomach expands with deep inhalations; you have released your muscles. You finally understand why you have strong stomach muscles: They have been making fists for years. You notice other tension areas have loosened: Your shoulders and jaw give in to gravity; the tip of your tongue drifts naturally to the roof of your mouth; your toes unfurl.

Only a few people know I am taking Prozac. Not only do I feel guarded about revealing I am "on something," I am also ashamed. Medicating oneself for an illness of the mind is socially unacceptable. Unfortunately, most of the general public remain ignorant about the effects of antidepressants. My illness is one more secret to which I have learned to adapt. I am used to keeping secrets. I am a lesbian, a recovering alcoholic and I take medication for depression. Some might call me a social misfit.

Depression is common, and for women it is twice as common as for men. Depressed men often turn to alcohol and are labeled as alcoholics. According to recent studies middle-aged depressed women are the heaviest drug takers in our society.[2] My mother was depressed, but never diagnosed. My father is a recovering alcoholic. Like many American families, mine passed on the same patterns from previous generations: shame, low self-esteem, abuse.

I told a friend who distrusts medication that I was taking Prozac; I shared this with her because I thought I could educate her about the physiology of depression. She believes diagnoses of mental illness are based only upon impressionistic evidence, not on facts. Psychiatrists push medication, she said, which doesn't solve the real problems from which one may eventually recover.

Those were opinions I once shared. I told her that for years I had resisted the idea that I need medication. I believed the common notion that taking antidepressants was like trading one drug for another. I had already medicated myself with uppers, downers, hallucinogens and many other street drugs since I was a teen. I felt an odd transformation as I promoted Prozac. I had stepped over a crack in the earth; there was no turning back to my old beliefs, yet I still possessed a sense of unease.

The generic name for Prozac is fluoxetine hydrochloride. It works by increasing the availability of serotonin, a neurotransmitter, in the nervous system. It can improve one's mood and mental alertness, increase the desire for physical activity and improve sleep patterns.

You go to the dentist for a checkup. A weekly newspaper's readers' poll has recently named her "best dentist" in the area. You congratulate her. She asks if you are on any new medication. You don't remember being asked that in the past. You hesitate, remember the side effect of dry mouth, wonder if there's a deadly link between Prozac and Novocain, and decide to be honest. "How many milligrams are you taking?" she asks without skipping a beat. She recommends an over-the-counter fluoride mouth rinse. "Are you using a fluoride-based toothpaste now?" she asks. "No, I'm not because of the controversy around it." She says that the controversy is an old one. "Talk about controversial," she says loudly in a room with other open-mouthed patients, "Prozac is one of the most controversial drugs around. Who knows, you could go out and kill someone." You want to say, "Better hope it's not you." She cleans your teeth silently, wants you back next week for a filling. You never go back.

Understanding depression's biological manifestations has been essential to my eventual acceptance of using medication. I accept the depressive-needs-medication-like-a-diabetic-needs-insulin analogy. Antidepressants enhance the output of serotonin, which in turn influences hormones, especially cortical hormones, which regulate mood, sleep, sexual activity, appetite, circadian rhythm, anxiety, motor activity and cognitive function.

The circadian rhythm is the body's day-night rhythm, and mine was confused: I had been part of the cricket world, chirping all night long, hiding from the hot sun by day. Depressive relapses are most common in spring and autumn when the amount of daylight changes significantly. This is most likely because the body's circadian clock parameters become de-synchronized. I had always wondered why an increase in suicide occurs in the spring, when the winds are warm and rebirth beck-ons. I, too, had felt an unexplainable heaviness between winter and summer. Visions of the outdoors and exercise floated in my head as my body lay wooden on the bed. I never thought I would have the courage to kill myself, but I did fantasize about how I would do it. I tempted the courage to emerge by thinking of jump-ing off bridges or scenic overlooks.

When the economy is in a depression, the dollar has little worth. When the body is in a depression, the ego has little worth, and rewards are sought on the black market: alcohol, Pringles, long naps in the early evening, which sink the body into an even lower state.

The most debilitating aspect of depression is uncontrollable ruminating. You cannot stop thinking about what may have an-noyed you that day; how your lover is forever leaving open the closet door; how worthless you feel. Antidepressants are effective in controlling that perpetual skip in the record, and the central nervous system is then freed from internal stress. Mood elevation is a secondary effect of the drug. The body returns to its natural tendency toward a sense of well-being.

It is not known what triggers depression: biological, psycho-logical or sociological factors. I may have been born with a bio-logical predisposition to depression, but it is more likely a residue from growing up neglected, abused and shamed. Serotonin dys-function is also common in people who are chemically dependent, hypoglycemic, autistic, obsessive-compulsive, violent, suicidal, bulimic-anorexic and schizophrenic.

A barrier seems to have been lifted from your brain, enabling you to do chores and errands without the usual painful process of building motivation. Evenings are spent at the library, biking or visiting friends. You begin to let beauty back into your life. You admire the neighbors' fine-trimmed lawns.

For every one hundred adults and adolescents, six are clinically depressed. The happy news is that depression is treatable, and Prozac has a 60 percent success rate. As I write this I have been on Prozac for less than a year. Roseanne and Dr. Shure said most people stay on medication for up to two years. Antidepressants rescue you from a rut and give your hormones a kick-start. Chemical reactions eventually resume normal function on their own, and medication is no longer needed. On my third monitoring visit with Dr. Shure I asked him how—if I had been depressed all my life—my hormones could ever work normally without medication. He said some people with chronic depression choose to stay on medication indefinitely. He's a smart man. If he would have told me that from the start, I may not have begun this journey. Now I am sold. I may even overlook troubling side effects in the future.

The phone rings at six on a Sunday morning. Your lover answers, mumbles a few words, hangs up. "That was some old woman trying to call her son in London." You laugh and laugh, imagining this poor woman on the other end thinking she's reached London. You realize you have awoken with a sense of well-being. All morning you are easily amused. "Quit laughing at me," your lover says. "I'm not laughing at you. You should be happy I'm even laughing," you say. "I'm not used to it," she says.

Prozac is known as a "breakthrough drug," not because it is more effective than older antidepressants but because it is easier to tolerate. Many people would rather suffer from depression than from the side effects of older antidepressants, which include drowsiness, weight gain and urinary retention. Prozac has been on the market only since 1987, however, so long-term effects remain unknown. The other day I saw a magazine cover that shouted, "Great News! The Pill is Safe." My mother was a member of the Pill generation; I am a member of the Prozac generation. Whatever the magazines say about Prozac forty years from now, I hope the rewards I feel today are worth the consequences.

Notes

1. Less common side effects of Prozac are abnormal dreams, acne, hair loss, dry skin, chest pains, runny nose, bronchitis, abnormal heart rhythm, bursitis, twitching, fibrocystic disease of the breast, urinary pain, conjunctivitis, anemia, low blood sugar and low thyroid levels. Fifteen percent of the people testing the drug before it was released had to stop taking it. In rare cases Prozac users have become violent, manic or suicidal. Two people have died from overdose.

2. *Newsweek*, March 26, 1990.

DENI ANN GEREIGHTY, R.N.

Awful Lot of Trouble

A Supersize Woman Deals with the Health Care System

In 1993, I injured my back at work. The injury was diagnosed eventually as a bulging annular disk. I had to make three doctor's visits just to get on "adequate" pain medication. My family practice doctor wanted to rush me back to work—I worked for a health maintenance organization (HMO) and had sick leave, and this was a Labor and Industries claim—but I was not well enough.

I had to fight to get an occupational medicine referral and aggressive physical therapy. I was out of work for four months. I was told I would never go back to my old job, as a floor nurse, but I refused to accept that. I had the absolute conviction I would return to my job. Being able to do my job was my ultimate goal. Having this focused and concrete goal also seemed to motivate the health care professionals who cared for me. My progress was measurable. My requests were appropriate to obtaining my goal. I was persistent and constant in the pursuit of my recovery and an active participant. I took responsibility for getting well. I did not lie down and whine that I was not getting better. I took purposeful and diligent care of my own recovery, and I told my doctor all the things I was doing in addition to her prescribed treatment and medication. I augmented her care, with acupuncture treatments, massage, homeopathy and Chinese herbs, all at my expense, and I did positive affirmations, visualization, meditation and floor exercises every day.

I went back to work with horrible sciatic pain, after submitting to an epidural injection of steroids. This was done by a doctor outside the HMO, under fluoroscopy/direct visualization. There was a great deal of concern about my size, as the fluoroscopy table was rated only up to 320 pounds, and I was over that. They spoke about this within my hearing, which was insulting; there was far more concern about the table than about me, I felt. Eventually, my doctor got them to use the table, and the procedure was done under visualization and not "blind." The table did *not* break!

The sciatic pain was due to my right sciatic nerve running through my piriformis muscle; when I hurt my back, the piriformis went into a spasm from which there was no release despite aggressive physical therapy: massage, ultrasound, heat and so on. Finally, the occupational medicine doctor tried a small injection of anesthetic into the piriformis muscle itself, and in thirty seconds, I was sciatic-pain-free permanently! That really should have been a first-line treatment, and it was done with a tiny needle, almost pleasant compared to what else I had endured.

I was on muscle relaxers and nonsteroidal anti-inflammatory drugs for months afterwards. But I have been back at work, full-time, at my original job for over three years. It was the hardest thing I have ever done, but the good news is my recovery was the most complete my occupational medicine doctor had ever seen.

I did not know in advance if any of the things I tried would help me get well. I believe it was a combination of all of them, as well as my insistence that we work toward my full return to work, that brought about the healing. I think I could have easily become permanently partially disabled. It was up to me to determine how I would wind up. While I experienced my first seconds of freedom from pain during acupuncture, I had to decide every day to keep forging ahead, knowing that I was doing all I could for myself.

And, I believe there were lessons I had to learn: I had to be assertive, to demand the care I needed, which is hard for me to do with authority figures. I also had to use the correct language; for example, saying something impaired me so that I could not do my job meant the doctor paid more attention.

I learned that recovery is not linear, although I had expected it to be. I had to fight everyone and everything to return to my temporarily able-bodied status. Walking is still uncomfortable and easily brings on back spasms, which require me to sit. I have had to accommodate this change in my abilities, but I celebrate the return of the vast majority of my mobility. I did not need surgery.

I have found it essential, in times of a health crisis or when a "workup" is needed, to have a second person with me, an advocate. That person can assist me in being assertive, calm me, ask questions I forget or don't think of, clarify points, and help me get information and options explained in understandable language. She can also validate how I was treated as a patient and as a person. I have had my partner along, but a friend you are willing to share medical information with would work also. A patient has the right to have an advocate with them during medical appointments and in the hospital. Nurses are trained to be patient advocates, and if all else fails while in the hospital, find a registered nurse (RN) who seems sympathetic and is not incredibly busy and ask her to be your advocate for the immediate problem. Do not overuse or abuse your RN, however, as they are a rare find lately.

I was brought up to save all my medical problems for one

doctor's visit but in practice, that has not worked well for me. I have found that a medical visit needs to focus on one problem, with all its ancillary ramifications for self-care and follow-up. If a second problem is brought up, the first one may be forgotten or neglected. Writing down your questions beforehand and bringing in any journals or charting on different regimens or drug therapies will help you communicate more effectively with your care provider. I try to bring the doctor a good history of the problem, a list of measures I have tried to alleviate the problem and an idea of the outcome I want.

The more detailed history you can give, with what helps and what makes the problem worse, the easier it is for the medical provider to understand the problem and validate what you have tried. It also shows that you are observant, cooperative and motivated, all characteristics that make the provider interested in putting thought into your problem and tailoring a solution that is appropriate for you. Everyone "should" be treated equally, but it does not work that way. You have to contribute to creating favorable conditions for your care.

How does being a lesbian figure into my provider-patient relationship? Well, I am "out" depending on who my provider is and if it matters in my care. I introduced D. as my partner at the infertility clinic, but as my roommate while being worked up for sleep apnea. I am "out" to my family practice doctor and gynecologist. When I needed stitches in my hand in the ER, information about my sexuality was not important for my care.

Once when D. took me to my HMO's emergency room, she went to admitting and explained she was my partner, with a medical power of attorney and so on. Despite the fact that the HMO provides medical coverage for domestic partners and has openly gay staff, D. was hassled and told she could not admit me! She was not allowed to make corrections to things like medications being taken or my mother's maiden name, once she was allowed to sign the forms, and she was listed as an "other" under relationship. I called and wrote letters about the situation once I was well, but what one encounters probably depends on who is on duty at the time.

Sometimes being prepared with creature comforts makes a health care visit more tolerable. Pack a lunch and a good book if you know it is going to be an all-day affair. And having a positive attitude helps invoke a similar response in your provider; a nasty patient gets less assistance, thought and care in my experience, even if her attitude is justified. Your advocate may be able to help smooth things over if anything unpleasant happens.

I also do not accept negativity or information I do not believe is true for me from health care providers. One therapist told me that all my progress with other therapists and my successes with positive affirmations had to be thrown out the window. I was to listen only to her and buy a book she recommended. I would have fallen for her spiel except that she condemned positive affirmations and I knew they had helped me recover from my back injury. Instead I sought out a former therapist I trusted. He was so thrilled I had achieved so much since I had last seen him two years before that I was truly impressed with it myself. He helped me do a reality check and decide her brand of therapy was not for me.

It has been a hard lesson to learn, but I have had to fight for everything I need in my life. I thought going to the doctor would be a simple thing. The conflicting information I have observed as a consumer and as a provider (even in an integrated system) makes me realize the amazing amount of energy each person has to expend to obtain appropriate care. Staying well is a high priority in my life, but as is true in many things, I have to pick which battles I fight in obtaining my health care. Sometimes, retaining my inner strength to fight on another day is all I can hope to do.

I try to be very clear about what I need when dealing with the health care system, especially as a supersize woman. Doctors often relate every health problem to my weight, even though many thin people have the same problems. For example, several women in my nursing unit had herniated disk injuries around the time I injured my back; the others, two of whom needed surgery, were thin. Of the four of us, I took the longest to return to work, partly because the enforced immobility quickly impaired my endurance. But bed rest or limited activity makes even thin, healthy people lose muscle rapidly. Asking your doctor how a thin person would be treated or what would be done to treat your condition if you lost weight may be useful. Sticking up for equal treatment may be difficult, but women of size have the right to supportive, quality health care just as everyone else does. If there are no gowns big enough on the shelf, ask for some. If the scale only goes to 350, ask for it to be adjusted with weights so that it goes up to 450 pounds. If you don't want to be weighed, say so. I have found it very difficult to do, but I feel much better if I make my wishes known.

I have struggled with my weight since my early teens, but I refuse to feel bad or to diet ever again. Instead, I have gone to two fall Fat Women's Gatherings, sponsored by NAAFA (National Association to Advance Fat Acceptance). These all-women events have changed my life, empowering me in a multitude of ways in the last three years. I have learned not to hate my body, to be happy with who I am and with what I have. I have been encouraged to open up my soul to writing again.

Being a supersize woman, I have never had any sympathy for women who diet constantly to lose the same ten pounds over and over. I have promised myself that I will not play with numbers; "I'm a better fat person at 220 pounds versus 340 pounds" is not a valid statement.

I realized that being alive means that I win. Instead of feeling that I should not exist, I can claim my space and my right to be. Positive affirmations, love, Goddess religion, a fat, fat-positive dyke therapist and sheer stubborn determination have gotten me to where I am, accepting myself and creating my life the way I want it to be. I still battle fear, sadness, depression and feeling incompetent on some days, but I get up the next day. A very difficult lesson was that a horrible day or week does not mean my life is over. If my partner and I fight, it does not mean we are going to break up. I am very proud of myself for having learned this.

There are dreams I had for my life I will not fulfill. That is okay! I am dreaming new, updated visions for my life. I spend a good deal of time and energy on exploring what I want and who I am. It is hard work, to tear down walls and erect bridges, to dare to be alone in new territory. But anger and adventure fight depression, although, it does not happen linearly. There are always waves that push me back, but sometimes these waves drop pearls. Changing my inner voice, how I talk to myself, via positive affirmations has wrought major changes in my life. Believing a fat woman is okay is incredibly powerful. I'm feeling a lot more confident and competent these days. I'm in control of this life, and I'm going to relish the journey, good and bad. I have proven that I can do what I set my mind to do.

I have recently been diagnosed with diabetes. Despite the fact that my father was diabetic and that his mother is diabetic, I know my mother will say, "If you hadn't eaten all that sugar and candy, you wouldn't have developed diabetes." Fortunately, I know diabetes is not caused by eating sugar. The first week after my diagnosis, I was in shock. Then I focused on not being able to stick my finger to test my blood sugar and on how I hate to exercise. I can see the first lesson of this part of my life coming: Do I forge ahead with determination, hope and the conviction that I can take good care of myself, or do I flounder around finding ways to sabotage my life? I have spent the last two days calling people who will support me emotionally, and those I know who have diabetes. I was surprised to find out how much emotional support, resources for networking and information on alternative therapies I received.

I went away for the weekend, by myself, to a hotel at a natural hot springs, for peace of mind, to reflect on my life and the major changes I was undergoing. I sat on my balcony at 2 A.M., looking out over three pools. I lit a candle, and, spontaneously, mentally did the following ritual. Doing it physically works well if you are not experienced at visualization and familiar with this form of psychic work.

Encircle yourself and your surroundings, such as your room, with blue-white light, and draw a chalk circle if it helps, three times three, which is nine times, or nine circles. The light is protection, impenetrable, stronger than steel. This is your sacred space, apart and between the ordinary worlds in which you live. Nothing has the power to harm you there. Feelings and memories can be taken out and examined safely, perhaps even death, without their previous power over you.

Mentally or physically, rap, tap or knock on each of the four walls or boundaries, invoking the four directions and acknowledging their corresponding elements: *East* lends the strength of *air*, hurricanes and tornadoes. *South* lends the strength of *fire*, wildfires and New Year's bonfires. *West* lends the strength of *water*, tidal waves and ocean depths. *North* lends the strength of *earth*, mountains and earthquakes.

Ask each element to guard you from harm and bring wisdom, keeping you in touch with the powers of our Mother Earth. Call the Goddess within you to come forth, your spirit self, apart from any religion you might believe in; your soul will answer.

Within the circle, I cried, holding the little doll that symbolized my vulnerable self. I talked to her of what I had hoped for out of life and where I should go from here. I relaxed and just allowed myself to simply be for a while in the stillness. I reviewed recent major decisions and found I still agreed with them. I grieved for the things I would therefore lose. I sang a round that embodies my belief in the interconnectedness of life and death, the concept that all life is change.

We all come from the Goddess,
And to Her we shall return,
Like a drop of rain,
Flowing to the ocean.

Then I said these positive affirmations to myself: I am calm, strong, healing, whole, myself, safe, wise, at peace, within my body, secure, okay, grounded, healthy, pain-free, flexible, together, clear-headed, integrated, accepting, complete.

After a time, I thanked and dismissed my guardians, knowing that I had respected myself and the earth that gives us life. I opened the circle and did some deep breathing. Then it was time to eat a snack, as a way of grounding energy.

I am always changing, and growing, a product of my experiences. I know I am learning the lessons life sends me and doing all I can to safeguard my health. I can do what I set my mind to do. I accept myself as a fat dyke, and that is power indeed! Acceptance of who I am, determination to create what I desire for myself are what I will carry in the spiraling dance of my life.

EVELYN C. WHITE

Spit and Image
Notes on Black Lesbians, Silence and Harm

Several years ago I was invited to address a gathering of the National Black Gay and Lesbian Leadership Forum. I spoke about the public images of Black lesbians and how they affect the emotional contours of our lives. Following is my text, which I have revised and expanded considerably for this book.

This is an important health issue because all too often the reality of Black lesbian life is rendered invisible. Taught in a racist and homophobic culture that it is not safe to reveal our authentic selves, we are rarely what we appear to be on the surface. In the words of Black poet Paul Laurence Dunbar we "wear the mask." The masking is a survival technique that has served to protect us from our oppressors and helped us to maintain bonds, albeit false ones, within the African-American community. It has also helped to foster distortions about our identity that often keep us in struggle with ourselves and with other Black women.

It is only fitting that we are gathered today in a meeting room, that for the purposes of this conference, has been renamed in honor of Pat Parker. For the late poet Pat Parker was a legendary force in the Black lesbian community. She lived in the San Francisco Bay area, as do I.

I knew Parker—not well, but we would periodically run into each other at concerts, readings or sporting events. Of course I knew of her exquisite poetry, especially *Jonestown and Other Madness* and its haunting refrain, "Black folks do not, Black folks do not, Black folks do not commit suicide." I also knew of her widespread reputation as a hell-raiser.

The general sentiment, in our community, was that if there was any kind of fracas involving Black lesbians, Parker was likely to be involved, if not the ringleader.[1] Indeed stories about Parker's rowdiness were legend. I heard several firsthand myself. For example, a woman I dated when I first moved to the Bay area told me that Parker had once plied her with Johnnie Walker and then pressured her to run down an ex-lover with whom there was bad blood. My friend said she thought better of the idea as she was weaving drunkenly through traffic. Everybody knew that Parker had a wild, crazy, iconoclastic, nonconformist, kick-ass streak. She let it all hang out. That was the image that co-existed with Parker's reputation as a masterful and mesmerizing poet.

I heard about her breast cancer diagnosis in 1987 just as I was beginning to compile *The Black Women's Health Book*.[2] I had always planned to include a piece of Parker's writing in the collection. When she died in June 1989, I decided that, if possible, I wanted a previously unpublished piece by Parker in the book. I wanted something that readers had not seen and that would honor her legacy as a pioneering Black lesbian writer.

I contacted Parker's literary executor and arranged to visit Parker's house to go through her papers. Parker lived in a tree-lined suburb outside of Oakland in a neighborhood resplendent with ranch houses and well-tended lawns. When I pulled into her driveway, I immediately thought: "This is just like *The Brady Bunch*. Who would believe that Parker—hellion that she was—would live in such a staid mom-and-pop community?" When I entered the house, there was an even stronger *Leave It to Beaver* vibration: school pictures of Parker's daughter, Anastasia, in the living room, a coffee maker in the kitchen, neatly hung potholders and grocery coupons under colorful magnets on the refrigerator.

It was the epitome of domestic bliss.

The literary executor directed me to Parker's writing studio, a wood-paneled room off the kitchen. When I walked in, I stopped in my tracks, completely dumbfounded. There was not a stray paper clip, a crumpled-up piece of paper, a dog-eared book or an ink-stained pad in sight.

The room was such a contrast to the reputation that Parker had out on the street that it was difficult, in that moment, for me to reconcile the image before me. So I diplomatically asked the executor if Parker, knowing that she was terminally ill, had gone through some kind of "pre-death, get your house in order, going to meet your Maker" transformation that would explain the fastidiousness I saw. "Not at all," the woman replied matter-of-factly. "This is the way Parker always kept her writing room. She was very, very organized."

The woman left. I spent the afternoon in the room perusing Parker's papers, journals and files. As I sorted through the documents, I remembered a student job I'd once had working in the archives at Wellesley College. The order and attention to detail I noted in Parker's study rivaled what I'd seen as I processed the papers of Wellesley's privileged graduates.

One of my most vivid memories from that day is of the file folder labeled *Anastasia.* Carefully placed in annotated, chronological order were the report cards, health records and crayon drawings of Parker's child. All the files were just as meticulous, all the way back to the letter Z. They were not doodled on or thrown in the file cabinet all wild and crazy, as are my files.

Scanning the wall-length bookshelf, I realized that Parker's hundreds of books were all in alphabetical order by author. "She must have been a Virgo," I thought, still unable to reconcile the calm serenity of the room with my memories of Parker in a grass-stained softball uniform, "selling wolf tickets" as she downed whiskey at the local bar.[3]

But the fact is that, contrary to her public image, Pat Parker (who was an Aquarius) had created and clearly thrived in a quiet and orderly sanctuary. She did not just raise hell.

As I left her home (with the previously unpublished poem "Massage") and drove back to the city, I was mindful of the difference between *real* Black lesbian life and the images many of our friends, families and co-workers have of us. I thought about the misperceptions people might have about me and how necessary it is for me to speak the truth about who I really am.

For in the absence of speaking, Black lesbians will continue to suffer the pain of being misread, of having our silences distorted, demonized and misunderstood. We will be misunderstood by our oppressors, who in the words of Audre Lorde, "never meant for us to survive," and perhaps, more painfully, by our mirror reflections.

Memories of my afternoon in Parker's study have been pivotal as I've struggled to heal from a wounding exchange I had with another Black woman that evolved from a deep and complex place of silence. Dana (not her real name) was a new friend, a woman I'd met while on a leave from my newspaper job and with whom there appeared to be mutual sexual energy and attraction. We were two Black women delighted to befriend each other as we worked on our respective projects thousands of miles from home. We met for dinner. We went to the theater. But mostly we had many long and laughter-filled conversations in her apartment during which we shared intimate and revealing stories about our lives.

For instance, I told Dana, as odd as it might sound, that I'd made a personal vow never to make love with a Black lesbian who had not read *The Color Purple*. Because to my mind, I figured a sister who had yet to read Alice Walker's magnificent novel might be struggling with issues of self-love and affirmation that I would find cautionary in an intimate relationship. In subsequent conversations during which Dana spoke quite emotionally about some of her interactions with Black women, I was led to believe that she understood why I had taken my *Color Purple* stance.

Several months after *The Color Purple* conversation, Dana and I slept together. For me, the encounter was pained and confusing. "I want to make you angry," she said repeatedly, as we flailed on her bed. Deeply disturbing, her words were an unheeded warning that we should not have been intimate in those moments, and for my error in judgment, I take full blame.

Overwrought and completely drained by the intensity of the evening, I still tried to connect with Dana in a meaningful way before I left her apartment the next morning. It was not easy. Much to my dismay I found myself re-engaged in the drama and madness of the previous night.

Wearing a white terry cloth bathrobe, Dana pulled me toward her for a farewell kiss after I made it clear that I absolutely had to leave. As I attempted to move out of her embrace, she took my right arm, locked her eyes with mine and said: "Guess what?" "What, Dana?" I answered, giving her my full attention despite my rising despair and exhaustion.

"I've never read *The Color Purple*," she said. "I haven't seen the movie either." Tossing her head back, she began to laugh maniacally.

Dana's words hit me with the force of an assassin's bullet. Although I remained upright, my inner spirit was crushed by the willful cruelty of the blow, and emotionally, I collapsed, like a rag doll. Then calling forth all the self-love and compassion (so much of it awakened in me by the life and literature of Alice Walker) that I could, I returned Dana's gaze and replied, "Well, you probably intend to." I turned and walked out.

Dana's derisive laughter trailed me down the corridor as she stood, in her white robe, leaning against the doorway. I was so shattered by the incident that I feared I would keel over while waiting for the elevator. Holding the banister for support, I descended the four flights of stairs in a numb swirl. When I arrived home, I ripped off my clothes and ran a hot bath in which I sat for hours and sobbed.

I am still weeping about my friendship with Dana. I weep because part of my soul was lost in the aftermath of lying naked with another Black woman. And I know that my pain, in varying shades and degrees, has been experienced by multitudes of other Black lesbians, including, I'm certain, Dana herself. The loss is connected, in tangible ways, to the silences we keep about who we really are and the depth of our vulnerabilities.

Upon reflection, it's clear to me that Dana and I never really *knew* each other, because despite our sisterly sharing we continued to "wear the mask." I've thought, since that evening, what a difference it might have made had I told Dana more of the details behind my *Color Purple* philosophy. Might it have made a difference in her response to me that morning had I told her that a former lover, using my admiration of *The Color Purple* as an example, had once berated me for "reading too much" and then to get my "priorities straight" fucked me with such ferocity and aggression that I had black and blue bruises all over my brown body the next day?

Would Dana have treated me more gently had she known that my movement toward her bedroom that night was not driven by wanton lust but rather by a sincere desire to comfort and soothe?

I know that because of my silences, Dana had misread me, astoundingly, as a woman scheming to toy with her emotions. Indeed, during one of our many lengthy, freewheeling, late-night conversations, I remember that she referred to me as a "Don Juana." I did not then, nor do I now have the slightest idea of what she was talking about. For a seductress, I decidedly am not. I can barely watch a love scene in a movie without blushing with embarrassment. I am by nature a very quiet, private and delicate person, especially with regard to sexual expression—which is precisely why *The Color Purple* assault by the ex-lover had such a profound impact on me. Still, somehow, I suspect because of my writing achievements and so-called prominence in the Black lesbian community, Dana got the impression that I was a lady-slaying Mack Daddy.[4] While I knew her "Don Juana" comment was completely off the mark, I stayed silent. And my silence led to additional silences and secrets on both our parts that culminated, ironically, in a tumultuous sexual encounter that left me with feelings of shame and humiliation I doubt I will ever fully resolve.

What I do know is that, for now, the thought of being intimate with another Black woman fills me with abject terror. And, I know that, among Black lesbians, I am not alone in this feeling. In fact, a friend in whose loving embrace I found solace after my nightmarish evening with Dana wrote me a letter that has helped me better understand the havoc we wreak upon each other.

> I don't believe that we Black women intrinsically know and understand each other simply because we are Black and female. In fact, I think we have refused to look and stand under each other's gaze for so long—that there is much we do not know and understand. There is so much anger, there is so much desire for love and power and there is much fear and despair. There is also desire to be known and desire to be shown how to be happy. That those desires have been thwarted and twisted as we have fashioned our lives is very complicated—covered by layers and layers of pain and expressed in codes that are hard to unravel. We dare and taunt each other, we too often refuse to keep faith with each other and ourselves.

And so I share this saga, pitiful as it is, to keep faith with myself and my Black lesbian sisters. For I know, now, how easily Black lesbians are misunderstood and how often our silences get misread as coldness, ego-tripping or power. The truth is that many of us are silent because we are shy, sensitive, fragile and afraid. There were many times during the course of my friendship with Dana that I felt so exposed and vulnerable I could hardly speak. Contrary to the damning stereotypes about us as strong and invincible Rocks of Gibraltar who can endure any burden and withstand any pain, I believe that most Black women are deeply wounded and very, very small. As June Jordan aptly notes, "None of us has ever known enough tenderness."

For a long time after my ill-fated night with Dana, I experienced extreme mental and physical distress. I became frightfully phobic about encountering her in public. And in what I believe was a psychosomatic response to being symbolically felled by cruel words, I developed a kind of spinal paralysis that made it difficult for me to walk. I tried to conceal these afflictions and, not surprisingly, they did not go away. Sessions with a chiropractor and a psychiatrist who specializes in trauma have helped steady me. I also sent Dana—inscribed with sincere words of thanks for the good parts of our friendship—a copy of *The Color Purple.*

But the most important part of my healing has evolved from reflecting on my afternoon in Parker's study and the misrepresentation of our common Black lesbian identities. I know that it is only in speaking openly about the masks we wear and the masks that have been thrust upon us that I can truly honor her passionate refrain, "Black folks do not, Black folks do not, Black folks do not commit suicide."

A week before final selections were made for this book, I still had reservations about the inclusion of my essay. In fact, I'd contacted Jocelyn White (no relation), who'd had "Spit and Image" for nearly a year, and told her I wasn't sure I wanted it printed in its present form. My concern was not so much about the details of the story, but rather an uncertainty about whether I'd rendered it in a manner that would be of real use to readers. I kept asking myself: What is the point?

Then, I met feminist legal scholar Catharine A. MacKinnon and was subsequently sent, by a mutual friend, a speech she had delivered in the aftermath of the Anita Hill–Clarence Thomas hearings. Among many other brilliant points she raised in the speech, MacKinnon posed the following questions:

> *I wonder, if what makes it possible to perpetuate abuse is the dead certain belief—the ground certain belief like gravity—by both the perpetrators and victims that it will never enter the public domain? . . . What does the way women are treated when we speak about abuse in public do to our ability to feel sane, as well as our ability to be sane?*

I realized, while reading MacKinnon, that so much of the misery that exists between Black women ossifies in our bodies and spirits because the experiences never meet the air. And we count on that. We depend on "Hush, children" and "Peace, be still." Of course, Audre Lorde was among the first to trailblaze this territory. But it was MacKinnon's pointed and particular legal discussion about injury and "the public domain" that has made it easier for me to publish this still unfinished and extraordinarily complex story.

Secondly, at about the same time I was considering withdrawing this piece, I met, in a foreign country, a woman with whom I developed a friendship very similar to that which I'd had with Dana. We spent a lot of time together, laughing, joking and sharing many of the intimacies of our lives. I had brought my essay abroad, in hopes of giving it a major revision or scrapping it completely. I was leaning heavily toward the latter.

One day I asked my friend if she'd look at the piece, adding, "Every time I think about it, I want to kill myself." After reading it, she offered a few vague and cursory remarks. I didn't feel the least bit slighted as I was totally sick of the essay by this point. We went on to other things.

The last night I saw this woman, we were hanging out in my hotel room after a sumptuous dinner by the sea. It was the perfect ending to a truly wonderful adventure. Before leaving, my friend took my hand and whispered softly: "You know, there's something I've been wanting to tell you the entire trip, and I've been really worried about how to say it, but here goes—I've never read *The Color Purple*. That's something I've definitely got to do."

Tears welled in my eyes, as I realized, though we'd never discussed it, how much my friend had been moved by my essay. And I was touched, incredibly, by my understanding that in exposing herself to me, my friend had revealed both her awareness of my vulnerability and the depth of her own self-esteem. Her loving gesture caught me completely off-guard. Indeed, I was as dumbstruck by her words as I'd been previously by Dana's. But whereas before I'd felt bludgeoned by duplicity and disrespect, this time I felt washed in comfort and love. It was as if a wound, that had been gaping open for five years, was gently sutured.

After a tender embrace, my friend returned to her bedroom. I slowly undressed and got into bed. As the surf roared outside my window, I thought about the grace that has imbued my Black lesbian life, and fell gently and gratefully, asleep.

Notes

1. I want to make it clear that I am not suggesting that Pat Parker was involved in violent or abusive intimate relationships. I am speaking exclusively of public interpretations about her.

2. Evelyn C. White, *The Black Women's Health Book: Speaking for Ourselves* (Seattle: Seal Press, 1994).

3. "Selling wolf tickets" is Black slang for aimless talking, flirting, bullying, bluffing or intimidating someone.

4. "Mack Daddy," Black slang for hustler, is commonly used to describe a male who makes aggressive attempts at seduction.

ANONYMOUS

Battering
One Woman's Story

This is, perhaps, not what you think. It is the other side.

It lasted four years. There were always two of us, of course. But only after it was finally over between us, did I find a healing circle to help *me*. That was close to fifteen years ago.

Counselors shake their heads. A tough group, they say. They don't seem to *want* to heal. I don't tell them my story, how for two years I was desperate with need. How every time I called, I was told there were not enough women for a group yet.

Please, they'd say, call again in a few months. Hang in there.

But I was already crazy with pain. I might not survive "a few months," I thought.

Why did I stay?

I stayed because I loved you. It was you who had stopped loving me. I stayed because I believed it was not mine to leave.

Why did I stay?

I stayed because mere anguish was not reason enough to leave.

I am tough. I am a dyke. I can take it.

Why did I stay, when it became so clear, at least to others, and at last even to me, that you held some part of me in contempt. Why did I stay?

Don't you see, it wasn't mine to leave.

Why did I stay? Why did I lay my hands upon you, forcing you away?

Why did you corner me, time after time after time? Why did I shove you in anger and then, because it felt good, push you again? Why did you cringe?

Of course you cringed, and I hated myself for it. But I hated you for it, too: Why didn't you stand up and deal with it, like a woman?

Why did I yell at you, crazy with pain, the muscles of my neck standing out in high relief, torrents of bitterness spilling from my mouth, spitting out foam and truth, lies and anger, and the hatred I had come to bear, why did I lie?

I actually spit on you, on how I felt you had twisted love to mean, put up with this forever. Meaning, you said, that it wasn't your fault if you didn't know yourself. That I robbed you of your being to explain yourself to you. That it was all very well for me, me with the language, to say my truths so clearly that you had no room to hide, but you had your own truths even if you didn't know them. I had no right to steal them from you and turn them into the light. They were yours, and if they were your secrets, even from yourself, so they were, and I had no right to them. They were not mine, your secrets. You had a right to your own ignorance of yourself.

Why did *you* stay? Why *did* you stay?

I stayed to force you to bear witness to your own truth. Thus is violence a need to control. I stayed, sipping bitterness for years, called into places I never dreamed I would agree to enter.

Ripping your shirt with the fist of my hand. Spitting in your face. Grabbing your arm, not in kindness but in anger, your flesh so mortal beneath my fingers. I wanted to kill you. I wanted you to stop. I wanted you to love me. I wanted you to tell the truth.

Why didn't I leave? Yes, why didn't I?

I am on the phone, at work, and here it is again between us. But I can't stop, and you don't or can't, and so on and on it goes. Why don't I leave? I hang up, press my head against the doorjam. I am drained. I know I should leave. But it will be more than two years before you finally do.

■

I have colleagues here, and that, finally, is the hardest humiliation, that there are days I can't stop crying, can't answer the quiet questions, are you all right? Are you sure? In my corner, at my desk, weeping into my hands, I cannot stop. The pain is burying me.

I am ill. I drive hundreds of miles to seek healing.

I find karate. It becomes a spiritual discipline, and I have some small hope again.

Eight weeks later, I injure myself, and no matter what I do, I can't go on.

I am ill, and every morning on the half-hour bus ride, I weep, my half-hour of weeping, a public mourning. We have fought, and my words have been as vicious as knives. Who is this stranger I have become?

We live in a large city. I search the papers endlessly. Someone, someone must have a cure, a group, a program for me. I swallow the word *batterer, abuser,* like just another bitter pill. Where is the group that will heal me? Who can see why this is a matter of life and death?

We have been in therapy together, but don't talk much about this condition. The therapists want us to make it. They want this love story to have a happy ending.

The lie again: that all is well. Everything is under control. Only we can't stop fighting. I only want you to love me. What do you want? Perhaps you only want to love me. But don't.

■

In the secret places of our life together, you continue to torture me. Did you know what you were doing? I thought you did. Maybe you didn't. Maybe you didn't know it was torture. You were surprised at the abuse, and then you hated me. No wonder. I hated myself. I crossed a line so fundamental, it would take years of hard, weary labor to get back on the other side.

That is the story I want to tell.

■

Once I crossed that line, it was like pushing a boulder up an unforgiving hill to get back on the proper side again, to trust myself again. And even when I knew I was together again, back on the safe side of the line, some would never believe it. They thought they knew how easy it could be, how seductive, to slip over that line again.

How can I explain it? The journey over that line, from the safe side to the violent side, is like a fish trap: Going one way is easy; getting back is anguish, can seem impossible. Sometimes is impossible.

I worked hard. I didn't know if it was possible. But I got back. Now I know where that line lies for me, and I believe I will not cross it again. Two of my three lovers since that time believe that entirely. One was not sure. The therapist from the healing circle did not believe me.

You will, perhaps, not believe me either. But here it is: I am mortally afraid of that line, and what it means in my life. Perhaps the world would change if we could teach simply this: *We bear the cost of our own footsteps. We bear the unimagined costs of our own decisions. We walk in our own footsteps, forever.*

I cannot tell you, reader, what to do if you inhabit those places. You have your own truths, you will travel your own paths, and nothing can be done about it. I know. I know.

I know what it feels like to act in ways you believe in your deepest soul to be wrong.

I put a note in the women's bookstore: Will chop wood for free. I wanted the clean bite of blade into wood. I didn't want to smash dishes in anger as they kept telling me to do. At least I wanted to build something from this illness. I wanted healing.

Three long years later, I would meet a woman in the therapy

group that finally came together (the first anyone had heard of for lesbian batterers). This was after it was all over between us (although as you can see it is still not completely over for me). She was a tall, slender, attractive woman. Carefully groomed. Very reserved. She controlled everything about her self, even her eyes, which were carefully measured. Small, delicate jewelry. A fine haircut. Carefully, beautifully dressed. A dyke with looks to die for. To die for.

She couldn't stop either. She was there because she wanted to stop, she said. But her voice was dead. Her soul was carefully under control. She didn't trust herself with children.

Another woman said she couldn't help it. The image—and I don't know whether it was hers or mine—was of her being tied and tortured, with words, in the middle of the kitchen floor. She would finally strike back. Battering.

Is it like this for men? I don't know. In my case, I fought back. I did it with shoving and spitting and grabbing and slapping. I did it in my living nightmares, with anger and finally contempt and sometime even hatred. I did it in towering rages, and the violence was in me, and I believe I must have been terrifying. Could you finally hear me, then? It might not have stopped there, I know. I have heard about it: the baseball bat across the ribs, the face shoved into the hot burners of the stove. Swearing, crying. "Stay back, stay back, I swear I'll hurt you."

I remember walking and crying, crying out loud down the long, shabby streets, walking in the icy streets, the cars between me and the houses with silent eyes, between me and the children, the families with ordinary problems. Sobbing out loud, breaking down, wanting to rip every mirror off every car. Wanting to go crazy from this pain. But wouldn't. Wouldn't. Wouldn't. Behind me, the long line of rearview mirrors, all carefully left intact. Crying even harder. Destroy destroy destroy destroy. Wailing. I could destroy it all.

I didn't.

I was crazy with pain.

Another picture. At a community concert, I am up in the stairwell, choking on tears. The stairwell is crowded with women. The women are so polite. They ignore me. The women are so . . . normal. No one is struggling with self-control.

I am dying from the pain inside. There is a black eagle tearing at my brain. I am in the kind of pain that is just one fine breath from unconsciousness. I live on the edge of this blackout, in that heightened pain, for two years. It is in my back, the disc that failed, that no one can treat. It is in my soul, the line that blew, that I stepped across, that no one can treat.

■

Why didn't I leave? You had already left, in spirit. Why wouldn't you leave in body? Leave me leave me leave me if you feel that way, if you don't feel that way. *Why won't you leave?* since you seem to hold me in such contempt, a poor specimen of life, unable to be whole, be good, be right. Like you. You seemed to believe you were always right. Although you often said, "I could be wrong." But you never said out loud you thought you were. My point of view did not appear to affect you. You had your own world.

Sometimes it was my most exquisite form of vengeful torture, to love you anyway, whether you wanted me to or not.

Once I destroyed my room. I tore down the curtains and broke things in my pain. Me, who couldn't stand the ugliness of our lives, your papers all over everything, everywhere, the poverty of color and shape and form, my room my only sanctuary of peace.

And I destroyed it. It could have been you. It would have been you. Instead it was me. Killing some part of myself for fear of that line, that line I had already crossed. And it was unthinkable: I who know that women, we women, hold the key to all life, that any future we have we must walk to on our own feet with our heads high. I who believe in women the way I have never believed in men, who believe and believe and believe.

What have I done? Why couldn't I stop? Why couldn't I simply walk away?

I walked in the Take Back the Night marches for my own reasons. They were just as true as any of yours. Or yours. Or yours.

Why did I stay? Because I continued to believe it was not mine to go, and it almost killed me. Why did I stay? I wanted to make you see your own story. Or what I perceived to be your own story. So in the end, it was about force. It was about control.

Why did you treat me so? I felt you treated me badly. I heard you say you cared. I listened to the word not the action. I believed you meant what you said. Perhaps I refused to remember that you didn't always know your own truths.

The worst time? One spring when we traveled all through the night. I had already driven through much of the previous night to pick you up at your mother's house, as we had arranged. I thought, get in late, sleep some and leave.

But at your mother's, the day kept going on and on, and still you would not leave. And all day I was angry. I would try to leave without you. No, just a little while longer, you would say. I would say—or did I only think?—I have to do this, don't you see? I have be back in the morning. I have to be there—eight, nine, ten hours of hard driving away—in the morning. Early in the morning. I don't want to drive through the night. I am tired. I am unstable. I don't want to drive all night.

We drove all night.

I don't want to discuss the difficult things between us, here in this truck, in the night, in the night now thinning to morning. I don't want to talk at all. I am tired. I didn't want to drive all night. I am at my wits' end. This is stupid. This is dangerous. I don't want to talk about issues and the hard things between us. Not now at 5 A.M. We're almost there. Will you please *shut up*. I don't want to do this.

Will you stop? Will you *stop*? *Stop. Stop. Stop stop stop stop stop.* I will stop. I will stop you, do you hear, I am pulling this truck off the road and now you are afraid, now you are afraid, but now it is too late because I *will* stop you I swear I will. I will find a quiet, lonely place, and yes, yes, I will, I will stop you, you viper, you whore. Who do you think you are? You have no right to do this; you have no right to do this. I will stop you. I can whisper it now, and you will hear me because by now you are terrified, and I am glad. I will stop you.

I drive off onto some sandy road, and I try to pull you out of the truck, and I swear I will kill you.

I would have killed you right there in the early morning light. And you saw it; somehow you escaped me, drove away, left me standing there. So then you were the one who got away. The survivor. The battered one. The one at risk?

■

The truth of this story is that there are two women at risk here, and both of them need help. Some of us who have crossed this line know it. Some of us don't. Some of us care. Some no longer do.

Some years later, after it was all over between us, I was involved with someone else. She knew the story because I had told her. My therapist thought she knew me. She didn't. She told my then-partner—we already had years between us—that she was at risk from me.

She wasn't.

Yes! I had been angry with her at times. *Yes*! I spoke loudly in that anger. In fact, I yelled. My partner said she was afraid and wanted a session between us, each with a therapist. I said, yes, of course I will do this. I knew my anger for a clean one, and said so. Yes, it felt good to be able to just be angry, to not be afraid to be angry. It was healing. She was so dear to me, had made it safe for me to have my feelings. Had made it so safe. Can you even imagine what that was like for me? How precious? And I was so, so careful to be clean. It wasn't even hard. There was no reason not to be. There was no desperation there. And so I allowed myself at last to be angry. And it felt good. I knew myself, and I knew my anger. And I knew it was clean.

Reading this, you ask: How could anyone trust you? It's too risky.

But I always told the truth of what I knew. I knew when my anger was dangerous. I knew when it was not. And I cared about the difference.

How could anyone trust that? you ask.

Ask yourselves. Do you tell the truth? Do you know who you are when you are angry? Do you know when you have ceased to love? Do you play at forms of love because women are supposed to be loving? Do you cover yourself with lies of convenience? Do you hide from yourselves?

Let me tell you this: I am angry if you don't see that *two* women are at risk here, and both of them are precious to us. I am angry if you buy the simple forms. Battered: to be pitied, supported, held. Batterer: to be shunned, judged, jailed.

Some admire the batterer, I am told. The batterer, they say, is exotic, powerful, erotic. Do women that batter feel erotic and powerful? I can only speak for myself. In that one moment in the early morning light, yes, I felt powerful. In fact, I felt like a god, invincible. Perhaps that was erotic then. I don't remember, although I do remember the heady sense of power. But well before that moment, and ever since, I have lived intimately with shame. I am covered in shame. And it doesn't matter that I am a woman of peace, because I live in shame and I have been silent. And it doesn't matter that I do good works, because I can never be pure again. I answer for my actions every time anyone thinks I have done them wrong. I abase myself. I am covered in shame and want to be whole, and this is the path I walk.

For me, perhaps, it has been a death of the erotic. I don't feel erotic. I don't feel powerful. I am grateful that I feel at all. That I lived to finally tell this, my own story, one woman's story. For others it will be different. We badly need these stories. We need these stories if our communities are to survive, if we are to learn how to deal with anger, with betrayal. If we are truly to learn about forgiveness, learn how and who and when to trust. How to keep our families safe.

■

I was trapped. In those four years so many years ago, this is how it was. I thought it was over. I thought it was resolved, but it wasn't; it could never be over, it kept coming back. Like this: I would remove myself from our heated argument and go to my room. You would follow me. Don't come in, I would say, pleading inside and out. You would come in. I would hold my breath and hold your eyes, fascinated as a mongoose before the snake. You would come in, quietly, your affect would be something like peace. No, not peace. Reason. Reason! We are locked in primal battle, and you come with the sword of reason! I don't believe it. I didn't believe it. What are you doing? This is the calm reason of the torturer, the quiet voice, the cloth over the razor. You enter my den. You walk up to me, huddled in my corner. I try to escape, and you block the door. In the end, I rip you from my door. I grab your arm, I push you, I shove you. You resist. I make you leave my door. I pull you away from my door. I hurl you from my door, hurting you. I run away.

You run after me. Do I want you to run after me? Yes. No. No!

Yes! . . . I don't want to leave you, I love you. Yes. Please. Take me back, take me back. I don't want to leave you.

How many victims figure in this story? And victims of what? And how many perpetrators?

Why didn't I leave/I bore witness

Why didn't I leave/It wasn't mine to do

Why didn't I leave/To force you to be honest

Why didn't I leave? Because my love didn't leave, and I didn't know about safety. I didn't know I could leave you to save myself. I thought the only way to be honest was to stay to bear witness, to stay until you left.

Why didn't I leave? Because, I think, I believed it would change, because I believed you would love me. Because I believed you would see me. Because I believed you would see yourself.

I didn't leave because I thought it was more important to bear witness than to care for the living, to be kind, to myself, to you. Because I had not learned, yet, those important lessons, that in the end it is kindness that will save us. And now I have survived to tell about it.

Why didn't I leave?

Looking Forward

■ DEBORAH BOWEN, DIANE POWERS AND
■ HEATHER GREENLEE

Lesbian Health Research
Perspectives from a Research Team

The authors work together on a breast cancer risk counseling study for lesbians at the Fred Hutchinson Cancer Research Center in Seattle. Deborah Bowen is a behavioral scientist at the Fred Hutchinson Cancer Research Center and an associate professor in the Department of Psychology at the University of Washington. She holds a doctoral degree in health psychology. Diane Powers, a project manager at the Fred Hutchinson Cancer Research Center, holds a master's degree in applied psychology. Heather Greenlee, a field representative at the Fred Hutchinson Cancer Research Center, holds a bachelor's degree in anthropology. What follows is an excerpt from on ongoing discussion on lesbian health research. It includes their initial entry into research, doing lesbian research in a biomedical institution and funding lesbian health research.

Diane: I first became interested in research when I was an undergraduate and took some classes that involved very classic behaviorist research with pigeons. When I was in graduate school I had the opportunity to do some qualitative research that looked at the experiences of forgiving another person. I was really excited about doing research that was relevant to people's lives, but the opportunities were limited as the focus of my graduate program was training psychotherapists.

Deborah
Bowen, Diane
Powers and
Heather
Greenlee

■

300

Because I am a lesbian and have an interest in the well-being of lesbians and gay men, I did my clinical training at Seattle Counseling Service for Sexual Minorities, a mental health agency that serves the lesbian and gay community. After a number of years working solely as a clinician, I'm excited to be doing research again, because it can make a positive difference in the health and well-being of other lesbians.

Deb: I've always been a pretty curious person. In college, I realized that doing research was a way to ask questions that got me out of my own experience and helped me to understand the experiences of other people. I like the parts of a research career and an academic career that allow me to ask questions and explore the answers, figure out what they mean and then go on and ask the next question. I like finding out answers in a way that balances the subjective and objective views of the world. I've been interested in and have done a lot of women's health research, but this has been my first experience doing lesbian health research, primarily because there weren't any opportunities in my graduate program or in my academic position to do that kind of research.

Heather: Since I was a kid I've also been interested in asking questions and figuring out the answers. My specific interest in women's health research came into focus when I was in college. In one of my anthropology classes, we read a book that explains in detail how traditional Western medicine has a really warped idea of women, their bodies and treatment of them. I was just coming out as a lesbian and started to read the history of how lesbians have been mistreated by the medical and psychological fields. This made me really angry.

One of my personal solutions was to get involved with current research that was improving how we understand women's health in general, and lesbian health specifically. I found a local research project that was interviewing lesbians with life-threatening illnesses. They asked me to analyze part of their data. At first I was really excited about working on the project, but then I started seeing problems with the structure of the study. The researchers were straight, they were asking the wrong questions, and they weren't asking for community involvement. When I told them what I thought, they got very defensive and didn't think I was in a position to voice my opinion.

When I graduated, I still wanted to do lesbian health research, but in a more supportive environment. I brought a group of local lesbians together to start a project on interviewing lesbians with cancer. One of those women was Deb. Things snowballed, and now I'm working with both Deb and Diane on a lesbian and bisexual women's study on breast cancer risk. I love it!

Deb: We've managed to form a nucleus of people at our institution who can do this kind of work and are interested in lesbian health research. In the approximate eight years I've been here, we've had very out lesbian and gay faculty, and I think that has played a large role in the research institution's openness. People at the institution understand issues of concern to lesbians and gay men: domestic partnership policies, AIDS and disability policies and other progressive employee policies. I think that the open atmosphere—supported at all levels, from the head of our institution to the head of our cancer prevention group to our co-workers—sets the stage for asking questions about lesbians and about the health of lesbians. We probably wouldn't have been able to do this kind of research here without first having this relative openness.

We have a fellowship program that brings in junior scientists to receive further training in cancer prevention research, both physician and postdoctoral fellows. We have been able to support two lesbians on these fellowships, and both of them have been interested in doing lesbian health research. Because of support at all levels, from the human resources department through the

Deborah
Bowen, Diane
Powers and
Heather
Greenlee

■

302

scientific group at the research institution, to having the right people in place at the right time, we've been able to form a group that will continue lesbian health research.

We wrote our first proposal to study four separate issues in lesbian health. It wasn't funded, but the idea led to a conference sponsored by the Community Liaison Group within the research institution. The conference brought scientists and staff together with community leaders and members of the lesbian community to discuss lesbian research opportunities and future collaborative efforts in lesbian health research. The conference achieved its goals, in that it showed the community that the institution was willing and interested in doing lesbian research, and showed the research institution that lesbians were willing to sit down and talk with an institution from the dominant culture. It was a pivotal event in forming a working group around lesbian health.

We began some research in breast cancer risk information provision to family members of breast cancer patients and realized we needed some extra funding to particularly study lesbians. That led us to apply for funding from the National Institutes of Health (NIH) and the Office of Research on Women's Health. That support was the final factor in forming a group of people with the skills, training, background and motivation to do lesbian health research.

Diane: That's a good overview of how we got where we are, the historical steps that led to the opportunity we have to do lesbian research about breast cancer risk, but that summary made it sound as if it were easy.

Deb: You're right. That overview smoothed over all the problems we ran into: people who are homophobic, review teams that are homophobic, people who wonder why we would bother to study lesbians at all. We've also run into lesbian community members who don't trust us.

One of the difficulties in doing lesbian research is finding the resources. A lot of the grant sources that traditionally fund lesbian activities don't necessarily fund biomedical health research. So, we turn to more traditional biomedical funding agencies. The biggest one, of course, is NIH, and they don't give money for lesbian research either, for several reasons.

Since we don't have a national sex survey that has appropriate sampling methods, we don't know how many lesbians there are in the United States. When you try to convince a review group about the importance of research on a given population, somewhere along the line you need to say, "And they are this much of the general population, and that is a big enough group to focus money and research on." We can't quite do that yet in the lesbian health field, and that holds us back. Given that the conservative right is slowly chipping away at the 10 percent figure, and more recent nonpopulation-based but nonetheless existing surveys have come up with prevalence figures of 1.5 and 2 percent of the population, we end up not being able to convince review groups that there are enough lesbians to bother spending money on.

Diane: Do you think that politics plays a role, too? I'm thinking of the National Endowment for the Arts. It seems that anything that deals with sex or is considered by conservative forces in Congress to be outside the mainstream is under fire. Congress is reluctant to give federal money to anything that could be seen as offensive by conservative groups. Do you think that plays into it?

Deb: I think it does in two ways. One is direct heterosexism, and one is covert heterosexism, which I think we deal with a lot now. The more bigots you have at any level of the review process, the less likely you are to get funded. That's the NEA route. People like Helms and other far right/new right folks consciously attack funding for issues, whether it be in art or science, that are gay

Deborah
Bowen, Diane
Powers and
Heather
Greenlee

■

304

or progressive. Covert heterosexism is a little harder to combat, because the target is a bit more amorphous. Review committee members say that there are not enough lesbians or that lesbians are not different from heterosexual women because they want to downplay the importance of lesbians and the need for attention to lesbian issues. This covert heterosexism is harder to fight because it is not outright bigotry.

When we submitted our initial lesbian health grant, I called the project officer, who is the administrator at the National Institutes of Health who coordinates the review. I offered, as did folks at NIH, to produce names of experts in lesbian health because we wondered if that type of expertise was available on the review committee. We offered to give names and curriculum vitaes of people with expertise in lesbian health who would be able to scientifically evaluate the merit of the grant. The project officer became extremely upset and said, "How dare you accuse me of bigotry?" and "How dare you accuse us of providing biased reviews?" Actually, that wasn't my intent at all.

NIH published the names of the members of the review team, and we didn't recognize a single name as being an expert in women's health, disadvantaged health issues, lesbian health or the like. We were offering to provide expertise in an area that had perhaps never been reviewed by this committee, and the project officer wouldn't listen to either the person from NIH or myself and wouldn't let us help him provide appropriate reviewers. So there may not be reviewers who have a knowledge base to review lesbian health grants. And of course nobody wants to hear they are not able to review lesbian health grants because they might be accused of bigotry. So you are stuck. You need somebody at the NIH who can help these reviews along by saying, "Gosh, I don't know anything about lesbian health," and not be threatened or worried that you are trying to smear them. It is not just an issue of knowledge either. Lesbian and gay rights and lesbian and gay health are not easily discussed, so you end up not even being able to improve the situation on some sort of reasonable basis.

Diane: So, what happened when you got the reviews back?

Deb: The reviewers had a very difficult time, not so much understanding the design of the four studies we had proposed, but
understanding why we would want to bother studying lesbian
health in the first place. Again because of the perception that the
lesbian population is too small to bother studying, too small
to make it worthwhile to put government money into lesbian-
specific public health issues. We try to tease out how much of a
review is heterosexist bias, how much is ignorance and how much
is accurate and constructive scientific feedback that we can use
in putting together our next grant. One of the things we read between the lines was that people simply don't know how to talk
about lesbians and lesbian health. They don't even know how to
frame the questions, so they avoid it. In that review, we sensed
a lot of "I don't want to deal with this stuff. We don't even understand why you are dealing with this issue, so we are refusing
your grant, partly because of the scientific issues in each of the
four studies, but also because we don't want to touch the whole
issue."

We realized we have to do a lot of background work, internal
work at the NIH and background work with the committee to get
one of our grants funded, because the reviewers will not necessarily be informed about or even sympathetic to why the issue is
important. We have to do a lot more homework with the review
committee, by writing all kinds of grants that use the word lesbian and have lesbians in them and by reiterating why lesbians
would be important to study, before we assume that a good grant
will get us funded.

Diane: It wasn't very long ago that this same attitude was taken
about women's health in general. The common attitude was that

Deborah
Bowen, Diane
Powers and
Heather
Greenlee

■

306

women's health was not substantially different from men's health. When women objected to being excluded from health research, the response was that the research being done with men could be applied to women, too. Researchers said they were excluding women only because it was simpler, but that the research results were valid for both men and women. It seems some of that is coming into play here. In the same way that women were told that their health needs were no different from men's, lesbians are being told that their health needs can't possibly be different from those of heterosexual women.

Deb: That is a good point. The history of lesbian health research in some ways parallels the history of women's health research and the history of minority health research. When you have a dominant culture and almost all research is done on that dominant culture—in this case, the culture of white male heterosexual health—then anything that deviates from the dominant culture, that normative perspective you have set up, is less important and less able to be discussed. As the newest kids on the block, I think we have had to do that for women and people of color, and we are having to do that for lesbians. I think there are a lot of parallels.

Heather: Deb, knowing that we face so many difficulties in getting lesbian health research grants funded, why is it important to get NIH funding rather than to go out and do this research on our own?

Deb: I've learned in doing research that you can work on a shoestring budget, but good research—good design, careful methodology—often costs money. I've seen projects where the proportion of quality improved dramatically when more money was put into them, when money was invested in doing good methodology and in having an effective computer tracking system, in doing all the things we want to do when we do good research. NIH provides something like 80–90 percent of the research funding in this country, and the United States is relatively flush with research money compared to other countries. To solve some of the problems we have had in lesbian health research we need to get research funding to do good, solid, methodologically sound studies. I think that is the next step, and I think it will solve a lot of the sampling problems we have had to date in the field.

Diane: Is it true that the majority of lesbian health research done so far has been either unfunded or underfunded? What problems has that created?

Deb: I think the lesbian health pioneers in the 1980s—Mays and Cochran, Stevens and Hall, Ryan and Bradford, all the folks who did early lesbian health research—probably were underfunded. Nobody then was giving out $100,000 grants to do lesbian health research, so they probably did it very much on a shoestring budget. Research was done by word of mouth: You and twenty of your best friends got folks together and did a survey. That those surveys exist is somewhat of a miracle given the climate at that time and given that nobody was thinking about lesbian health research at the NIH.

Those surveys were critical in understanding what lesbian health is and could be, but I think the sample was incredibly biased. For example, if you get most of your subjects in bars, because that is where surveys could be easily handed out to three or four hundred lesbians at a time, then you may have a sample of people who drink alcohol in larger amounts than the general population of lesbians might. So when you see rates of alcoholism among lesbians set at 40–50 percent and rates of alcohol consumption set at 70–90 percent, you should wonder if that is true or a result of the way the information was collected.

The National Lesbian Health Survey, which surveyed lesbians

Deborah
Bowen, Diane
Powers and
Heather
Greenlee

■

308

and women who came to music festivals and national marches, showed alcohol consumption rates of about 10 percent. So when you compare not only the high rates of drinking among lesbians in the early surveys to the rates of heterosexual women, but also to the two lesbian surveys and find such a disparate prevalence, you wonder, "Who are we getting in our surveys, and what is the 'real' or 'true' rate of drinking and alcohol consumption?" The answer is critical is because these kinds of risk factors are measured to understand a population's risk of, say, breast cancer. If we don't know the risk factor prevalence, we can't begin to judge a population's risk. If we could prove that lesbians were at higher risk for breast cancer, we could loosen up moneys to research that issue and to provide services, but we can't loosen up the money until we come up with the documentation, and we can't come up with the documentation until we get a representative sample of lesbians, meaning one from which we can generalize to the whole population of lesbians in the United States. We don't have that yet.

Diane: Are any researchers around the country moving in that direction?

Deb: I don't know of any plans for surveys, but I do know that folks have been talking about better methodology. The Office for Research on Women's Health tried to put together a working group on methodologies in lesbian health last year. I think that the Lesbian Health Research Institute (July 1996) will bring together the right people—lesbians who have been thinking about this. Again, it will take hard work to get somebody to fund such a survey, because good methodology is very expensive. We've got to work on the problem of bothering to do lesbian health research at all before we get to the question, "How can we get a better representative sample?"

I think some of the data collected in the Women's Health Ini-

tiative (WHI) might help us as well. The WHI is the largest research project ever done—largest in terms of number of people
and largest in terms of money spent on a research project. The
WHI recruits women in forty-five clinical centers around the
country to answer some pretty fundamental questions about
women's health, and we thought, as we were designing the WHI
questionnaire battery, that we really ought to include a measure
of sexual orientation. This would be a golden opportunity to look
at lesbian health if we included a measure of sexual orientation.
So the behavioral committee, composed of the behavioral scientists from the key clinical centers, drafted questions and worked
through the larger steering committee to get them approved.

It was a pretty bloody battle: Reaction ran the gamut from
"Why bother studying lesbians, they are just like heterosexual
women?" to "I wouldn't ask my wife these questions, so I'm not
going to ask my participants these kinds of questions." Again, it
took people on the inside of the WHI, people in the NIH who put
pressure on other NIH officials, grassroots folks who wrote letters and folks from the National Center for Lesbian Rights, the
National Lesbian and Gay Health Association and others to write
letters and put pressure on the NIH. It took a combined effort to
get two simple questions about sexual behavior and current and
past sexual behavior of the participants on the questionnaire. The
fear was that the presence of those questions would make the
participants throw out the whole questionnaire and drop out of
the WHI project. That was a completely unfounded fear. As it
turns out, those questions are not a problem: Almost everybody
answers them.

Now that we have these questions in place, we will be able to
look at a less biased sample of lesbians and heterosexual women
and compare their risk factors for breast cancer. That will really
set us forward in lesbian health and in trying to discover whether
or not lesbians have a higher risk for breast cancer.

Deborah
Bowen, Diane
Powers and
Heather
Greenlee

■

310

Diane: The WHI questionnaire may make it easier for future researchers to include sexual orientation questions in national studies. If they get the argument that the questions are too offensive, they can refer to the response to the WHI.

It would be exciting if sexual orientation would become a standard demographic question like income or race. These beginning battles may help pave the way to that goal.

But, in addition to convincing the NIH and our research colleagues of the importance of lesbian health research, we also need to convince the lesbian community. There may be a tendency to draw conclusions from our own and our friends' experiences, and to interpret those observations as global truths, when they may not be. We need to convince the lesbian community as much as the scientific community that we have to do research to really understand what lesbian health is, where the needs are and how lesbians are different.

Deb: Lesbians need to hear that we must have a knowledge base to convince biomedical institutions that they have to pay attention to lesbian health issues. Scientific and medical communities look at data, and on the basis of data, they make decisions. If there is no data on lesbian health, or if there is limited or perhaps biased data on lesbian health, then we don't have the support to argue for particular services or treatments or public health prevention activities.

Heather: When we hosted the Cancer and Cancer Risks Among Lesbians Conference in December 1994, I wrongly assumed that the women who attended would be just as excited as we were. Throughout the conference, however, there was a definite sense of mistrust. The women wanted to know if there was any possible way for lesbian health research to be used against lesbians. Given the history of lesbian interactions with the health care field, that mistrust is understandable; but, I thought that because we are lesbians and we are the ones who are going to do the research, that we would be trusted in a way that other researchers aren't. I was wrong.

We were continually questioned of whether we were telling the whole truth and whether we were too biased because we were a part of the research institution. They questioned whether we would just repeat truths we heard in the system without really thinking about them, and they questioned whether we would be honest with them. I think this is probably a very functional concern in an oppressed community that continually doubts what it's told by members of the mainstream community or dominant culture. At the conference, this concern was something we had to keep working around, because it was obvious that the community members didn't trust us, although we weren't completely part of the dominant culture because we were working as lesbians.

As lesbian researchers, we got caught in the middle. We were in a no-woman's-land between the mainstream biomedical institute where we work and the people from our community. We had to explain why we were trying to serve as a link. There was distrust from both sides: The institute was saying, "Why do you need to do this research in the first place? Why do you need to bring these people to the research institution?" And the people from the community were saying, "Why do you need to bring us to this institute? Why do you want us here? What is our community going to get out of this? How is this going to be used against us?"

Diane: I think the community members saw how the research institution could benefit from their participation, but not how they could benefit. That may go back to that desire to jump right into programs or public health interventions without first getting a solid understanding of the issues and needs. A lot of the community members were community activists, and maybe some of that comes from being an activist. You want to get out and be active. I think they could clearly see the benefit to us but were

Deborah
Bowen, Diane
Powers and
Heather
Greenlee

■

312

skeptical of the benefit of research to them.

Heather: The roots of this mistrust are understandable because many lesbians have encountered extreme homophobia in the area of health care. When lesbians have encounters with homophobic providers, it feeds a general distrust of all medical professionals. For example, many of us have experienced our partners not being recognized by health care professionals in the same way that a spouse is, as an important source of support and an integral part of our lives.

Diane: There is also a long history of heterosexist bias in the delivery of health care. When most health care providers ask a woman if she is currently sexually active, they really want to know if she is sexually active with men. If a woman says "yes" but doesn't offer the information that she is a lesbian, the assumption is that she has sexual intercourse with men. If this isn't clarified during the interview, the health care provider may make erroneous judgments about her health care and risk for various diseases based on heterosexist assumptions.

Heather: At the Cancer and Cancer Risks Among Lesbians Conference, a lot of lesbians, including many lesbian health care providers, were not aware that mammography techniques have improved to the point that only a very small amount of radiation is involved, so small that it poses no real risk. A myth that came up consistently was that mammography causes breast cancer. Some women didn't want to get them, and some providers said they can't or won't recommend getting a mammogram to their patients. So, there is a direct distrust of the effects of biomedical screening techniques on health.

Overall, though, the conference was quite a powerful experience, and I think people were able to take home some useful information, ideas and agendas. One of my favorite aspects of the conference was listening to women talk about the prevalence of "alternative" forms of medicine within the lesbian community. Many attendees, including myself, prefer to use more holistic and so-called alternative modes of healing. Because there is so much distrust of mainstream organizations within the lesbian community, many lesbians have turned to alternative health care as a mode of care that meets more of their needs. Women at the conference wanted to see mainstream medical research recognize the benefits of alternative medicine and funnel funds to research on holistic cancer treatments. Some of us who have studied alternative medicine are interested in studying ways of creating bridges between alternative medicine and Western medicine.

Deb: This idea of bridging is visionary, but I don't think it happens very much, and I don't think the lesbian community has seen it happen. For example, a friend of mine has had cancer and has had to sift through the treatment options in the dominant culture—mastectomy, chemotherapy, radiation—and in the alternative culture—fasting, micronutrient sorts of treatments and so on. The idea of using both types of treatments doesn't receive much support anywhere: Western medicine (or allopathic) folks completely dismiss the idea that these "natural" or "alternative" or nonallopathic methods can work, partly because of bias and partly because, in general, the nonallopathic treatments don't come through the traditional paths of research that the decisions of allopathic medicine are based on. The nonallopathic medicine folks are in some ways equally resistant to bringing in allopathic treatments or joining forces with allopathic medicine. They feel they are going to get swamped or overruled, and that their treatments won't work in the presence of allopathic treatments. That may be true, but it leaves a community who is very interested in the alternative, nondominant culture forms of healing confused at best.

I had a friend who died of breast cancer recently who struggled

Deborah
Bowen, Diane
Powers and
Heather
Greenlee

■

314

with this for the year and a half after she was diagnosed. She had a relatively late stage breast cancer, and she decided she was not going to have a mastectomy, but was going to use fasting and micronutrient sorts of treatment: The cancer had already metastasized and had spread to her lymph system and other organ systems. An oncologist at the research institution talked to her and convinced her at least to get a mastectomy. Her allopathic physician and her naturopath made very little attempt to work together to try to help her. The tug of war began immediately upon diagnosis and left her to wade through Medline (which she was not trained to do) trying to make sense of the information by herself instead of with a team or group interested in her health who would try to do the best they could by merging fields.

So the bridge idea is visionary, but it doesn't generally happen. The lesbian community is often left rejecting allopathic medicine, and I'm not sure that is the wisest choice. The conference was a microcosm of that dilemma—that a community that is not from the dominant culture and has been a victim of oppression and bias tends toward nondominant culture forms of healing, and sometimes that is not in its best interest.

Diane: Part of the problem is that while the medical establishment is duking it out with the alternative health folks, each side trying to exclude the other, their patients just want help with their health problems. I noticed, both at the conference and elsewhere, that most lesbians take a practical approach. They feel that neither side has all the answers, and they don't really care as much about the philosophical arguments or who creates a blend or how that happens, but just want to know what choices are out there and what works and what doesn't.

Deb: One of the difficulties of being a lesbian in a biomedical institution is that, by their nature, biomedical research institutions are part of mainstream medicine, and mainstream medicine is very conservative. It is cautious, and it requires proof, which is a reasonable requirement, but that means new ideas are not adopted easily. In addition, biomedical research is part of the medical-industrial complex, and so it is very conservative. There is a huge amount of money involved, corporate money in addition to research money. I think a lot of the same forces that drive a very conservative culture drive a very conservative field. Being a sexual minority in mainstream medicine is a bit like being a fish out of water. In some ways the two cultures don't mix at all. That makes it hard to get lesbian health research accepted; it also makes it hard on a daily or hour-by-hour basis to be just who you are in an institution that in some ways denies who you are.

Diane: Another factor is that the research institution also relies on donations from the community, so I think it operates with an eye to not offending the community, wanting to make sure there is a positive image—whatever that means.

Deb: Part of it is money, but part of it is that we do research with the public, and so, even if people don't give the institution money, they give it their time in the form of research participation. The argument goes like this: If the research institution was seen as sort of a "lesbian haven," then maybe people would hesitate to become associated with it as part of a research study. The institution, therefore, wouldn't be able to do the research with real people in real-life situations. Therefore, we would not be able to answer the important public health questions we want to answer. So it is partly money, but it is also the reputation of the research institution in the community. There is no evidence of a negative effect on the institution by including lesbians in research. Therefore, we have to work to convince the institutional leaders of the value of doing so.

Another difficulty is that research and biomedical institutions are hierarchical. Science lives and breathes by hierarchies of

Deborah
Bowen, Diane
Powers and
Heather
Greenlee

■

316

people and ideas. When you try to apply some sort of feminist process to this work, you end up running up against the hierarchical system of the institution. I think all three of us have struggled with that a bit. When you try to work more collectively, without such power dynamics, you interact with the research institution system and your ideals begin to break down. You end up not being able to work in a more egalitarian, feminist fashion. You have to mold yourself to the perspective of the institution.

It's also hard to work back and forth on an equal basis among people with different knowledge bases. When people don't all know the same things, the knowledge differences can lead to power differences. Power and knowledge hierarchies at the research institution make it difficult for a lesbian who wants to include feminist ideals in the way she works.

Diane: I agree. I had never been a manager before I came to the research institution, and since coming here I've taken a lot of the management classes, which have been excellent and really helpful for me. Some of them have been fairly visionary, including one class that used a text that drew from the principles of quantum theory, but still there is a feeling of traditional systems of hierarchy. Deb and I have always been committed to creating a working environment among our research group that is as feminist as possible within a major biomedical research institution. I think most of the time this works really well. Everyone is expected to contribute their particular expertise, knowledge, experiences and personal strengths to the group's efforts without much concern for what their job title is.

We also try to work very collaboratively, with consensus as a goal. One example is a booklet on breast cancer risk that our research group wrote. Everyone in our group comes from a different training background and position within the study. During the creation of the booklet, all members of the team, from the scientists and medical experts to myself, the study manager, and

Heather, who at that time was the project's administrative assistant, contributed substantially to the writing, design and layout of the booklet based on our areas of knowledge and interest. Heather did quite a bit of the initial writing, adapting complicated medical language into a more accessible form, explaining risk and designing graphics to illustrate the points of the group. The group members then jumped in and contributed their own particular expertise and ideas for making the booklet better. We spent several months revising, rewriting and always going back to the group for input. It was impossible to come to complete consensus, so Deb had to take the last remnants of conflicting feedback and make some decisions about the best direction to go. Even though the approach we took meant more work for everyone, I think everyone agrees that the booklet is better than it would have been otherwise and that we all feel we were able to contribute as much as we wanted regardless of job title.

Heather: As a person with a job that the research institution hierarchy views as a support position, I feel fortunate to be able to reap the benefits of working in a system where Deb and Diane are trying create a nonhierarchical environment. This supportive and creative environment makes my job more rewarding and makes me want to put more effort into it. I really don't have to deal with the rigid hierarchy. On the other hand, I see Deb and Diane trying to interface our island of nonhierarchy with the existing hierarchical structure. I see this when you deal with other faculty members, project managers and the administration. You have to switch back and forth between people who want to work in a nonhierarchical setting and people who don't believe in that at all.

Deb: I am pretty vulnerable when I try to switch back and forth between two worlds. It gets to me faster than anything else. I try to keep some kind of separation between the two worlds, but I can't. I make mistakes in each because I bring pieces back and

Deborah
Bowen, Diane
Powers and
Heather
Greenlee

■

318

forth. It's like time travel in science fiction. I can't keep the two worldviews apart. I can't keep a more egalitarian, open, respectful mindset when I work in a hierarchical setting where things are very competitive and brutal. I think it is very difficult not just for lesbians but for all women to work through emotional issues as well as scientific issues. It is almost impossible at a biomedical institution because emotion is not the currency of dialogue. The currency is competition and productivity and how much money have you brought in and how many papers have you published. There is no attending to any sort of larger or different perspective.

My first years here were very different. It was my first job after graduate school, and there were times when I thought I really wouldn't make it—"make it" meaning stick around and continue doing the kind of research I wanted to do. There are folks in pockets that are, even at places like the research institution, very conservative and will stop at nothing to interfere with your professional life and your personal life if your belief systems clash with theirs.

When I first came here, I worked for a person who had beliefs that were very right-wing and very antilesbian. I don't think he knew I was a lesbian, and I didn't know what his beliefs were when we began working together, but after two years our differences were pretty obvious. He spent the next year trying to fire me or get the director to fire me or at least undermine my position to the extent that I couldn't work anymore at the research institution. He didn't succeed because I switched to another work group and found people who were interested in the same type of science I was interested in and would be supportive of who I was while we were working toward a more common scientific goal. My first position was a pretty dangerous place to be in the beginning, and that type of experience is probably not uncommon for lesbians when a policy and track record of inclusiveness doesn't exist in the workplace.

Diane: It's great to work in a group where I'm not the only lesbian. At some meetings, the majority of us sitting around the table are lesbians, and that's a real different experience. It's nice not to be isolated or put on display as the token homo.

Heather: As I said earlier, when I was in school, I was studying lesbian health and wanted to pursue this into a graduate program. One of my advisors told me I shouldn't because my topic of interest was "too close to home." I was told I wouldn't be able to offer a comprehensive analysis of what was going on in the lesbian community because I myself was a lesbian and my bias would taint my work making it worthless. Now I'm working on a funded lesbian-specific project, both of my supervisors are lesbians, and we are doing "good" science. This climate is much more welcoming, open and comfortable. That advisor was obviously wrong.

Deb: A feminist analysis would be that no one can be objective. Objectivity is in the eye of the beholder. Philosophers have talked about that for the last twenty or thirty years. In fact, being a lesbian has advantages in doing lesbian research. A junior fellow here is a lesbian and is trying to decide how "out" to be as she applies for academic jobs. Unfortunately, I think she may be subjected to real bias in academic settings if she puts lesbian health research on her vitae. I think the academy hasn't really accepted women's studies and lesbian health research for example; it is still very conservative and very competitive and very tight, and it doesn't easily open up to lesbians as an "out" group.

There may be a danger professionally to getting pigeonholed. In a place like the research institution, you rely on collaborations with colleagues, even unfriendly collaborations, but you rely on working with other people on grants and on having collaborators working with you on your grants. There is always the danger that people will simply not work with you anymore. I don't think that

Deborah
Bowen, Diane
Powers and
Heather
Greenlee

■

320

has happened at the research institution since starting the lesbian research track, but at other academic institutions it could be a problem.

Heather: Where do you see us going over the next few years? Will we be able to continue doing lesbian health research—asking the types of questions we want to ask and working in a feminist environment?

Deb: As long as there are questions to ask and answer about lesbians' health we will try to continue doing that. Diane has already mentioned one goal: to include sexual orientation in standard demographic questions on all surveys and research projects. We will soon have the data to identify good inclusive questions that measure our current definition of sexual minority. We will encourage our colleagues to use these questions in their research projects, as a normal part of asking about a person's background. That way, we can learn about lesbians at every opportunity. I think we have to be open to the idea that the construct of "lesbian" when narrowly defined as a woman who defines herself as a lesbian, is not perhaps as useful as a broader understanding of sexual orientation.

We also need to tackle the issue of breast cancer risk among lesbians. Data from national studies will help us there. We need to figure out if lesbians have a higher risk for breast cancer as a group than heterosexual women, and why. We need then to figure out what to do about it.

A third activity for us is to continue figuring out how to work together in a way that enriches our lives as lesbians. This is difficult to do in the best of times in this country, but even harder in a world like the biomedical research institute. There are ethical and moral issues that can become clearer when one is a lesbian, and we could use these to inform our questions and our relationships. This is a difficult task, but one that we must try to accomplish.

NANCY A. BROWN

Finding Health Information

Might it be that the more health information women
acquire the more power they have and their greater
their authority over their own bodies?

—Janice L. Nusbaum, *My Body: Women*
Speak Out About Their Health Care

The 1990s are being hailed as the beginning of the Information
Age. The Internet is linking millions of people worldwide and
making vast amounts of information available at a keystroke,
including health information. You can even "see" a physician
electronically: A site on the World Wide Web provides a second-
opinion medical consultation, a written report based on information entered on an online questionnaire. Resources on the World
Wide Web (which, unlike the text-only gopher[1] Internet resources,
also offers graphics, sound and video) grow exponentially every
day. Attempts to catalog these resources are underway, but the
task is overwhelming. You may find that minutes quickly become

hours as you search for online health information.

Searching through print information can be no less daunting. Health information in print comprises everything from peer-reviewed scholarly medical journals to women's magazines at the grocery store checkout counter. Whether you're looking for health information on the Internet or in a bookstore or library, here are several questions to keep in mind: How do I decide if this information is valid? How do I know the person providing it is reliable? Is this information the most current available? Too much is at stake—our physical and emotional health—to blindly accept what we read and hear about health care issues. Even if we do our own research, the answers may not be clear. It is not uncommon to read of major clinical trials or academic research studies that contradict each other. Is estrogen a factor in breast cancer or not? Is caffeine really bad for you, or is it harmless if drunk in moderation? Finding the answers for ourselves can be a bewildering process when those who are supposed to know cannot seem to agree.

Where do we start this research process? What kind of information can we expect from our health care providers? Where can we find health information easily and inexpensively? The following sections answer some of these questions and direct you to sources you may not have known about.

Background

Peruse any large bookstore and you'd find several shelves of books devoted to women's health. This is a recent phenomenon. In 1973, *Our Bodies, Ourselves* by the Boston Women's Health Book Collective was the first book written by women to frankly examine women's health issues—it even included a chapter on lesbians. Until very recently, health researchers paid scant attention to women's health. Women were (and still are) often patronized by male physicians, their questions and concerns frequently discounted or ignored. Most health research projects (led by men) used men as their subjects, and the results were assumed to apply to women. Thus, there was little published literature specifically on women's health. Women's physiology and emotional and mental health, much less possible differences for lesbians and women of color, were not being addressed.

With increasing demands from feminist activists over the past thirty years, health care providers and health researchers have begun to pay more attention to the particular health issues of women. The National Institutes of Health (NIH) is funding research in women's health, resulting in more published literature, and women of color are being recognized as having their own health issues. Over the past decade, many women have entered the health care field in all specialties of traditional and alternative medicine, providing the consumer with more opportunity to find women, and even lesbian, providers. Finally, women activists are demanding and developing funding, support and information on health issues that affect women, including breast cancer, heart disease, HIV and drug abuse.

While attitudes toward health care for women in general have changed, the situation for lesbians today is much the same as before. In the past, lesbian patients were rarely able to come out, fearing homophobic reactions from their usually male physicians. There was the added stress of being assumed heterosexual and treated accordingly. A 1992 review of lesbian health care from 1970 to 1990 found that not much changed: Lesbians questioned on the quality of their health care over those years still found themselves marginalized and ignored, and many times their health care providers focused more on a "cure" for their lesbianism than their original complaint.[2] The author concluded that health care providers need to be educated about lesbians as health care consumers. A 1995 study found that, unfortunately, a high proportion of lesbians still do not seek health care because of previous homophobic reactions from health care providers.[3]

Our Rights as Patients

What does all this mean for lesbians wishing to find health information? There's good news and bad news. The increase in information for women in general makes it likely you'll find what you're looking for on specific women's health issues walking into a library or bookstore. The bad news is, not surprisingly, you won't find much on lesbian health issues. It's the old Catch 22: Rigorous scientific studies require a large number of people to validate their findings; therefore not much will be published on lesbian health issues until more lesbians come out to their providers with their specific problems. But, lesbians will not be willing to come out to their providers until there is a safe, comfortable atmosphere in which to do so.

This requires that we be our own advocates in seeking (and sometimes demanding) health care information from our providers. Who has not had the experience of walking out of a physician's office feeling frustrated, feeling as if you were rushed through the appointment or that you did not get the information you needed to understand your problem? The American Medical Association (AMA) Council on Ethical and Judicial Affairs has published a list of patient's rights that it feels are essential. The first of six rights concerns information:

> The patient has the right to receive information from physicians and to discuss the benefits, risks and costs of appropriate treatment alternatives. Patients should receive guidance from their physicians as to the optimal course of action. Patients also are entitled to obtain copies or summaries of their medical records, to have their questions answered, to be advised of potential conflicts of interest that their physicians might have and to receive independent professional opinions.[4]

Here are a few things you can do to get the information you need from your provider:

1. If possible, find women health care providers who will create a comfortable atmosphere for your coming out as a lesbian and for discussing your health concerns. Many women, lesbian or heterosexual, find it much easier to talk about health problems with another woman. Many urban gay/lesbian organizations provide lists of lesbian and gay health care providers. Word of mouth is often a good source: Ask your friends if they have a provider they can recommend.

2. It is important for lesbians to come out to their health care providers. (Remember, physicians are required to respect patient–physician confidentiality.) It not only gives the provider an important piece of information concerning your care (for example, not having to ask questions about birth control), but makes it more probable you will get the health information you need. If you feel any judgment or homophobia from your provider, try to find another one.

3. If you don't understand, ask questions! Some providers, though skillful with diagnosis and treatment, may lack communication skills. If you are continually put off by your provider and are finding yourself stressed not only from your illness, but from your interactions with your provider, inform her that you will seek another provider unless you can get your questions answered. We have a right as health care consumers to be treated kindly and with patience, whether the provider is an hour behind in her appointments or not.

4. If you are dealing with a traumatic illness and feel you cannot hear what the provider is telling you or are too upset to remember, either tape your session or take a friend with you who can more objectively hear what the provider is saying.

5. Ask your provider if she can recommend any literature or other

resources about your illness. If you read something contrary to what your provider has told you, call and clarify.

6. If your provider has no literature, use one of the methods described in the next section to find your own information, and then discuss it with your provider.

However you find information, make sure it is from a reputable source. There are always people who will try to exploit others' illnesses and anxieties. Advertisements in popular magazines, 800 numbers advertised on television, or online Web pages that promote a quick cure for anything should be suspect. Look for information provided by credentialed authors from reputable organizations or agencies.

Lesbians must learn to be their own best advocates in finding health information. We cannot assume that health care providers will give us all the information we need to stay healthy. The Information Age is beginning to provide myriad ways to educate ourselves about our physical, mental and emotional health. That we as lesbians have to dig a little deeper, try a little harder, is nothing new.

Health Information Resources

Libraries

Public libraries can provide a wealth of free information on women's health. If they do not own the book or magazine you need, they can often get it for you from another library (sometimes for a small fee). Directories of health agencies and organizations are also available. If you do not know where to start looking or are intimidated by computer resources in the library, ask the librarian for help.

Those of you in or near urban areas are in luck. Many large

hospitals and medical centers are opening consumer health libraries as part of their services. Specialty libraries on heart disease, cancer, diabetes and other diseases are not uncommon. Many hospitals across the United States are adopting the Planetree Hospitals' philosophy of consumer-advocated care. Part of that care includes packets of health information from Planetree Resource Centers, which are open to the public. The centers also sponsor lectures and seminars by experts in many areas of health care. Planetree Resource Centers are currently found in San Jose and San Francisco, California; The Dalles, Oregon; Fort Morgan, Colorado; Derby, Connecticut; Seattle, Washington, and Moline, Illinois.

If there is a hospital or medical center in your city, chances are it supports a health sciences library. Smaller rural hospitals are also required to provide some sort of resource for health professionals. Most of these libraries will not allow the public to check out books and materials, but usually allow in-house use for research. Librarians may not be able to do research for you, but will usually point you to the appropriate resources. Access is generally free to major medical databases on easily searchable CD-ROMs. State-funded major medical center libraries are required by law to serve their state's population. Most will charge for librarian-generated database searching, but anyone can use the library and its resources. Call these libraries to find out their public-use policy before venturing a visit.

Organizations and Hot Lines

Many organizations offer free or nominal-cost information on a variety of health subjects. There are few resources specifically for lesbians, so most of the sources listed here are for women in general; gay and/or lesbian resources are asterisked (*). Absence of a particular subject here does not mean a resource does not exist. There are hundreds of organizations covering almost every health issue; unfortunately, all can't be listed. The resources here are meant to give you a starting place and help you think creatively about where you might find other health information. You are your own best detective!

Oftentimes one resource will lead you to another. Ask agencies or organizations you contact if they know of other places to call or if they have free information they can send you. Many of the publications will have references listing more sources of information. Or write the National Health Information Center (NHIC, P.O. Box 1133, Washington, DC 20013-1133) for its free list of toll-free numbers for health and public service organizations.

Phone numbers and addresses have been verified, where possible, as of early 1997. Contact information for some agencies and associations may change when their leadership changes. The general listing is followed by resources specifically for AIDS, alternative health, breast cancer, cancer, disabling conditions and minorities.

General

Al-anon, (800) 344-2666, 8:00 A.M.–6:00 P.M. EST, M–F.

Alcoholics Anonymous (AA) World Services, (212) 870-3400, 8:30 A.M.–4:30 P.M. EST; Spanish Services (212) 964-2560.

Allergy Information Line, (800) 822-2762. Written materials on asthma and allergies; physician referrals. Sponsored by the American Academy of Allergy and Immunology.

Alzheimer's Association, 919 N. Michigan Ave., Suite 1000, Chicago, IL 60611, (800) 272-3900. An information and referral service.

American Association of Retired Persons (AARP) Women's Initiative, 601 E St. NW, Washington, DC 20049, (202) 434-2277.

American Council of the Blind, (800) 424-8666 or (202) 467-5081, fax (202) 467-5085. Information and resource lists on blindness and referrals to rehabilitation organizations, research centers and chapters.

American Heart Association, 7320 Greenville Ave., Dallas, TX 75231. To find a local office, call (800) 242-8721. Free materials on heart disease, risk factors, diet and other information on heart disease.

Arthritis Foundation Information Line, (800) 283-7800. Information about arthritis and referrals to local chapters.

Centers for Disease Control and Prevention (CDC) National Sexually Transmitted Diseases Hotline, (800) 227-8922.

Children of Aging Parents, Woodbourne Office Campus, 1609 Woodbourne Rd., Suite 302A, Levittown, PA 19057, (215) 945-6900. Information on caregiving.

*Community Health Project, 208 West 13th St., New York, NY 10011, (212) 675-3559. Provides a wide range of medical services to gays and lesbians in the New York area. World Wide Web: *http://www.chp-health.org/*

Crohn's and Colitis Foundation of America, Inc., (800) 932-2423, (800) 343-3637 (warehouse) 9:00 A.M.–5:00 P.M. EST. Educational materials on Crohn's disease and ulcerative colitis; referrals to local support groups and physicians.

Depression Awareness, Recognition and Treatment Program, National Institutes of Mental Health, D/ART Public Inquiries, 5600 Fishers Lane, Room 15C-05, Rockville, MD 20857, (301) 443-4513, 8:30 A.M.–4:30 P.M. M–F.

Endometriosis Association, (800) 992-3636. A 24-hour recording; leave name and address to have information sent.

Fibrositis Association, P.O. Box 1483, Dublin, OH 43017, (614) 764-8010. Information on fibrositis or fibromyalgia.

*Gay and Lesbian Medical Association (GLMA), 273 Church St., San Francisco, CA 94114, (415) 255-4547, e-mail *GayLes Med@aol.com*. Referrals to physician members for the public. Publications available, including *Journal of the Gay and Lesbain Medical Association*. World Wide Web: *http://www.glma.org/*

Hearing Helpline, (800) EAR-WELL or (703) 642-0580, 9 A.M.–5 P.M. EST, M–F. Sponsored by the Better Hearing Institute. Information on hearing loss and hearing help. Implements national public information programs on hearing loss and available medical, surgical, hearing aid and rehabilitation assistance for millions with uncorrected hearing problems.

Hysterectomy Education Resources and Services (HERS Foundation), 422 Bryn Mawr Ave., Bala-Cynwyd, PA 19004, (610) 667-7757. Non-profit referral service for women who want to know how to avoid a hysterectomy, find other options or learn of the consequences of a hysterectomy.

Jewish Women International, 1828 L Street NW, Suite 250, Washington, DC 20036, (202) 857-1300. Membership organization that supports Jewish women, children and youth. Material available on health issues.

*Lesbian and Gay Aging Issue Network, American Society on Aging, 833 Market St., Suite 511, San Francisco, CA 94107, (415) 974-9600. Promotes programs and policies to improve the quality of life for older lesbians and gays; newsletter available.

*Lesbian Services/Lesbian Health Clinic, Whitman Walker Clinic, 1407 S St. NW, Washington, DC 20009, (202) 797-3585.

National Arthritis and Musculoskeletal and Skin Diseases Information Clearinghouse, Box AMS, 9000 Rockville Pike, Bethesda, MD 20892, (301) 495-4484, 8:30 A.M.–5:00 P.M. EST. Includes information on osteoporosis.

*National Association for Gay and Lesbian Gerontology, 1290 Sutter St., Suite 8, San Francisco, CA 94109.

National Diabetes Information Clearinghouse (NDIC), 1 Information Way, Bethesda, MD 20892-3560. Information, educational and referral resource for health professionals, people with diabetes and the general public.

National Eating Disorders Organization, 6655 S. Yale Ave., Tulsa, OK 74136, (918) 481-4044.

National Headache Foundation, 5252 N. Western Ave., Chicago, IL 60625, (800) 843-2256. Free information on headache causes and treatment; free newsletter.

National Health Information Center, Referral Specialist, P.O. Box 1133, Washington, DC 20013-1133, (800) 336-4797 or (301) 565-4167, fax (301) 984-4256, e-mail *nhicinfo@health.org*. Helps both professionals and the general public locate health information through identification of health information resources, an information and referral system, and publications. The NHIC staff refer inquiries to the most appropriate resource. They do not diagnose, make referrals to health care professionals or recommend treatment for medical conditions. Publication list is available as well as lists of many other government health information sites on the World Wide Web and a list of toll-free numbers for health information. World Wide Web: http://nhic-nt.health.org/

National Insurance Consumer Helpline, (800) 942-4242, fax (202) 223-7896. Information and answers to questions on life, health, auto and home insurance. Free consumer publications. English- and Spanish-speaking operators.

*National Lesbian and Gay Health Association, 1407 S St. NW, Washington, DC 20009, (202) 939-7880, fax (202) 234-1467. Sponsors a yearly international conference on lesbian and gay health, including HIV/AIDS.

National Mental Health Association, 1021 Prince St., Alexandria, VA 22314, (800) 969-6642, fax (703) 684-5968. Free information on over two hundred mental health topics, including clinical depression, warning signs of illness, and women and stress. Referral service to mental health organizations and providers.

National Multiple Sclerosis Society, (800) FIGHT-MS, fax (212) 986-2981. Twenty-four-hour message line; staff members available from 11:00 A.M.–5:00 P.M. EST, M–Th.

National Osteoporosis Foundation, 2100 M Street NW, Suite 602, Washington, DC 20037, (202) 223-2226.

National Women's Health Network, 1325 G Street NW, Washington, DC 20005, (202) 347-1140.

National Women's Health Resource Center, 2440 M Street NW, Suite 325, Washington, DC 20037, (202) 293-6045.

North American Menopause Society (NAMS), University Hospitals, Dept. of OB/GYN, 2074 Abington Rd., Cleveland, OH 44106, fax (216) 844-3348 (fax written requests for information).

Office of Minority Health Resource Center, P.O. Box 37337, Washington, DC 20013-7337, (800) 444-6472, fax (301) 589-0884, e-mail *info@omhrc.gov*. English- and Spanish-speaking operators available. Information on minority health topics for consumers and health professionals. Materials, referrals and sources for technical assistance. Extensive list of programs and organizations for African Americans, Hispanics, Asians, Native Americans and Pacific Islanders. World Wide Web: http://www.omhrc.gov/

Older Women's League (OWL), 666 11th St. NW, Suite 700, Washington, DC 20001, (202) 783-6686 or (202) 638-2356. National advocacy membership organization dedicated to obtaining social and economic equity for mid-life and older women, with special emphasis on health care, retirement, income, employment and housing. Free and for-purchase materials.

Panic Disorder Information Line, (800) 647-2642, 24-hours/day. Sponsored by the National Institute of Mental Health. Educational materials on panic disorder symptoms, diagnosis, referral and treatment for health care and mental health professionals and the public. Lists of additional resource materials and organizations that can help callers locate a treatment professional. Spanish-speaking operators available.

PMS Access, (800) 222-4767, fax (608) 833-7412. Sponsored by Madison Pharmacy Associates, Inc. Information, literature and counseling on premenstrual syndrome. Referrals to physicians and clinics in the caller's area.

Rural Information Center Health Service, (800) 633-7701, TDD (301) 504-6856. Information and referrals to the public on rural health issues. Free literature searches.

*Senior Action in a Gay Environment (SAGE), 305 7th Ave., 16th Floor, New York, NY 10001-6008, (212) 741-2247. Social services provided by an intergenerational staff of professionals and volunteers: drop-in center, homebound services, socialization and education workshops, services for older people fighting HIV/AIDS.

WHAM (Women's Health Action and Mobilization), P.O. Box 733, New York, NY 10009, (212) 560-7177, e-mail *wham@listproc.net*. Direct action group "committed to demanding, securing and defending absolute reproductive freedom and quality health care for *all* women." Resources available mostly via the Internet: For their online newsletter, send a message on the Internet to *listproc@listproc.net*; leave the subject line blank, and in the body of the message type SUBSCRIBE WHAM [YOUR NAME]. World Wide Web: *http://www.echonyc.com/ ~ wham/*

Women's Health Information Center, Boston Women's Health

Book Collective, 47 Nichols Ave., West Somerville, MA 02172, (617) 625-0271.

Women for Sobriety, P.O. Box 618, Quakertown, PA 18591, (215) 536-8026. Information on self-help groups nationwide.

AIDS

AIDS Information Newsletter, c/o Michael Howe MSLS, Editor, AIDS Information Center, VA Medical Center, San Francisco, CA 94121, (415) 221-4810 x 3305, email: *hivinfo@itsa.ucsf.edu*. Electronic newsletter at *gopher.niaid.nih.gov/* (listed as the "VA AIDS Information Newsletter"). Includes information on women and AIDS.

AIDS Treatment Data Network, (800) 734-7104. Provides treatment counseling and referrals to men, women and children and their care providers. The office is located in New York City.

*Black Gay and Lesbian Leadership Forum, 1219 S. LaBrea Ave., Los Angeles, CA 90019, (213) 964-7820, fax (213) 964-7830. Articulates the voice of the African-American community that is HIV-infected. Support groups, treatment updates, holistic counseling and treatments.

Communicable Diseases Center (CDC) National AIDS Hotline, (800) 342-2437, Spanish (800) 344-7432, TDD (800) 243-7889, 8:00 A.M.–2:00 P.M. EST. Information for the public on prevention and spread of HIV/AIDS, including description information, risks, referrals, publications and more.

*Lesbian AIDS Project (LAP), c/o Gay Men's Health Crisis, 129 West 20th St., New York, NY 10011, (212) 337-3532.

National Native American AIDS Hotline, (800) 283-2437. Sponsored by the National Native American AIDS Prevention Center.

Printed materials and information about AIDS and AIDS prevention in the Native-American community.

National Resource Center on Women and AIDS, Center for Women's Policy Studies, 2000 P St. NW, Suite 508, Washington, DC 20036, (202) 872-1770, 9 A.M.–5:30 P.M. EST, M–F.

Sisterlove, Inc., 1432 Donnelly Ave. SW, Atlanta, GA 30310, (404) 753-7733. Non-profit organization established to provide education and support by women for women who are at risk for or who are already infected with HIV. African-American women receive particular attention within Sisterlove's culturally appropriate programs. Education, housing, support, advocacy and empowerment are provided to women and their families.

Alternative Health

American Association of Naturopathic Physicians, 2366 Eastlake Ave., Suite 322, Seattle, WA 98102, (206) 323-7610. Provides a referral service for physicians in caller's area.

American Chiropractic Association, Information Resource Center, 1701 Clarendon Blvd., Arlington, VA 22209, (800) IRC-8448 or (703) 243-2593, e-mail *AmerChiro@aol.com*. Information free to members; charge for nonmembers.

National Acupuncture and Oriental Medicine Alliance, P.O. Box 77511, Seattle, WA 98177-0531, (206) 524-3511, e-mail *76143.2061@compuserve.com*.

National Association of Acupuncture and Oriental Medicine, 433 Front St., Catasauqua, PA 18032-2506, e-mail *AAAOM1@aol.com*.

■

Breast Cancer Organizations

African-American Breast Cancer Alliance (AABCA), P. O. Box 8981, Minneapolis, MN 55408, (612) 825-3675. Member-supported advocacy group for women with breast cancer, their families and the black community. Extends beyond Minneapolis to include regional and national networks.

Community Breast Health Project, 770 Welch Rd., Suite 370, Palo Alto, CA 94304, (415) 725-1788, 9:00 A.M.–4:00 P.M. PST, M–F, fax (415) 725-5474, e-mail *CBHO@Forsythe.Stanford.edu*. Grass-roots, patient-driven educational resource center for all concerned about breast health and cancer; clearinghouse for information and support, providing newsletter; volunteer opportunities for breast cancer survivors and friends dedicated to help others with the disease. Services are free.

National Alliance of Breast Cancer Organizations, 9 East 37th St., 10th Fl., New York, NY 10016, (800) 719-9154 or (212) 889-0606, fax (212) 689-1213, e-mail *NABCOinfo@aol.com*. Not-for-profit, membership resource that provides individuals and health organizations with accurate, up-to-date information on all aspects of breast cancer, and promotes affordable detection and treatment; networks more than 370 organizations dealing with breast cancer. World Wide Web: *http://www.nabco.org/*

Reach to Recovery, c/o American Cancer Society, 1599 Clifton Rd. NE, Atlanta, GA 30329, (404) 320-3333.

SHARE: Self-Help for Women with Breast Cancer, 19 W. 44th St., No. 415, New York, NY 10036-5902.

Sisters Network, 8787 Woodway Dr., Suite 4207, Houston, TX 77063, (713) 781-0255. African-American breast cancer survivors group that provides emotional and psychological support and a national newsletter; chapters in several states.

Susan G. Komen Breast Cancer Foundation, 5005 LBJ, Suite 370,

Dallas, TX 75244, (800) 462-9273 or (214) 450-1777. Advances research, education, screening and treatment of breast cancer. Information on breast health care and breast cancer.

Y-ME National Breast Organization, 212 W. Van Buren St., Chicago, IL 60607, (800) 221-2141 or (312) 986-8338. Extensive list of medical and support resources nationwide. Resources for women of color, lesbians, older women, economically disadvantaged women, women with disabilities and others with special needs.

Cancer

American Cancer Society, Cancer Helpline, 1599 Clifton Rd. NE, Atlanta, GA 30329, (800) 227-2345 or (301) 929-8243. Publications and information about cancer and coping with cancer. Referrals to local chapters for support services. World Wide Web: *http://www.cancer.org*

Cancer Information Service, (800) 422-6237, 9 A.M.–4:30 P.M., M–F. Sponsored by the National Cancer Institute. Answers cancer-related questions from the public, cancer patients and families, and health professionals. Spanish-speaking operators available.

CANcer Patients ACTion Alliance, 26 College Place, Brooklyn, NY 11201.

National Cancer Institute, Cancer Information Service, 9000 Rockville Pike, Bethesda, MD 20892, (800) 422-6237.

National Coalition for Cancer Survivorship, 1010 Wayne Ave., Silver Spring, MD 20910, (301) 650-8868. Founded to provide psychosocial support for survivors of cancer. Links individuals, organizations and resources, provides a national voice for the media, addresses issues of concern for survivors, and works to reduce cancer-based discrimination in the workplace. Newsletter available.

*National Coalition of Feminist and Lesbian Cancer Projects, c/o The Mautner Project, 1707 L St. NW, Suite 1060, Washington, DC 20026, (202) 332-5536. Dedicated to helping women with cancer, their caregivers and partners in the D.C.-Baltimore area. Sells technical assistance manual ($10) on how to start a similar organization, and presents workshops for and provides information to policymakers.

Disabling Conditions

Handicapped Media, Inc., (800) 321-8708 (Voice/TDD). Provides information, referral services and advocacy.

Health Resource Center, One Dupont Circle NW, Suite 800, Washington, DC 20036-1193, (800) 544-3284 or (202) 939-9320, fax (202) 833-4760, e-mail *heath@ace.nche.edu.* Operates the national clearinghouse on postsecondary education for individuals with disabilities and learning disabilities.

Job Accommodation Network, (800) 232-9675 (Voice/TDD) or (800) 526-7234 (Voice/TDD); in Canada, (800) 526-2252, fax (304) 293-5407. Sponsored by the President's Commission on the Employment of People with Disabilities. Ideas for accommodating disabled persons in the workplace and information on the availability of accommodation aids and procedures. Services available in English, Spanish and French.

Medical Rehabilitation Education Foundation, (800) 368-3513. Medical rehabilitation information and referral service for help in locating reliable rehabilitation facilities throughout the country.

National Clearinghouse on Women and Girls with Disabilities, Educational Equity Concepts, 114 E. 32nd St., Suite 306, New York, NY 10016. National directory of services for women and girls with disabilities.

National Rehabilitation Information Center, (800) 346-2742 (Voice/TDD) or (301) 588-9284 (Voice/TDD), fax (301) 587-1967. Research referrals and information on rehabilitation issues and concerns. Spanish-speaking operators available.

Minority Resources

National Black Women's Health Project (NBWHP), 1237 Ralph David Abernathy Blvd. SW, Atlanta, GA 30310, (404) 758-9590.

National Black Women's Health Project (NBWHP), 1211 Connecticut Ave., Suite 310, Washington, DC 20036, (202) 835-0117, fax (202) 833-8790. Self-help and advocacy membership organization committed to improving the health status of Black women. Free and for-purchase health information materials.

National Caucus and Center on the Black Aged, 1424 K St. NW, Washington, DC 20005.

National Latina Health Organization, P.O. Box 7567, 1900 Fruitvale Ave., Oakland, CA 94601, (510) 534-1362.

National Native American AIDS Hotline, (800) 283-2437. Sponsored by the National Native American AIDS Prevention Center. Printed materials and information about AIDS and AIDS prevention in the Native-American community.

Native American Women's Health Education Resource Center, P.O. Box 572, Lake Andes, SD 57356, (605) 487-7072, fax (605) 487-7964, e-mail *nativewoman@igc.apc.org*. Health education materials for distribution to Native American audiences: reports, posters, pamphlets and videos on several topics, including AIDS, cancer prevention, fetal alcohol syndrome, diabetes and reproductive health. For a publications order form, e-mail *nativewoman@igc.apc.org*. World Wide Web: *http://www.nativeshop.org*.

Office of Minority Health Resource Center, P.O. Box 37337, Washington, DC 20013-7337, (800) 444-6472, e-mail *info@omhrc.gov.* Extensive list of information on subjects such as adolescent health, parenting, urban health and hundreds of agencies for minorities, particularly African Americans, Asians, Hispanics, Native Americans and Native Hawaiians. World Wide Web: *http://www.omhrc.gov/*

Online Resources

Those of you with a computer and modem and access to the Internet will have a never ending source of information, particularly if you have a World Wide Web (WWW) browser. A word of warning, however: Anyone with a computer and an idea about health care can post cures for cancer, the common cold and obesity "available for just $19.95 on your Visa card." Your best bet is to stick with information provided by colleges, universities, hospitals and other well-known health organizations and agencies. Also, check to make sure the information is updated on a regular basis. (As a check, look for a "last updated" notice or a "what's new" area.) Many people post Web pages and then leave them, so the information may not necessarily be current. Common sense is a necessity when searching on the Web.

The following is a small sample of the kinds of information available on the Web. The first three resources are well-known search engines, which provide text word-searching. For instance, if you enter the words "breast cancer," the search engine will list hundreds of sites (Web, gopher and ftp sites) that provide information on breast cancer.

Search Engines

Alta Vista

http://altavista.digital.com

Open Text
http://index.opentext.net/
Click on "Power Search" for more refined searching.

Yahoo!
http://www.yahoo.com/Health

Web Pages

Acupuncture Information: http://www.acupuncture.com/

The Alternative Medicine Homepage
http://www.pitt.edu/ ~ cbw/altm.html

American Association of Naturopathic Physicians (AANP)
http://infinity.dorsai.org/Naturopathic.Physician/
List of naturopathic physicians in the United States, naturopathy in Canada, naturopathic medical schools.

Atlanta Reproductive Health Centre
http://www.ivf.com/index.html

Avon's Breast Cancer Awareness Crusade
http://www.avon.com/about/awareness/frame.html
Dedicated to educating women about breast cancer and, particularly, to providing low-income, minority and older women access to early detection services. List of cancer support groups for each state.

Breast Cancer Information Clearinghouse
http://nysernet.org/bcic/

Cancer Information for Patients
http://www.kumc.edu/service/dykes/RRPAGES/patient/
pcancer.html

Community Breast Health Project
http://www-med.stanford.edu/CBHP

*Community Health Project, New York
http://www.chp-health.org/
Provides a wide range of medical services to gays and lesbians in the New York area.

Food and Nutrition Information Center, National Agricultural Library, Agricultural Research Service, USDA
http://www.nalusda.gov/fnic
Dietary guidelines, food data and much more.

*Gay and Lesbian Medical Association
http://www.glma.org

Infoseek Women's Health Page
http://www.infoseek.com/Health/Womens_Health?tid = 1221/
A directory of women's health issues including abortion, breast cancer, contraception, eating disorders, endometriosis, sexuality, infertility, menopause, pregnancy and childbirth.

Lists About Women's Health
http://umbc7.umbc.edu/ ~ korenman/wmst/f_hlth.html
Comprehensive list of discussion groups available on the Internet.

National Alliance of Breast Cancer Organizations (NABCO)
http://www.nabco.org
List of regional breast cancer support groups for each state, including phone numbers.

National Health Information Center
http://nhic-nt.health.org/
Health information referral service.

Office of Minority Health Resources
http://www.omhrc.gov

OncoLink, the University of Pennsylvania Cancer Resource
http://cancer.med.upenn.edu

Sycamore Sexually Transmitted Diseases Web Page
http://med-www.bu.edu/people/sycamore/std/

Women's Health Interactive
http://www.womens-health.com
For women of all ages who want to learn about diseases, medical conditions or personal development issues that contribute to their quality of life.

WomensNet
http://www.igc.org/igc/womensnet/index.html
A comprehensive resource for women on the Internet; links to lesbian and gay resources, including health, world news and action alerts. Aims to support women's organizations worldwide by providing and adapting telecommunications technology to enhance their work.

Women's Wire
http://www.women.com/
A variety of news, including health information, by, for and about women.

Yahoo! Alternative Medicine
http://www.yahoo.com/health/alternative_medicine/
Index of information on alternative health.

Yahoo! Women's Health Resources online
http://www.yahoo.com/Health/Women_s_Health/
Index to information on women's health.

Print Materials

The following is a short bibliography of newsletters and books on women's health issues. Check your local public library or bookstore for these and other health-related publications.

■

Newsletters

Feminist Women's Health Center News, 633 East 11th Ave., Eugene, OR 97401, (800) 995-2286, e-mail *fwhc@efn.org*. Published quarterly, free.

Harvard Health Letter, P.O. Box 420300, Palm Coast, FL 32142-3000. Monthly, $32/yr.

Harvard Women's Health Watch, P.O. Box 420064, Palm Coast, FL 32142-9574. Articles on all aspects of women's health, in simple language. Monthly, $30/yr.

Menopause News, 2074 Union St., San Francisco, CA 94123, (800) 241-6366. Six issues per year, $24/yr.

Books

American College of Nurse-Midwives and Sandra Jacobs. *Having Your Baby with a Nurse-Midwife: Everything You Need to Know to Make an Informed Decision*. New York: Hyperion Press, 1993.

Arnup, Katherine, ed. *Lesbian Parenting: Living with Pride and Prejudice*. Charlottetown, P.E.I.: Gynergy, 1995.

Astbury, Jill. *Crazy for You: The Making of Women's Madness*. New York: Oxford University Press, 1996.

Ayers, Lauren K. *The Answer Is Within You: Psychology, Women's Connections and Breast Cancer*. New York: Crossroad Press, 1994. How to actively work for your own health rather than passively accept the disease.

Baron-Faust, Rita, with physicians of New York University Medical Center Women's Health Service and Kaplan Comprehensive Cancer Center. *Breast Cancer: What Every Woman Should Know*. New York: Hearst Books, 1995. Information on risk factors, treatment and prevention, including realistic ways to assess risk, how diet may reduce risk, mammography guidelines, biopsy techniques and surgical options.

Boston Women's Health Book Collective. *The New Our Bodies, Ourselves: A Book by and for Women*. 2d. ed. New York: Simon and Schuster, 1992. Over six hundred pages of information on the physical and mental health of women.

Carlson, Karen J., et al. *The Harvard Guide to Women's Health*. Cambridge: Harvard University Press, 1996. An A–Z guide that answers questions about all aspects of women's health and medical care. Topics include anxiety, depression, menstrual disorders, herpes, breast reconstruction and much more.

Clunis, D. Merilee, and G. Dorsey Green. *The Lesbian Parenting Book: A Guide to Creating Families and Raising Children*. Seattle: Seal Press, 1995.

Cotton, Deborah J., and D. Heather Watts, eds. *The Medical Management of AIDS in Women*. New York: Wiley-Liss, 1997.

Doress-Worters, Paula B., and Diana L. Siegal. *The New Ourselves, Growing Older*, 2d. ed. New York: Simon and Schuster, 1994.

Elias, Jason, and Katherine Ketcham. *In the House of the Moon: Reclaiming the Feminine Spirit of Healing*. New York: Time Warner, 1995. Helps women reclaim innate ability to heal and create wholeness. Interweaves traditional values with insights from ancient and contemporary thinkers, and offers natural remedies that can be used to complement conventional medical treatment.

Hepburn, C., and B. Gutierrez. *Alive and Well: A Lesbian Health Guide*. Freedom, Calif.: The Crossing Press, 1988. Although dated, this book is included because it is one of only a few dealing specifically with lesbians. Includes still-relevant information on nutrition, exercise, legal issues, lesbian mothers, sexually transmitted diseases and AIDS.

Hirschmann, Jane R., and Carol H. Munter. *When Women Stop Hating Their Bodies: Freeing Yourself From Food and Weight Obsession*. New York: Fawcett Columbine, 1995.

Hoffman, Eileen. *Our Health, Our Lives: A Revolutionary Approach to Total Health Care for Women*. New York: Pocket Books, 1995. Empowers women to use the health care system to full advantage, to understand female physiology and psychology, and to know what questions to ask. Topics include heart disease, cancer, diabetes, osteoporosis, menstrual periods, pregnancy and menopause. Includes some discussion of cancer in lesbians and attitudes toward lesbians.

Jacobowitz, Ruth S. *150 Most-Asked Questions About Menopause: What Women Really Want to Know*. New York: Hearst Books, 1993.

Kloser, Patricia, and Jane M. Craig. *The Woman's HIV Sourcebook: A Guide to Better Health and Well-Being*. Dallas: Taylor, 1994. Regarded as a leading authority on women and HIV infection, Dr. Kloser attempts to address women's questions and information needs regarding HIV.

Krotoski, D., et al., eds. *Women with Physical Disabilities: Achieving and Maintaining Health and Well-Being*. Baltimore: P.H. Brooks, 1996.

Kus, Robert J., ed. *Addiction and Recovery in Gay and Lesbian Persons*. Binghamton, N.Y.: Haworth Medical Press, 1995.

Lark, Susan M. *Women's Health Companion: Self Help Nutrition Guide and Cookbook*. Berkeley, Calif.: Celestial Arts, 1995. Written by a physician, the book attempts to provide complete information about all aspects of nutrition for women: foods to eat, foods to avoid, vitamins, minerals and herbs for female health problems, food preparation and recipes and so on.

Lark, Susan M. *Treating Menstrual Cramps Naturally: Effective Natural Solutions for Discomforts Most Women Face.* New Canaan, Conn.: Keats Press, 1996.

Love, Susan M., with Karen Lindsey. *Dr. Susan Love's Breast Book.* 2d ed. New York: Addison-Wesley, 1995. The revised edition reflects new developments in breast care, screenings, diagnosis, treatment and research. All chapters are updated, including silicone implants, imaging techniques, genetics, risk factors and prevention.

Maleskey, Gale, and Charles B. Inlander. *Take This Book to the Gynecologist with You: A Consumers' Guide to Women's Health.* New York: Addison-Wesley, 1991.

Martin, April. *The Lesbian and Gay Parenting Handbook: Creating and Raising Our Families.* New York: HarperPerennial, 1993.

Northrup, Christiane. *Women's Bodies, Women's Wisdom: Creating Physical and Emotional Health and Healing.* New York: Bantam Books, 1994.

Notelovitz, Morris and Diana Tonnessen. *Essential Heart Book for Women.* New York: St. Martin's Press, 1996. Heart disease discussed from a woman's viewpoint, with recommendations made from studies on women. Includes illustrated explanation of normal heart function and easy-to-understand discussions of heart disease risk factors, diagnosis and risk reduction.

O'Leary, Ann, and Loretta Sweet Jemmott, eds. *Women and AIDS: Coping and Care.* New York: Plenum Publishing, 1997.

PDR Family Guide to Women's Health and Prescription Drugs. Montvale, N.J.: Medical Economics Data, 1994. Illustrated consumer health guide on women's health topics including common diseases, menopause and rape. Includes a full color drug-identification guide.

Puretz, Susan L., and Adelaide Haas. *The Woman's Guide to Hysterectomy: Expectations and Options*. Berkeley, Calif.: Celestial Arts, 1995. Addresses common fears, second opinions, diagnostic tests, outpatient procedures, preparation for surgery, postoperative care and sex and sexuality.

Ries, Andrew L., ed. *Shortness of Breath: A Guide to Better Living and Breathing*. St. Louis: Mosby, 1996.

Schneider, Beth E., and Nancy E. Stoller, eds. *Women Resisting AIDS: Feminist Strategies of Empowerment*. Philadelphia: Temple University Press, 1995. Essays documenting and analyzing impact of AIDS on women and women of color in particular.

Schwartz, Ann. *Listen to Me, Doctor: Taking Charge of Your Own Health Care*. Aspen, CO: MacMurray and Beck, 1995. A cancer survivor offers help on how to be assertive in taking charge of your health care. Discussion of second opinions, health insurance, getting referrals, what makes a good doctor and much more.

Snyderman, Nancy L., and Margaret Blackstone. *Dr. Nancy Snyderman's Guide to Good Health: What Every Forty-Plus Woman Should Know About Her Changing Body*. New York: William Morrow, 1996.

Stoppard, Miriam. *Woman's Body*. London: Dorling Kindersley, 1994. A good book for teenage girls. Includes a frank discussion of sexuality and several photographs of the female body. Deals with every physical aspect of being a mature female.

Villarosa, Linda, ed. *Body & Soul: The Black Woman's Guide to Physical Health and Emotional Well-Being*. New York: HarperPerennial, 1994. Discusses the physical, emotional and spiritual health of black women. The editor consulted black female scientists, academicians, health care practitioners and writers.

Vliet, Elizabeth Lee. *Screaming to Be Heard: Hormonal Connections Women Suspect . . . and Doctors Ignore*. New York: McEvans Press, 1994. Vliet, a doctor and director of a women's health care center, believes that hormones play a significant role in women's health. Varying levels of estrogen, progesterone and testosterone can be linked to depression, chronic fatigue, migraines, fibromyalgia, bladder problems, heart disease and cancer. She defends hormone replacement therapy as a preventative treatment, provided it is individualized and integrated with alternative therapies.

White, Evelyn C., ed. *The Black Women's Health Book: Speaking for Ourselves*. Seattle: Seal Press, 1994. More than fifty black women write about health issues that affect them and the well-being of their families and communities. Topics include fibroids, benefits of breast feeding, skin color issues, menopause, evolution of African-American diet, non-Western healing and the Tuskegee Syphilis Study. Includes excerpts from works by bell hooks and Toni Morrison.

Yntema, Sharon. *Vegetarian Pregnancy*. Ithaca, NY: McBooks Press, 1995. A sensible, trustworthy guide for women who want to enjoy a healthy pregnancy on a vegetarian diet.

Zabbia, Kim Howes. *Painted Diaries: A Mother and Daughter's Experience Through Alzheimer's*. Minneapolis: Fairview Press, 1996.

Notes

1. "Gopher" sites, a distributed document search and retrieval system which allow users to browse and retrieve documents, still exist. While accessible from the World Wide Web, they typically have an address beginning with "gopher://" Some Web browsers can read these files directly, that is, interpret them as text and display them

without having to use a more complex method for downloading them onto your computer to read with another program.

2. P.E. Stevens, "Lesbian health care research," *Health Care for Women International* 13, (1992) 91-120.

3. Katherine O'Hanlan, "Lesbian Health and Homophobia: Perspectives for the Treating Obstetrician/Gynecologist," *Current Problems in ObstetricsGynecology and Fertility* 28, no. 4 (1995) 93-136.

4. American Medical Association, *Patients Bill of Rights: Fact Sheet*, Dept of News and Information, AMA, 515 North State St., Chicago, IL 60610, (312) 464-4443.

The author wishes to gratefully acknowledge the research assistance, support, and all-around good humor of an exceptional librarian, Ms. Madelyn Hall.

▨ SHARON M. DAY, RITA SHIMMIN PULIDO,
▨ VERONICA MATOS AND LETITIA GÓMEZ

▪ The Future of Our Health

The four sections of this piece and the following piece were originally presented as a panel discussion on the future of the lesbian health advocacy movement at a 1995 meeting of the National Lesbian and Gay Health Association in Minneapolis. Panelists included Sharon M. Day, Executive Director of the Native American/Indian AIDS Task Force; Rita Shimmin Pulido, HIV Program Services Director, Lyon-Martin Women's Health Services in San Francisco; Veronica Matos, Assistant Director of Health Services at the Los Angeles Gay and Lesbian Community Services Center; Letitia Gómez, a National Gay and Lesbian Health Association board member and Executive Director of the National Latino and Latina Gay Organization (LLEGO); and Marj Plumb, a health policy consultant for the National Center for Lesbian Rights, a Lesbian Health Fund (a project of the Gay and Lesbian Medical Association) advisory board member, a National Policy and Resource Center on Women and Aging national advisory board member and a member of the Washington, D.C.-based Lesbian Health Advocacy Network.

Sharon M. Day

Good morning. Welcome to the land of the Ojibwe and to the headwaters of the Mississippi River.

▪

351

Sharon M. Day,
Rita Shimmin
Pulido, Veronica
Matos and Letitia
Gómez

∎

I want to introduce my remarks with a short piece of history that will frame my comments and is the lens through which I view the world. These stories have been handed down generation by generation by my people.

Long before Europeans set foot on North America, my people migrated from the eastern seaboard based on a prophecy. Seven generations ago, seven spiritual people visited the Anishinabe and presented them with seven prophecies. One prophesy told of the coming of Europeans. The Anishinabe were told to avoid contact with the Europeans even at the cost of giving up their homeland on the east coast. They were instructed to move west until they came to a place where food grows on the water. The rivers and great lakes provided a natural migration route, and they continued on until they came to places where food grows on the water. The food I am talking about is the grain we call mahnomen, which you call wild rice. Another prophecy given to my ancestors was that in seven generations great changes would occur. It would be a time when the people would be given a choice to take one path or another. One direction would lead to death and destruction and the other to peace and harmony among all people. Today, we are in the seventh generation that my ancestors spoke of and as an Ojibwe lesbian I feel a sense of urgency. Ojibwe or not, we all should feel a sense of urgency about our position in the current health care system in this country.

If I were designing a lesbian health movement, it would be inclusive in many ways, and I would start from scratch. I would transform the current health care industry in this country from a crisis-oriented system to a proactive preventive system that included the following:

Prevention and health promotion services would be provided to everyone. They would be designed by the communities they are to benefit, and health promotion would include issues of identity and sexuality. We would all be encouraged to explore racial and ethnic identities, and our sexual identities would be a source of joy and strength.

A lesbian health movement would actively work to eliminate racism and sexism. A lesbian health movement would strive to eliminate poverty, because poor diets and the lack of adequate food are at the root of many chronic illnesses in this country. In my family everyone over the age of forty is living with diabetes—except me. It is far more cost-efficient to provide adequate nutrition up-front to prevent diabetes, heart disease and other illnesses than to provide renal dialysis or bypass surgery once people have suffered through years of poverty.

A lesbian health movement would pay attention to the environment. Those of us who suffer from asthma and other chronic lung diseases are the "canaries in the coal mines," giving the danger signal that the air we breathe is being poisoned by toxins spewed out into the environment. We should be able to drink the water from our taps without worrying about infection and we should be able to eat the fish we catch in our lakes and rivers. And our children should be able to play in their homes and their backyards without being poisoned by lead.

A lesbian health movement would include in its mission advocacy for fair, affordable, safe housing for all of us.

All of these issues would be considered and undertaken within a lesbian health movement.

Considering that my ancestors left their homelands based on a prophecy, I think some of them must have been uncomfortable, skeptical or even downright resistant about the idea of moving. So the community leaders and the spiritual people must have worked hard to convince those that were reluctant that it was in their best interests, and the best interests of the community, for everyone to join in this journey. We must work as diligently to educate ourselves and each other.

Today, even though we understand health care in its present form doesn't meet our needs as lesbians—or as Natives or Latinas or African Americans or Asian Americans—it is still frightening

Sharon M. Day,
Rita Shimmin
Pulido, Veronica
Matos and Letitia
Gómez

■

354

to confront the system and demand change. We need to educate ourselves as consumers, educate health care providers and then work with public policymakers to mold health care reform to include those issues I have just listed.

If I were designing a lesbian health care system, I would continue the practices of my people and make sure that they were folded into health care policies. After five hundred years of genocide, our survival can only be attributed to the healing practices of our own medicine people. Yet, we are unable in most cases to access these healers today because Western medical practitioners have not validated our healing practices under a microscope. We must educate our community members so they will become aware of these historical facts and act accordingly. A little bit of poison sugar-coated is still poison.

Native people saw illness as having two distinct causes: one, something that came from outside of the body, the other, an imbalance within the individual. Each required its own treatment. And when someone was treated, everyone was involved in the healing.

Lesbians, Native people and people with HIV are provided with little support in, and in fact are actively persuaded against, using traditional health practices from their communities. In my agency only the people living with HIV who are the most tenacious, stubborn and sensible demand that their physicians refer them for methods of pain management besides prescription drugs. This usually requires a visit with a psychiatrist first, but occasionally they get the referrals for "alternative therapies." One case manager who practices traditional healing has a poster that reads "Just say no to Western medicine," and that would be the first public campaign I would run in a lesbian health movement.

People in every hemisphere are suffering from the effects of Western medicine. Viruses are rampant, and bacterial infections are resistant to antibiotics. When I was growing up my dad would tell my mom that if any of us—and there were thirteen of us—

had a fever they would do everything they could to bring it down. Only if they couldn't reduce the fever would we go to a doctor for antibiotics. My dad would say, "The more they take, the less they work." Recently our state epidemiologist said the same thing. It's time to search out other methods of healing, and it's time we begin to heal ourselves and restore health in our communities.

Rita Shimmin Pulido

A lesbian health movement that includes me is going to have to be something that doesn't have an expectation of what I should be. A lesbian health movement that includes me is going to have to be different from any of the models I've seen to date. I haven't seen anything that works for me yet. So it can't be anything that we've seen together, yet.

Many people would say I came unprepared today. They would say I am unprepared because I don't have a piece of paper and an outline and an agenda for you; because I'm walking around without a mike, raising my voice, moving my body, not reading calmly from a prepared speech. Well, I have prepared for fifty-one years for this moment. It's fifty-one years of preparedness you are seeing now.

My father came to this country as an immigrant. A Filipino. And some of his countrymen had to read signs to him that said: FILIPINOS AND DOGS, KEEP OFF THE GRASS. My mother is an African woman—centuries of history on this land, which I don't need to recount, I hope. If it doesn't mean something to you when I say my mother is an African woman, if that doesn't make you shift in your seat, then you need to do some studying.

A lesbian health movement that includes me has to include anybody who's uncomfortable right now by the way I am present-ing and what I am saying. But if this is making you uncomfort-able—get ready, because this is nothing. This is nothing compared to what's out there and—guess what—what's inside each of you

Sharon M. Day,
Rita Shimmin
Pulido, Veronica
Matos and Letitia
Gómez

■

356

right now, that's not loose yet, that's tight and closed down.

I hate to give the man press, but Newt Gingrich said, "America is the only nation sophisticated enough, complicated enough, large enough to lead the human race." He said that. It was in the *New York Times*. And in the same article he said, "English must be our common language because without English there can be no civilization." When I hear things like that I want to *scream*. I mean really scream. I mean fall down on the floor and cry. I also laughed like you are. I laughed, too. But you know what—how come there hasn't been anything said in the press about these statements? How come nobody said, "What the *fuck* are you talking about?" How come it just happens in our newspapers, like it's okay for someone to say that in this country? Do you know it is okay for someone to say that in this country?

A lesbian health movement that includes me means that everyone in this room as an individual—you, you, you, you—would stand up if you heard that and *scream*. If you didn't stand up and scream, then I'm not moving with you. Then I'll have to find a movement someplace else. Because that's not okay with me.

If I am making you uncomfortable by either the loudness of my voice or by anything—that's okay. It is not my agenda to make you uncomfortable. It is my agenda to express myself. Every day I struggle to have an experience of myself. Why? Because every day, out there, there is this whole network of systems set up to say to me, "You will not have an experience of yourself! You will have an experience of a white, male heterosexual"—anything but who I am. And you know what? I don't know who I am, and I love it. Because what I am is constantly changing. It's constantly changing. I don't know what I am going to say two seconds from now. How could I? If I have to know what I am going to say from moment to moment, then I feel clamped down, shut down and shut up.

It is not my intention to make anyone uncomfortable. I want a place where I can feel like I can get up and be who I am. And that's what a lesbian health movement would be to me. And everywhere I go, when I stand up and say how I feel, like this, because I happen to be full of emotion, people say the loudness in my voice hurts them. I'm told to sit down or stand behind the podium. I'm instructed to state an opening thesis and supporting statement. I can't do it.

So a lesbian health movement that includes me has got to have a new paradigm—a different model. We haven't seen it yet. And that's what we have got to create together.

Veronica Matos

Let me get a little personal. I'm originally from Puerto Rico, and like many of us I'm a displaced Puerto Rican. I've been living in Los Angeles for the past six years. Politically I identify myself as a baby dyke, not because of my age or the way I look, but because these woman [on the panel] have been doing this work for three of my lifetimes put together, so I consider myself a baby dyke still. I live with my son, who promised me that as a surprise he was going to get me Cat Woman, because I need a friend.

Now, I'm here to finish the sentence, "If I were to design a lesbian health movement, it would look like . . . " And if I were to practice what I'm going to preach, I would pick up this mike and go and talk to Dorothy, I would take the mike and go to Yvette and to Eunice, and I would let them tell me what a lesbian movement needs to look like. But logistics-wise I would be shot dead by the people who want everything to go on tape, so I'm going to speak from what I think Dorothy, Yvette and Eunice would tell me about what this movement needs to look like.

The first thing is ownership. The most critical part of any movement, and I don't care what movement it is, whether it's the Newt Gingrich movement or our movement, the most critical part is the constituency. It is for all of us to remember that it is the Eunices, the Yvettes and the Dorothys whom we are working for.

Sharon M. Day,
Rita Shimmin
Pulido, Veronica
Matos and Letitia
Gómez

■

358

Inevitably when we navigate on the streams and the rivers the community is left out. The constituency I say I'm representing is nowhere in sight. Whether it's a big ship like a national organization or whether it's a little boat like the one I'm in charge of, my number-one priority is working hard, making sure that there's ownership by those people I say I'm providing services for, that they feel that they own those services. I see myself as a pawn. It is not me—it is the women. I need to make sure that all these women have ownership of what it is I'm facilitating for them, and that ownership is going to lead to responsibility.

It's also important to have a collective goal. If we don't have a goal, we are just going to react: If there's money in HIV, we are going to react so that the agenda becomes HIV-focused. If we have a collective goal, then it's my constituency's agenda I'm going to fight for—not react to some funder. Having their goal in my sight will help me in developing programs. It is not my movement, it is Dorothy's movement, it is Eunice's movement and it is Yvette's movement.

Finally a movement should have a strategy, I won't use the word "structure" because I don't want you to know I'm a control queen, so I'll use the word "strategy." Our movement needs to have a clearly defined strategy: a strategy that will help us foster a sense of ownership so that we know who owns the movement; a strategy that will help facilitate the development of a collective goal and sense of direction; and a strategy, and this is very important, to ensure that the movement is a lot more than individual players. When I put that idea in the context of big ships and little boats we need to make sure that the movement is a big tanker with a crew, who owns it and takes responsibility for it. And if one woman disembarks for whatever reason, the tanker still keeps going. That versus having a movement which is made up of a big ship called *Veronica*, and when *Veronica* sinks, there's no more movement. We need to move away from the movement being dependent on individual players because we need to give the ownership of the movement to the constituency, because five or ten years from now, when I've stopped doing this and have married the woman of my dreams and we have a family to raise, I want to be sure the movement has not stopped, that there's someone behind me carrying on.

One strategy we need to have is what I would like to call "baby dyke baton passing." I want to make sure that the baton goes to another baby dyke who is going to speak for her consituency, who is going to be a pawn for all those other woman out there. We need a movement that ensures that this is not about individual players, so that when a leader leaves the community, members are not asking, "So, what happened to the movement?" and the response is not, "Well, Veronica's gone, so there is no movement."

If it were up to me to design what a lesbian movement should look like, rather than its being "big ships and little boats," it would be a body, whether it be a body that looks like mine, a body that looks like yours, a body like Lettie's, or a body like anybody else's here. A body that can't work without the head or without the toes either. Parts working together to form a healthy whole.

Letitia Gómez

We were each asked to address what a lesbian health movement would look like if we could design it. In my mind it would look something like a campaign. We have many of the parts now: We have individual activists, we have community-based organizations, we have grassroots groups and we have national organizations that are beginning to address the issue of lesbian health. So we have some parts, but we need others.

First, we need to make lesbian health a priority within our organizations. We also need to do planning; many times we jump into something without really thinking about long-term objectives. Funding is something we have begun to pursue very

Sharon M. Day,
Rita Shimmin
Pulido, Veronica
Matos and Letitia
Gómez

■

360

assertively at the national level, but with the move to give the states block-grant money, our efforts to seek funding will need to move even more aggressively on the state level.

Education. We need to educate our funders and our consumers that our health is a priority. Lesbian health wasn't a priority for me—I was off doing other things and not thinking of myself, what my needs were as a lesbian and what my health issues were. Now I'm getting older, and the bones are starting to do funny things. We need to decide our health is important.

Technical assistance. It's wonderful that the Centers for Disease Control is providing the opportunity for lesbian outreach to be a part of its state-by-state screening program, but I hope technical assistance is a part of the effort, for example, perhaps periodically bringing the four sites together or sitting down with them early on to look at what lessons have been learned already, providing them with resources and periodically checking in to see what they can be doing better. And evaluation in any program is essential. It's something that many of us perhaps are not very good at, but we need to work at it.

We have grassroots activists working on lesbian health issues on the local, state and national levels, we have national activists working on the national level, and we have community-based groups as well as national organizations working on lesbian health issues, but many times only because lesbians in those organizations have added lesbian health to their own plates, not because it has been a priority for the organization. So our organizations need to incorporate lesbian health as a priority—a lesbian health project should not just have a staff person assigned to it but it should receive funding as well. And if the organization, for whatever reason, cannot or doesn't want to give lesbian health priority, let's look around for other organizations that could take this issue on and that we could support.

The education that has been done already is important, but, as we have seen this weekend and certainly with the Lesbian

Health Roundtable last year and the work the Lesbian Health Advocacy Network has done, materials have been developed that should be shared, because when you go visit a funder or a state legislator, you need to leave that person with something: They need to see that work has been done.

I want to share with you a model of an organization I work with. When we started LLEGO we were very clear that the strength of an organization like ours is at the local level—it's not in Washington, D.C., necessarily. We have over the years begun to develop a network of gay and lesbian Latino organizations that are doing work in their communities; we count on them for input and for feedback because they are the ones who are doing the work; they are the ones who are putting together local programs. I can't possibly imagine that I would tell them how to do anything. But I can help them, perhaps by finding resources for them and dollars; it's very important for national organizations to be available to provide technical assistance and also be available to hear what's going on, on the local level.

I'm very excited about the potential of the lesbian health movement. As a follow-up to this conference, perhaps next year, we could provide some "how to" sessions: how to write a grant proposal, how to approach your state legislature, how to develop a program. Those are skills I think we need to develop. We can learn a lot of lessons from those of us who have worked in the AIDS movement and not reinvent the wheel, but there are things particular to us we need to model for ourselves.

MARJ PLUMB, M.N.A.

Blueprint for the Future
The Lesbian Health Advocacy Movement

Largest study of women—ever—will include lesbi-ans

Four breast cancer research studies funded by feds to include lesbians

CDC establishes special outreach initiative to ensure low-income lesbians receive free Pap smears and mammograms

Gay and lesbian docs start the Lesbian Health Fund—over $100,000 donated for lesbian health research in less than two years

NIH to publish guidelines on how to research lesbian and gay youth suicide

First Lesbian Health Research Institute held July 1996 to begin articulating a lesbian health research agenda

CDC holds first government-sponsored meeting on lesbians and HIV

Lesbian Research Network founded to assist lesbian researchers from all disciplines

Foundation and Clinic Consortium merge to form first D.C.-based national lesbian and gay health organization

Didn't see those headlines in your local lesbian and gay newspaper or your favorite queer magazine? No one did. Hundreds of advances have been made throughout the country on behalf of lesbian (and gay) health since the early 1990s, but with limited attention from the media. Despite the lack of headlines, there has been an explosion of grassroots organizing and activism, and on the national level, lesbian health issues are being included within federal health department programs at unprecedented levels.

The Lesbian Health Advocacy Movement

Like other communities with poor access to the health care system, the lesbian and gay community has had to build elements of its own health system to survive. Throughout the country, health-related service programs for the lesbian, gay and bisexual communities have sprung up: youth programs, elderly programs, substance abuse and mental health programs, cancer care projects, HIV prevention services, smoking cessation classes, hotlines, primary care clinics and community services centers. National coalitions include organizations working on the issue of lesbians and HIV, lesbian and feminist cancer projects and service providers working with lesbian, gay, bisexual, transgender and questioning youth. Lesbian and gay health professionals—

doctors, nurses, social workers, physician's assistants, addiction professionals and gerontologists—have formed their own national organizations. Two cities (San Francisco and New York) have an office of gay and lesbian health in their respective public health departments and at least one for-profit health maintenance organization (HMO) has an office of gay and lesbian health. The annual lesbian and gay health conference attracts more than fifteen hundred lesbian and gay health professionals and advocates; a new lesbian and gay health organization (the National Lesbian and Gay Health Association) is operating out of Washington, D.C.; and the Lesbian Health Fund, a project of the Gay and Lesbian Medical Association, provides grants for lesbian health research and education.

There is also a burgeoning lesbian health advocacy movement. Advocacy, the active support of a cause, by and for lesbians and bisexual women is certainly not a new phenomenon. Lesbian and bisexual women (and some heterosexual women as well) have long advocated for lesbians and bisexual women on such health-related issues as domestic violence, reproductive health, breast cancer and HIV. In fact, many of the movements that address those issues have had lesbian and bisexual women in their leadership. Yet, for the most part, the health gains achieved for lesbian and bisexual women have been a result of our own efforts; we have researched ourselves, taught ourselves, cared for ourselves and funded ourselves. But the times they are "a-changin'."

Since the election of Bill Clinton to his first term as president and shortly thereafter the appointment of Donna Shalala as secretary of health and human services, significant national advances have been made on behalf of lesbian and bisexual women's health concerns, including access to the largest source of funding for health services and research in the United States—the Department of Health and Human Services (DHHS)—as well as to members of Congress.

Prior to the 1993 March on Washington (MOW), the National

Gay and Lesbian Task Force (NGLTF) organized a grassroots group of lesbians from across the country to begin preparing for the first known congressional briefings on lesbian health. Out of this effort came a definition of *lesbian* and a definition of *a lesbian health issue* that are still being used in meetings and organizing efforts within Washington, D.C., as well as throughout the country.[1] A lesbian health issue was defined as "diseases or conditions which are unique, more prevalent, more serious, and for which risk factors and interventions are different in lesbians and some subgroups of lesbians." What makes this definition effective is that it does not rely on prevalence alone to determine the importance of an issue to the lesbian and bisexual women's community. Diseases or conditions that do not appear to be at a higher prevalence for this community or for which data is not available, often because of the difficulty in reaching this population, can be considered lesbian health issues if they require a targeted intervention.

The definition of a lesbian took more time and work to develop because it was meant to offer the broadest possible description of the entire population of women who have at some point in their life or may in the future be sexual with another woman. The definition reads:

> A lesbian is a woman whose erotic desire and affectional preferences are directed at other women. Her sexual behavior ranges from exclusive homosexual behavior with other women to bisexuality to situational heterosexuality prompted by economic status, cultural factors or sexual desire. "Lesbian" is a social/political construct that not all women who partner with women are comfortable with. The process of choosing to identify with the term is highly individualized and fluid and is also affected by other social constructs, such as age and race. Women who identify themselves as lesbians do so in their teens, in young adulthood, in middle age and some late

Marj Plumb,

M.N.A.

■

366

in life. There are lesbians who never claim the identity.

Lesbians are as diverse as all of America. We share with other subgroups of women systemic barriers to access as women of color, poor women, sex workers, incarcerated women, single mothers, women addicted to drugs and alcohol, working-class women, immigrant women, youth and older women. In addition, all lesbians experience the stigmatization, marginalization and sometimes overt hostility directed at gay men, bisexuals and transgendered people in our society. As a family unit, lesbians are denied benefits enjoyed by hetero-sexual married couples, such as joint health care and parenting rights.

Finally, we are often forced to lie and hide our sexual de-sire for other women so that we can access the health care or social services we need. We also hide in order to guarantee the commitment and support of our biological families, our jobs, our neighborhoods, our children, our language and our access to valued cultural and religious institutions. Medically, socially and economically, the less room we have to turn around, the more problematic our crisis becomes as we balance precari-ously between the women and community we desire and the help and support we need. For many, the process of "coming out" is often dangerous and isolating.

In conjunction with the March on Washington, several lesbian health activists participated in an historic meeting between les-bian, gay and bisexual health advocates and Secretary Shalala. A series of recommendations were made to her, and the door to DHHS was opened to lesbian, gay and bisexual health concerns. Patsy Fleming, who was then special assistant to Donna Shalala (and then President Clinton's AIDS czar) was appointed the les-bian and gay health liaison for DHHS.

In February 1994 four national gay and lesbian organizations sponsored the first Lesbian Health Roundtable.[2] More than sixty lesbian and bisexual women's health activists met in Washington, D.C., to establish a lesbian health agenda and to meet with representatives of the Department of Health and Human Services and members of Congress. Roundtable participants met with directors and other staff at the National Institutes of Health (NIH), the Substance Abuse Mental Health Services Administration (SAMHSA), the Agency for Health Care Policy and Research (AHCPR), the Human Resources Services Administration (HRSA), the U.S. Public Health Service Office on Women's Health and the National AIDS Policy Office. At each meeting advocates gave a short briefing on lesbian health issues and then presented each department with a detailed list of recommendations on lesbian health.

After the roundtable, Washington, D.C.-based representatives of the national organizations and local D.C. health service organizations formalized their previously ad-hoc coalition into the Lesbian Health Advocacy Network (LHAN), which provides support for and coordination of lesbian health advocacy with federal agencies, Congress and mainstream national organizations. One of the first activities of LHAN was to meet with the directors of the women's health offices within each of the federal health agencies to follow up on the roundtable meetings. LHAN members provided education on lesbian health issues and underscored the need for each agency to begin working on the recommendations previously presented to them.

Some of these advocacy successes are truly remarkable. As a direct result of the roundtable, the National Institutes of Health (NIH) has funded four mainstream breast cancer researchers so they can broaden their studies to include lesbians. Also as a result of the roundtable meetings, the U.S. Public Health Service Office on Women's Health included a paragraph on lesbian health concerns in their new four-page publication called "Women's Health Issues."

Dr. Kate O'Hanlan (then president of the Gay and Lesbian Medical Association) and the National Center for Lesbian Rights began two letter-writing campaigns urging researchers to include lesbians in their studies. The largest study of women—ever—the Women's Health Initiative (163,000 women studied over a ten-year period), now includes questions about the gender of sexual partners, thus allowing researchers to compare data among women with different sexual behaviors. The study's lead researcher has also agreed to assist each of the forty sites of the study to actively recruit lesbian and bisexual participants.

The Harvard Nurses Study, the longest ongoing study of women's health, recently agreed for the first time to ask their study participants (127,000 female nurses) about their sexual orientation. So successful was the pilot test (only one participant complained—but she still answered the question!) that the Nurses Study researchers are planning to write a medical journal article on their experience.

The Centers for Disease Control and Prevention (CDC) has established a special outreach initiative to ensure that low-income lesbian and bisexual women receive free Pap smears and mammograms throughout all fifty states. This initiative has included hiring staff at the CDC to oversee the project, and funding four sites to begin pilot outreach projects that could be replicated in each state. The CDC has also recently held the first government-funded federal meeting on lesbians and HIV to discuss what is known about risk factors for lesbians and bisexual women, and what is known about female-to-female transmission of the virus.

Since 1992 we also have seen an explosion of grassroots lesbian health organizing. We have seen the development of a lesbian health bibliography that includes more than eight hundred citations on lesbian health; new lesbian health organizing in cities like Houston, Denver, Kansas City and Miami; two national lesbian health newsletters, and more lesbian health articles published in mainstream professional journals than in the previous twenty years.

A Unique Moment in Time

We are at a unique moment in time. We have a community more interested in health issues than ever before. We also have a community more knowledgeable about the health system and health terminology. We have greater access to the federal health department than under any other administration. Furthermore, the national interest in health (health reform in particular) is at an all-time high. This convergence of experience, access and visibility places us at a critical moment in time, a moment that will allow us to make massive advances in the development of a health care system truly responsive to lesbian and bisexual women's needs.

So where do we go from here? We know that all of these efforts, national and grassroots, are having an immediate impact on the health and lives of lesbians. More lesbians are getting Pap smears and mammograms, medical providers are being better trained in caring for lesbians, and the health system itself is beginning to question its rigid heterosexual assumptions. Unfortunately, we also know that the factors leading to the greatest health risks to our community cannot be eradicated without a more complete overhaul of the current health system; poverty and racism alone account for the greatest health threats most members of our community will experience. Once you include sexism, ageism and homophobia, it is easy to visualize spiraling levels of the uninsured, sick and dying. In the face of these issues, and the underlying economic assumptions that allow them to exist, the four recommendations listed here are not intended to cure the health system—just make it a little less lethal.

How We Do It

Each city or county throughout the country needs to have at least one lesbian health organizing project, service or agency.

These projects should be established under two organizing principles: 1) Be as autonomous as possible, and 2) engage the health system as often as possible. We have seen throughout the country that our individual organizing efforts to provide services by lesbians and for lesbians is effective and powerful. Grassroots groups have developed and implemented lesbian and bisexual women's health needs assessments and begun strategic planning for program development in many communities. Some efforts have resulted in new organizations specifically formed to address lesbian health. Some efforts have resulted in forming lesbian health projects within gay and lesbian organizations and even within mainstream health organizations. We must organize our own services to constantly engage the current health care system. There need to be lesbian and bisexual women's voices in the debates over changes in Medicaid and Medicare, in the movements to create national health reform and in local medical schools and public health departments.

The Lesbian Health Advocacy Network developed recommendations for the Department of Health and Human Services (DHHS), which I have edited for general use. I hope lesbians across the country will copy this list and meet with local public health directors to discuss it. When you do, ask them to adopt these recommendations. Go to the head of the research hospital in your area or to the head of the local health maintenance organization. Start somewhere—just get pushing—and don't be stopped!

1. Target lesbian and bisexual women as subjects in research initiatives. Analyze research data by the demographic characteristics of sexual orientation and sexual behavior as well as by age, gender, race and income level.

2. Undertake research to better understand those cultural conditions and socialization processes that affect lesbian and bisexual women's health and access to care differently than those affecting the issues of heterosexual women.

3. Include lesbian and bisexual women on funding review panels and internal review boards. Provide sensitivity training for review panels and internal review boards to reduce homophobia and increase understanding of lesbian and bisexual women's health issues.

4. Initiate efforts to increase access to health care for lesbians and bisexual women, especially those who are uninsured and underinsured, poor, from rural communities or isolated by virtue of ethnicity or race.

5. Provide sensitivity training for all health providers, staff, members of committees or boards and the general public to reduce homophobia and increase understanding of lesbian and bisexual women's health issues.

6. Include presentations of lesbian and bisexual women's health information and research at all conferences and meetings where women's health research, programs and policy are discussed.

7. Publish and distribute lesbian and bisexual women's health research, educational materials and resource guides.

8. Encourage medical schools to develop a sensitive, culturally competent and language-appropriate curriculum for lesbian and bisexual women's patient care.

9. Ensure freedom of choice of medical providers in any health insurance plan or health system (including HMOs).

National organizations need to recommit themselves to supporting the contemporary lesbian health advocacy movement.
National gay and lesbian organizations (such as the National Gay

and Lesbian Task Force, Human Rights Campaign, Black Lesbian and Gay Leadership Forum, National Center for Lesbian Rights, Latino/a Lesbian and Gay Organization and Parents and Friends of Lesbians and Gays) can provide a number of services to the lesbian health movement that would have an immediate impact on the ability of lesbians to organize in their communities. Many of these organizations have been involved in past lesbian health advocacy successes, but more could be asked of them and with community support more would be provided.

First and foremost, the national organizations need to commit to hiring paid staff whose full-time work is lesbian health. These staff should provide technical assistance to grassroots lesbian health organizers. If information is the key to organizing, then the more staff we have available to help local organizers hook up with funders, with researchers and with other organizations, the better our organizing efforts will be. Staff are also needed to represent lesbian health issues at meetings and conferences held by mainstream national organizations (such as the National Organization for Women, Planned Parenthood and the National Black Women's Health Project) and coalitions (such as the Campaign for Women's Health). Staff from our national organizations would also help maintain an active lesbian and bisexual women's voice in any congressional health care or health reform battle, especially in regard to issues such as the definition of the family, non-discrimination language, community clinic funding, benefits determination, cost and eligibility requirements.

National organizations can also help form a grassroots computerized lesbian health information network and assist in the acquisition of computer systems for lesbian health projects across the country so that access to information and support can occur more quickly. Distribution to local communities of lesbian and bisexual women's health information will increase the knowledge and awareness of lesbian health issues and would help many communities become aware of the volume of information already available. National organizations can also help coordinate letter-writing campaigns for the inclusion of lesbian and bisexual women's issues in health education materials, health education programs, medical school curricula, health research and funding proposals.

The lesbian and gay media need to be more responsive to the lesbian health advocacy movement and highlight our successes.

Only a handful of gay and lesbian newspapers or magazines throughout the country has provided any real coverage of lesbian health issues. A recent national Lesbian and Gay Journalists Association conference had no lesbian health-specific workshops or plenary speakers. The lesbian and gay media need to hire columnists with expertise in lesbian health, seek out stories on lesbian health issues, hold workshops in their local communities to train lesbian health advocates in accessing the media and pick up lesbian health stories from other lesbian and gay media sources.

Lesbian health organizing needs to reflect issues of race and poverty.

Most lesbian health activists would agree that homophobia is a health hazard. Homophobia in society causes everything from violence against gay people to reduced resources for HIV prevention and research. Homophobia within the medical system is cited as a significant reason lesbians do not get care and/or receive inadequate care. Eradicating sexism would be another shared principle within the lesbian health movement; we are all familiar with the stories of heart disease research that did not include women and how female patients are treated differently than male patients by male medical providers. Yet, as important as understanding and combating homophobia and sexism are, I honestly believe that we as a movement lack the recognition and understanding of the impact of racism on all of us.

It helps me in my own thinking about the future of the lesbian health advocacy movement to remember that we, as a social change movement, are not alone. We are not the first social change movement in the history of oppressed communities nor will we be the last. Lesbian and gay people are not the first to be called immoral, we are not the first to lose our children or our jobs, we are not the first to fight for legal freedoms, we are not the first to be killed for who we are, and we are not the first to be treated unjustly by the medical system. That should give us a sense of awareness of others' struggles. If we pay attention to our organizing principles now, we will ensure we are building this movement with consciousness—not cutting corners for the expediency of victories.

In June 1995, during the Lesbian Health Plenary at the National Lesbian and Gay Health Conference, I spoke on what I would like the lesbian health movement to look like in the future. I told a story from my youth in the suburbs of Chicago: As a young child I loved riding in the car with my father. He was a truck driver, and I felt very safe with him behind the wheel. But every once in a while, another car would get a little too close and I would let out a blood-curdling scream from the passenger's seat. My dad would laugh and say, "It's okay; it's on your side." My partner and I were discussing this story and realized the similarity between my father's joke and the lesbian and gay movement. Time and again we have seen this movement remain silent on issues of class and poverty and racism because they supposedly weren't "gay" issues. Welfare is being dismantled? "That's okay," we say, "welfare's not a gay issue; it's on your side." The North American Free Trade Agreement is bad for the working poor and unions? That's okay; it's on your side. Racism and anti-Semitism are on the rise? That's okay; it's on your side. Capital punishment is back, English-only amendments are flourishing, and the Contract with America will hurt the poor and the working class? That's okay, we respond, it's on your side. The passengers in our movement car come in many colors: white and black and yellow and brown; we come poor and working class, immigrant and enslaved. We are all in the car together. And we need to remember this single truth of car accidents, if one side takes a hit, the whole car takes a hit. Our movement must begin to reflect this reality and organize with the whole car in mind.

Lesbian health organizers need to commit to multicultural organizing principles.

In the spirit of encouraging direct action to multicultural organizing principles, I presented my own personal lesbian health movement manifesto during the National Lesbian and Gay Health Conference. I keep it in front of my desk to remind me, with each project, each phone call, each letter, that I have laid a path in front of me that I hope—combined with the paths of other movement activists—will build a truly effective and inclusive movement.

1. Every day I will act to stop racism. If I hear or see it, I will confront it. If there are people missing from the table, I will name them. If I participate in racism, actively or passively, I will take the time to understand my own behavior.

2. Every day I will act to end economic injustice. I will raise questions of access to meetings and events for poor people with limited incomes. I will make sure my programs are respectful and accessible to the poor. I will read more about poverty and its causes.

3. I will organize more inclusively around geographic region, age, race, class, physical ability, size and language. Every day I will take at least one action to build a network list that truly reflects the diversity of our community. I will never again say I do not know any young Native American lesbians or older lesbians of color from the Midwest. I will make it my job to reach out to find the diversity of our community and

participate in coalition building.

4. I will include more bisexual women in my lesbian health organizing. I will work more actively with bisexual women's health organizers to learn more about their health needs. I will strive to be aware of the similarities of our struggle and more conscious of possibilities for inclusion.

5. Every day I will speak out about gender identity. I will talk more about transgender issues and gender role-nonconformity. I will make sure that lesbians reflecting the span of gender (from butch-femme to androgyny to transsexuality) will be included in my organizing efforts no matter the risk to my project.

6. Every day I will speak about lesbian sexuality. What we do, how we do it and who we do it with are as essential to this movement as breathing air is to our lives. I will not bow to the repressiveness of government threats or our own movement's desire to be accepted as the "girls next door," to silence our sexuality, our desire or our edges.

7. I will not participate in "random acts of senseless diversity."[3] I will not invite the diversity of our community to a table or project without being willing to do the work of understanding the differences and being willing to work out the conflicts.

8. I will remember that "isms" happen. So often when an *ism* is charged, we rush to defend ourselves, to combat the charge. I will remember that it is the process that is undertaken that gives life to the movement and this process must not be suffocated in guilt or fear.

I challenge other lesbian health activists to consider your

individual participation in this movement. Together we can and will make a difference in the lives of all women who, briefly or for their entire lives, have loved, intimately, other women.

Notes

1. Parts of this article have appeared in previous documents, as I have borrowed generously from work I have collaborated on with others. I hope this gives voice to the dozens of lesbian health advocates and leaders who have worked on these documents as well.

2. The National Gay and Lesbian Task Force, the National Center for Lesbian Rights, the Human Rights Campaign Fund and the National Lesbian and Gay Health Foundation were the lead agencies that organized the roundtable. Local assistance was provided by the Mautner Project for Lesbians with Cancer and the Lesbian Services Program at the Whitman Walker Clinic.

3. I first heard this phrase from Scott Nakagawa while I was employed by the National Gay and Lesbian Task Force.

CONTRIBUTORS

ANONYMOUS continues to live in North America. She has finally discovered that even though, yes, she is tough, yes, she is a dyke and yes, she can take many things, she is not tough enough to meet the eyes of strangers who would know her only by this story.

MADELYN ARNOLD is a lesbian living with AIDS.

HELENA BASKET is thinking about having a zipper tattooed over the scar on her belly.

NANCY A. BROWN has a master's degree in library science and has been employed in the health sciences information field for almost twenty years. She has worked at major medical centers and at health research facilities, and is currently employed at the Telemedicine Research Center in Portland, Oregon, as a research librarian. An Oregon native, she has lived in Portland off and on for twenty years.

DEBORAH BOWEN is a health psychologist and faculty member in the departments of psychology and public health at the University of Washington and at the Fred Hutchinson Cancer Research Center. She has strong interests in women's health, lesbian health and the evaluation of public health interventions.

SHARON M. DAY is the executive director of the Native American/Indian AIDS Task Force in Minneapolis–St. Paul, and a playwright and artist.

RISA DENENBERG is a family nurse practitioner and health writer. She presently teaches, provides health care and writes in New York City. She was a co-director at the Feminist Women's Health Center in Tallahassee, Florida, from 1975 to 1988. She has been a volunteer provider at the Community Health Project in New York City since 1988, a member of ACT UP New York since 1988 and a volunteer member of the New York City Lesbian Health Fair Organizing Committee since 1990.

DENI ANN GEREIGHTY is a witch who lives in a house with three lavender bedrooms and a cat just outside of Seattle. She writes science fiction, Goddess-themed stories, lesbian novels and nursing-related articles.

LETITIA GÓMEZ is a member of the National Gay and Lesbian Health Association board and is the co-founder and executive director of the National Latino and Latina Gay Organization (LLEGO). She has been active in the lesbian and gay movement since 1981. She was a member of the Gay Chicano Caucus in Houston, Texas, and later helped to organize the first Latin Lesbian Retreat in Texas in 1987. With degrees in sociology, social work and urban studies, she has dedicated the past fifteen years to working on making gay and lesbian Latinos aware of the importance of their participation in the Latino and gay and lesbian communities. She believes our individual communities need to be strong and empowered to be effective in the larger movement.

HEATHER GREENLEE is currently coordinating a study at the University of Washington's Harborview Medical Center on the quality of the dying experience of persons with AIDS. In the fall of 1997 she hopes to begin a graduate program in naturopathic medicine and acupuncture. Her long-range goal is to open a women's health center that bridges nontraditional and traditional medicines to serve all women's health needs. In her not-so-spare time, she hikes, travels, gardens and remodels houses with her babe, Liz.

AMBER HOLLIBAUGH has thirty years of experience as a national organizer, educator, policy analyst, filmmaker and writer. She has worked as a theoretician and activist on issues including prisoners' rights, homophobia, women's rights, incest, domestic violence, rape, race and class oppression, and sexuality. For the last ten years she has worked as a health educator, as a pre- and post-test supervisor on New York City's AIDS hotline, in the New York City Commission on Human Rights AIDS Discrimination Unit and, finally, as director of the Lesbian AIDS Project at Gay Men's Health Crisis in New York. She is an award-winning film producer with fifteen years of experience in video and film production. She was co-producer/director of *The Heart of the Matter,* an independent documentary film focusing attention on women's sexuality through the prism of AIDS. The film won the Freedom of Expression Award at the 1994 Sundance Film Festival as well as a 1994 national premier on the PBS series "POV." She is an essayist and published writer.

SUSAN KRAJAC lives in Minneapolis with her lover and two large dogs. She has a B.A. in journalism from the University of Wisconsin and is currently working on a teaching certificate. Her poetry and articles have appeared in various local publications and nationally in the *Evergreen Chronicles* and the *Advocate*.

DEL MARTIN and **PHYLLIS LYON** are co-founders of the Daughters of Bilitis, the first national lesbian organization (1955) and co-authors of *Lesbian/Woman* (Volcano, 1991). They are members of Old Lesbians for Change and were delegates to the White House Conference on Aging (1995). They are Proud *Old* Lesbians.

RIVKA MASON is a proud, bold, bearded Jewish country dyke who presently resides in the Berkeley hills. She has made her living by planting gardens and by carpentry. At the present time her work is in the healing arts of Shiatsu, yoga, macrobiotic cooking and teaching gardening in elementary schools.

VERONICA MATOS is an assistant director of health services at the Los Angeles Gay and Lesbian Community Services Center. She was involved in women's issues early on as a developer of a domestic violence/rape crisis center and the women's movement in the South Pacific. For the past five years she has been involved in various aspects of HIV service provision, advocacy, activism and program development and planning. Her involvement in lesbian health includes her experience in helping to open the Audre Lorde Lesbian Health Clinic at the Gay and Lesbian Community Services Center in Los Angeles.

SALLY MIKULAS is fifty years old and lives in Seattle, Washington, with her partner Adrienne, their twenty-four-year-old goddaughter, two cats and a dog. She has sung second alto in the Seattle Lesbian and Gay Chorus for five of its six years and is very involved in her chorus family.

WENDY MORSETH is a native of the Pacific Northwest. She has published poetry, fiction and book reviews in alternative literary magazines and *Deneuve* (now *Curve*). She is a clinical psychologist in private practice in Portland, Oregon.

MERRIL MUSHROOM is now fifty-five, and the worst of all this is behind her. She is considerably less dense than she was thirty years ago. She still has an occasional hot flash in the Tennessee hills where she lives.

KATE O'HANLAN was born in the Shenandoah Valley of Virginia. She always knew she liked girls and knew how to hide that fact in kindergarten. Dr. O'Hanlan is an obstetrician/gynecologist specializing in pelvic and cancer surgery. One of the founders of the Lesbian Health Fund and past president of the Gay and Lesbian Medical Association, she has published in numerous medical journals, lectured at the National Institutes of Health and many medical schools and associations, and co-authored a report on anti-discrimination in medicine. Her goal is to reduce the homophobia she faced all her life, from family, friends and even from herself, so that her younger sisters and brothers in the world will have an easier time. She is in private practice at Stanford Medical Center and in her tenth year of marriage to Léonie Walker.

CAROLYN PATIERNO is a HIV/AIDS and sexuality educator and lives in New York City.

JANE A. PETRO is a plastic surgeon who lives, works and writes in New York state.

MARJ PLUMB is a longtime advocate and public policy analyst for lesbian and gay health issues and services. She has a bachelor's degree in public administration and a master's degree in nonprofit administration, both from the University of San Francisco. She is currently Director of Public Policy at the Gay and Lesbian Medical Association, Health Policy Consultant for the National Center for Lesbian Rights, a member of the advisory board for the Lesbian Health Fund (a project of the Gay and Lesbian Medical Association), a member of the national advisory board for the National Policy and Resource Center on Women and Aging, and a member of the Washington, D.C.-based Lesbian Health Advocacy Network.

DIANE POWERS practiced as a mental health therapist for seven years before entering the world of cancer research. She is particularly interested in the issues of breast cancer and lesbian health since losing one of her first dyke friends to breast cancer. Her passions include textile arts, women's basketball and her three cats.

LIZA J. RANKOW is a researcher, educator and activist specializing in lesbian health. She provides cultural competency trainings and technical assistance to state and federal agencies, medical professionals and queer activists and organizations nationwide. Liza is the author of numerous resource materials including the *Lesbian Health Bibliography*, a comprehensive document listing eight hundred books, articles and studies, and *Women's Health Issues: Planning for Diversity*, a curriculum and handbook on lesbian health for primary care providers. Her professional writing has appeared in the *Journal of Family Practice, Women's Health Issues* and the *American Journal of Public Health*. Her poetry has been published in *Bridges: A Journal for Jewish Feminists and Our Friends* and the anthology, *The Femme Mystique*.

RITA SHIMMIN PULIDO is the HIV program services director at Lyon-Martin Women's Health Services in San Francisco.

SABRINA SOJOURNER is an African-American activist, feminist writer and speaker, organizational development consultant, former legislative aid to Maxine Waters and the first U.S. Representative from the District of Columbia. She lives with her life partner, Letitia Gómez, and her son, Christopher Sasek.

JAN THOMAS, initially a social worker, has worked on environmental and peace issues as a communications specialist over the past ten years. Her great passions include Asian spirituality, poetry and harmony singing. She lives in the San Francisco Bay area in California.

VAL ULSTAD is board-certified in internal medicine and cardiology. She and her partner, Dr. Kathleen Ogle, a medical oncologist, live in Bloomington, Minnesota.

JULIE VAN ORDEN is currently surviving in Portland, Oregon, and has recently discovered a new use for unwanted shoulder pads (just be sure to remove the Velcro hooks first!).

EVELYN C. WHITE is a visiting scholar in women's studies at Mills College in Oakland, California. She is editor of *The Black Women's Health Book* (Seal, 1994) and author of *Chain Chain Change: For Black Women in Abusive Relationships* (Seal, 1994). Her writing has appeared in numerous publications including *Essence, POZ* and *Smithsonian* magazines, the *Wall Street Journal*, the *San Francisco Chronicle*, the *Seattle Times* and *Sojourner*. Her biography of Alice Walker is under contract with W.W. Norton.

WILLY WILKINSON is a writer and researcher. Though disabled with CFIDS since 1992, she plans on fully recovering and becoming a triathlete. She lives with the femme of her dreams in Oakland, California.

ANNE WYATT was born in Ashland, Oregon, in 1954. After completing a bachelor's degree in journalism, she tried law school but decided to switch to creative writing. After earning a master's degree, she pursued a doctorate in educational policy and management. In 1988, she was diagnosed with multiple sclerosis, and her real education began. She lives now with her partner and their sixteen cats and three dogs on Happy Lane in Eugene, Oregon.

INDEX

ABOUT THE EDITORS

JOCELYN WHITE practices and teaches internal medicine in Portland, Oregon. She has published widely in the medical literature and lectured nationally on lesbian health, medical ethics, and doctor-patient communication. She is a past president of the Gay and Lesbian Medical Association and is an editor-in-chief of the *Journal of the Gay and Lesbian Medical Association.* She teaches doctors, nurses and other clinicians to care for lesbians with respect and compassion and works for the day when no lesbian will be afraid to seek health care.

MARISSA C. MARTÍNEZ earns her living as a software engineer. Her writing has appeared in the *Americas Review, Raven Chronicles, Seattle Arts,* and others. Originally from San Antonio, she now makes her home in Seattle.

■

SELECTED TITLES FROM SEAL PRESS

The Black Women's Health Book: Speaking for Ourselves, expanded second edition, edited by Evelyn C. White. $16.95, 1-878067-40-0. A pioneering anthology addressing the health issues facing today's Black women. Contributors include Faye Wattleton, Byllye Y. Avery, Alice Walker, Angela Y. Davis, Audre Lorde, Lucille Clifton, bell hooks and Toni Morrison.

Lesbian Couples: Creating Healthy Relationships for the '90s, by D. Merilee Clunis and G. Dorsey Green. $12.95, 1-878067-37-0. A new edition of the highly acclaimed and popular guide for lesbians in couple relationships.

The Lesbian Parenting Book: A Guide to Creating Families and Raising Children, by D. Merilee Clunis and G. Dorsey Green. $16.95, 1-8780670-68-0. This practical and readable book covers a wide range of parenting topics as well as issues specifically relevant to lesbian families. Information on each child development stage is also provided.

The Me in the Mirror by Connie Panzarino. $12.95, 1-878067-45-1. This is the dynamic memoir of writer, lesbian and disability rights activist and artist Connie Panzarino, who has been living with a rare muscular disease since birth.

Ceremonies of the Heart: Celebrating Lesbian Unions, edited by Becky Butler. $14.95, 0-931188-92-X. An anthology of twenty-five personal accounts of ceremonies of commitment, from the momentous decision to the day of celebration.

Alma Rose by Edith Forbes. $10.95, 1-878067-33-8. A brilliant lesbian love story filled with unforgettable characters and the vibrant spirit of the West.

The Dyke and the Dybbuk by Ellen Galford. $10.95, 1-878067-51-6. A fun, feisty, feminist romp through Jewish folklore as an ancient spirit returns to haunt a modern-day London lesbian.

Latin Satins by Terri de la Peña. $10.95, 1-878067-52-4. Full of humor, tenderness and salsa, this novel tells the story of the lives and loves of a group of lesbian Chicana singers in Santa Monica, California—the irrepressible Latin Satins.

Ordering Information: If you are unable to obtain a Seal Press title from a bookstore, please order from us directly. Checks, MasterCard and Visa are accepted. Enclose payment with your order and 16.5% of the book total for shipping and handling. Washington residents should add 8.6% sales tax. Send to: Orders Dept., Seal Press, 3131 Western Ave., # 410, Seattle, Washington 98121. (800) 754-0271 orders only; (206) 283-7844 phone; (206) 285-9410 fax; sealprss@scn.org. Visit our website at www.sealpress.com.